D1346869

McGRAW

McGRAW

THE INCREDIBLE UNTOLD STORY OF
TAM 'THE LICENSEE' McGRAW

REG McKAY

BLACK & WHITE PUBLISHING

First published 2008
by Black & White Publishing Ltd
29 Ocean Drive, Edinburgh EH6 6JL

1 3 5 7 9 10 8 6 4 2 08 09 10 11 12

ISBN: 978 1 84502 240 2

Copyright © Reg McKay 2008

The right of Reg McKay to be identified as the author
of this work has been asserted by him in accordance with the
Copyright, Designs and Patents Act 1988.

The publisher has made every reasonable effort to contact copyright holders
of images in the picture section. Any errors are inadvertent and anyone who,
for any reason, has not been contacted is invited to write to the publisher so that
a full acknowledgment can be made in subsequent editions of this work.

All rights reserved. No part of this publication may be reproduced,
stored in a retrieval system, or transmitted in any form, or by any means,
electronic, mechanical, photocopying, recording or otherwise,
without permission in writing from the publisher.

A CIP catalogue record for this book is available from the British Library.

Typeset by Ellipsis Books Limited, Glasgow
Printed and bound by MPG Books Ltd, Bodmin

CONTENTS

To the victims

1

DANCE OF FEAR

The man with hunted eyes walked out into the sunlight and grimaced with fear. Before him were people calling for his attention. Men and women who wanted his life. His blood. He hunched his shoulders and took off.

His long-legged, staggering stride couldn't leave them behind. They called for him loud, asking questions, shoving cameras into his face. In his wake young men and women surrounded him, pushing the chasers away, smiling and staring. Still the chase went on through the streets of Edinburgh.

It was an odd place for the fugitive to be. Edinburgh, and in that place, that building, that court. Japanese tourists on the way to the Castle stopped and stared trying to work out who the man was. Some took photographs just in case.

He looked lost, afraid. Beside him a female friend led him by the sleeve, her calm stride keeping up with his wobbly rush with ease.

He made a sad sight. That body wracked and thin, a starved man among the muscled and fat. The shoulders hunched and stooped. A heavy weight resting on his shoulders. The hair, too big for his long, faint face. The suit too large for such a pained and wasted man. And those eyes. Those hunted eyes.

In there people would poison or stab him. Out here they would shoot him and kill him.

They reached a road crossing and the lights were against them. Our man looked flustered, lost as the traffic flowed thick and fast past him. He went to step out, his thick glasses and watery pupils letting him down. Or was it his need to escape?

A young woman held him back by the slightest grip on his sleeve. Whirled him round and pulled him back. He was helpless in this adult world. Reduced to being at the whim of anyone, just anyone.

Across the road more citizens stopped to watch. Who was that man, they wondered? The one in the over-large grey suit, whose shirt collar was three sizes too big, his cheekbones sunken and his eyes terrified? The one who looked like a prisoner of Dachau and walked liked a puppet who danced?

A terminal cancer patient in the last throes of his life? An escapee from a long-term mental hospital terrified by all that he saw? An old country boy taken to Edinburgh for the first time? For the last time?

The lights changed and while his followers growled at all around them he pranced across the road like Groucho Marx on speed.

His biggest mate reached out and smashed a camera. A young woman turned screaming and swearing at some men chasing in a car.

Soon they found their motors, piled in and drove off at speed. As the cars whizzed past, cameras zoomed and followed. Some people threw them the finger, others shouted and threatened. The man with the hunted eyes? He kept his head down like a fugitive on the hoof. Someone escaping some madness.

Who was he?

The most hated gangster in Glasgow. He was The Licensee.

2

THE THIEF

"Whit's your name?' The boy asking the question was around his height, good looking and gemme, as Glaswegians say. Cheeky, insolent, up for anything.

"Eh, Ah'm Tam," he replied nervously.

"John," his young enquirer added. "John Adams but you can call me Snaz."

"Snaz?" The other boy shrugged and smiled.

"It's my gang name. And this is Drew." The larger but younger boy beside him nodded his head and grinned. "Drew Drummond." Drew Drummond sounded like some kind of pop star like Buddy Holly. Like he'd made it up. And Snaz just sounded too savvy for words. A gang name? That sounded the bee's knees. Did he need one?

"Tam McGraw," he continued though he had just made the McGraw bit up. His family were called McGrow and the young-ster didn't like it. McGraw sounded a lot tougher. It was 1961 and boys wanted to seem tough back then. It was the time of Cowboy and Indian films, boxers as heroes, street gangs and men who had fought in the war telling their tales on street corners.

He was nine years old and it was his first day at Pendeen School. He shouldn't really be there. His family came from Calton but after his untimely entry to the world as the family set off for a summer break at Lennoxtown, there were just too many McGrows for their tiny tenement flat.

No problem. Tam got on well with his grandparents and a

3

casual arrangement to stay with them now and then in their home in Barlanark soon became a long-term plan.

It was good having two places to go. He could hang around the old streets of the Calton of a weekend and get up to all sorts of badness. By the next day he was out of there and not coming back for many days. Maybe even a couple of weeks. Hard to catch a baddy when he leaves town fast.

McGraw knew a lot of kids around Barlanark, it being the rule of the day that children played outside at kick-the-can, leavo, peever or one of the hundred street games that everyone knew. Then again there was always football. But this was his first day at Pendeen School and like all young kids he was a bit anxious. Maybe he should get a gang name? First he'd have to find a gang.

The three boys' eyes flitted around the organised chaos of the playground packed with bodies in various shades of grey and navy and rested on a kid nearby. He was with his mates and they watched too as he carefully prised open a brand new packet of Spangles. The smell of sugary fruit floated towards them and all three silently lusted for a sweet. Just one sweet. The boy wasn't even handing them round his mates and they could see why.

The arse of his brown trousers was worn through showing pants that used to be white but were now some version of charcoal grey. The knees of the trousers had been torn where he had fallen several times too many and old, dark bloodstains marked one leg where some wound had leaked. His jumper was a hand-knitted affair and made for someone much bigger than him and a pink-wearing girl at that. Even that was unfurling at the hem that hung over his thighs and the v-neck had been ripped. The ensemble was topped off with a flea-ridden crewcut to the bone and heavy leather tackety boots upturned at the toes. The kid's family was dirt poor, in other words. Anyone could see that. The Spangles were either a big treat or blagged from some nearby shop more likely. Why would he share them?

"They're mine." An older and much bigger boy was standing

close up to the lad pointing at the newly opened Spangles in his mitt. "Gie's them."

"Aye, so Ah will," replied the lad perhaps more keen on eating the fruit flavoured gems than he was brave.

"Think so?" The older boy rammed his knee into the boy's thigh, setting him grimacing and moaning. Now holding the sweets the boy's attacker turned to the other lads nearby. "Any of youse got a problem?" Looking at the boy writhing from his dead leg their answer was plain – silence.

"You okay?" Snaz asked the kid after a short while.

"Naw Ah'm no." Tears ran down his dirt streaked red cheeks as he rubbed at the injured thigh. "That bastard needs seeing to." Suddenly he was on his feet and off after his bully.

"FIGHT," the roar went up as one as happened in every school playground around the country almost every day. Young boys in shorts abandoned their games and rushed from every corner of the playground. Girls in their school skirts and others in whatever their parents could afford skipped excitedly and hung around at the edge of the crowd. In the centre of the melee the two boys stood trading punch for punch. The janitor was usually on watch, Pendeen not being the quietest of schools, but this was lunchtime and he'd slipped back to his house near the school for a quick sandwich. If he wasn't keeping an eye on the playground from his window this fight could run a wee while.

"FUCKING KILL HIM."

"STICK THE BOOT IN."

The crowd were in great voice. Well, everyone loves a scrap. Especially kids.

McGraw and his two new mates struggled, pushed and ducked their way through the crowd till they could see the action. The bigger boy wasn't having it all his own way. His smaller, skinnier opponent was ducking his wide swung blows and hitting him two or three times on the break, drawing blood from his nose and his lip. Still the battle went on with the sweet stealer becoming more and more desperate in his lunges. WHACK. At last he caught his opponent a good blow square on the side of his face. The little guy shook his head, stunned, almost going down then the big guy lunged at him again. No time for ducking, the wee man grabbed his enemy round the neck and the pair tumbled to the ground.

Rolling among the feet of the onlookers, if the janny didn't come soon the skinny kid was a dead man – anyone could see that. The big guy tried rolling over on him but only succeeded in ending up on his back. That's when the boots started going in. First one kid stamped on the big guy's face, then another shoe caught him a hard one on the cheek. Then more rained in. Down on the ground he couldn't see who was kicking him.

Small as his opponent might have been he wouldn't budge off his chest. The big guy was weeping now and failing to get to his feet. More boots caught him from his skull to his legs. That was it. Bellowing lumps of green snot he rolled over and stood up. Now the boots would stop.

"YE LITTLE CUNT," he roared and stamped down hard on his opponent, bursting his face open. "PRICK." He stamped on the wee boy's stomach again and again repaying him for the gang kicking he had just suffered.

"JANNY." No one needed to hear that twice. Fighting – even watching it – got the kids into deep trouble with the heidie. That meant the tawse and no one wanted that.

Kids scampered away from the scene as fast as they could. All bar one – McGraw. He was hanging around as if transfixed by the bleeding state of both opponents.

"He's fucking pure mental," Snaz said to Drew as they watched from the far end of the playground.

"Ye're no kidding," Drew agreed.

Eventually their new pal strolled up, his hands in his pockets and a smile on his face.

"Fancy one?" he asked holding out the disputed packet of Spangles.

"Did you lift those?" McGraw nodded.

"Well it doesn't look like those two would enjoy them now."

Behind him the two fighters sat slumped and crying on the ground, their faces splattered with blood and dirt. One held an arm as if it was broken and the other was trying to tell the janitor that he couldn't stand up. One of his legs wasn't working.

"That's fucking robbing."

"So?" McGraw smiled. "Fuck all wrong with a bit of thievery." He unwrapped a Spangle and shoved it into his mouth. "As long as you don't get caught."

3

RICH PICKINGS

McGraw had found his partners in crime. It didn't seem that way to him, Snaz and Drew Drummond at the time but partners in crime they were and would so remain for decades.

To start with they were just mates hanging around, playing the games, moaning about teachers, dogging school and avoiding a slap at home from some parent. But every now and then they'd choose a bit of devilment. Nothing big, just shoplifting sweeties, stealing from a house when the door was left open, taking off on someone's bike.

They were young, very young, and the world was there for the taking.

The early 1960s were an exciting time. Gangs were waltzing the street with axes in their hands. Money was better but always too little. Skirts were getting shorter, music was changing and, best of all, they were young. They could do anything.

"He's a prick that polis Dixon," McGraw had once offered, talking about the main character of a favourite TV programme of that time. "Whit the fuck's he doing walking the streets like that saluting and stuff?" His mates didn't say anything. They kind of liked *Dixon of Dock Green*. "Catch somebody that fat bastard? No fucking chance. Ah'd outwit him dead easy. And if no, Ah'd outrun him."

McGraw set about proving that he could outwit or outrun any Dixon or cops called Tom or even Harry. Too often he failed.

As McGraw hit the age of twelve and was moving on to the big school, his father died of cancer. In the few years following, some of his relatives blamed losing his old man on McGraw's behaviour. Why else would he take to stealing big time? What they didn't know was that he always had.

Teenagers don't steal bikes and pocket some sweeties from a local shop. Not according to McGraw. They now had the muscle and the brains to try harder jobs and score some decent loot.

The three set about tackling some of the many factories that littered the east end. They'd watch where slum clearance was at its height and target the isolated houses where people still lived – when the people were out, of course – with no neighbours to spot them at their badness.

Old women on their own abounded in Glasgow at that time, what with so many men killed in World War II, the heavy industry and bad habits of the city taking more than their fair share of lives. Most of them didn't have much and lived in the old rundown tenements that blitzed the city but they were easy prey. McGraw didn't stop to think of his grandparents or old relatives. What he wanted was their goods and take them he did.

Other kids were targeted too. Just the ones who presented no challenge and had something worth stealing. For this McGraw would sneak a free ride on a bus up to nearby Mount Vernon, the local rich area. A wander down the streets of that patch told you the people had money.

Big villas with cars in the driveway. Women with their hair covered in scarves and their aprons showing under the hem of their coats would hurry to and from houses to clean them up for a meagre wage, of course. Occasionally, a nanny would be seen out pushing a pram and taking a toddler by the hand. Money? The place reeked of it to poor boys from Barlanark. Then there were the kids.

A slap in the chops and a boot in the balls was mostly all it took and the comrades would run off with everything they could lift. McGraw went the farthest, usually on his own. Sometimes he'd strip them of their shoes, jacket and trousers if the gear was new and of good quality.

"Rich little bastards," he'd mumble, "their mammy and daddy'll just buy them some more." Then he was out of there in a flash and not coming back for a long while and not to the same street either.

The clothes and good leather school bags went to women who traded in such matters. The wages were handy but never that generous, with it taking two or sometimes three raids to earn a quid. That was reason number one McGraw wasn't fond of those kind of thefts but there was a more serious one.

The boy looked small, ineffectual and a do-gooder in his neat, private school uniform. Yet when he demanded his money he gave McGraw his answer by sticking the nut on him. A Glasgow kiss that almost blew him off his feet followed by a series of punches so fast and accurate that the wee man had to have been trained. Who would have guessed that such a posh kid was a boxer?

McGraw already knew he didn't like pain. Didn't like it at all. After that he was always tooled up. Just a leg of a chair or a handy half brick but tooled up nevertheless and quick to use them if he had to. Then there were the knives.

The streets of Glasgow had returned to an old theme – street gangs. They had never been away but now they grew and grew till battles between two took over whole areas leaving gutted and maimed boys in their wake. Too often dead boys were left too.

Unlike the razor gangs of the same streets of the 1930s, the 1960s crews preferred proper blades, chibs, knives – the sharper and longer the better. If you were a teenager it wasn't cool not to carry a blade. Who was McGraw to disagree?

While the gangs used their weapons in battle, McGraw used his in robbing people. Young public schoolboys or frail old women – it didn't matter. Not many argued when a chib was stuck in their coupon.

Still he preferred robbing warehouses, factories and shops with their bigger wages and was getting to be a dab hand at breaking and entering. That was all you needed in those days when security amounted to putting a strong lock on the door.

A dab hand all right but not that good. On the third time he was nabbed by the cops McGraw was sent down. He was still only a child but he was going to the closest to a jail the law allowed. His borstal days had just started.

4

BORSTAL DAYS

"Who's the new boy then?"

"Whit one?"

"The guy gabbing in the corner."

"Aw, him? He's from close to my patch."

"Well?"

"Dae ye want his right name or his real name?"

"Eh?"

"Well, ye see . . ."

"Just spit it fuckin' oot, would ye."

"We call him Hans, as in Hans Christian Andersen."

"Whit?"

"Ye know, fairytales and that." His companion was still looking at him as if he was speaking some long dead Chinese language. "He tells tales. Made up fuckin' fantasies like aw the time."

"Arsehole."

"Aye, so he is," he said not sure if his mate meant Hans or him. "Hans is his right name but his real name is Tam McGraw."

"A bit of an Andy Pandy then."

"Aye, then some. Always trying to make oot he knows the hardest gang leaders and has pulled the biggest jobs. Aw shite."

"So, whit the fuck is he daein' his borstal for? A bad fuckin' endin'?" The pair of them laughed at the teenager's wry line.

"Naw, naw. He's a tealeaf. A big fuckin' thief. Cannae fuckin' help himself."

"Even in here?"

"Every fuckin' place and from any fuckin' body."

McGraw had only been in Polmont Borstal for a few days but had already decided he didn't like it. The place was hard, harder than most adult jails and no mistake. The Labour Party were in power under Harold Wilson and they weren't about to make the error of being soft on crime and criminals, in spite of what some of their backroom policy boys and girls were telling them.

The death penalty might have been abolished, abortion introduced and even homosexuality legalised but if you broke the law you went to jail, simple as that. Home Secretary Roy Jenkins said as much.

Not that McGraw or the other inmates gave a hoot about politics. They were too busy surviving.

Harsh was a word that didn't match the place's grimness. It was an old jail with dank, dark, dungeons of cells that smelled of decades of fear seeping from frightened boys' bodies.

The teenagers had their hair shorn to the skull – a terrible humiliation in those long-haired trendy days – and were dressed in rough working clothes. Every day they'd be wakened at an hour few had seen before to run round the track regardless of the weather then end it all with a cold shower. Anyone slacking was given a slap and a kicking from the staff then trailed in front of the governor for punishment. Usually it was extra work of a mundane nature – cleaning the toilet floors with a toothbrush, raking up the leaves outside in a howling gale. Or more exercise – press-ups in the mud that went on and on, a run round the recreational area in the rain or snow – a run that never seemed to be coming to an end. Finally, the worst punishment – solitary confinement that went on for weeks regardless of the law of the land.

The screws weren't there to be helpful to the boys. They were there to bully and torment them. Exercise them till they dropped. Work their fingers till they bled and then work them some more.

Borstal wasn't meant to be therapeutic. It was meant to be a punishment and the kids' last time in jail. Some said that one out of two wasn't bad so they made that one as bad as it could be.

If the screws, the rules and the regime were a pain, there was much worse – the lads themselves. After all, the borstal housed the most violent, disturbed and damaged kids from all over the country who weren't about to treat each other like blood brothers.

Most of the inmates came from Glasgow, Scotland's biggest city and still with claims to being the Second City of the Empire. While that was handy for some kids in teaming up with guys they knew, it was a loss leader in that it always meant the place was stuffed full of their enemies. Enemies they hadn't even met.

In a city still keeping a tight grip on its sectarian roots, the first question often asked of a stranger was what school did they go to? It was an obvious ploy to find out if they were Protestant or Catholic. In borstal it was what gang are you part of? As in, do I embrace you or end you?

Every few city streets were the territory of some gang. The rest of the world might have been celebrating Love and Peace but Glasgow had broken out in street warfare – again.

On the outside, straying into someone else's patch was reason enough for them to chase you with blades and hatchets and, if they caught you, to use them on your body.

In borstal there were no patches. Just enemies slung together with one eye out for the screws, the other out for a chance to hurt you.

The young McGraw wasn't a gang member of any repute. He couldn't fight, hated to stand up to anyone and his few friends had escaped borstal. The only thing he did was gabbed and told tales. It was about to bring him bad trouble.

5

SUSSED

"I'm in the BarL Team." McGraw had answered the borstal question in the only way he could by naming his local gang. In truth, he did hang around with some of the BarL boys and even the women from the She BarL. Now there was a tough bunch of chib carrying dames but some were not bad looking and would let you go all the way if they thought you were tough or you gave them a few fags or even a wee present. He had always some ciggies on him and a wee present handy for just that purpose. Stolen, of course, out of somebody's house. Maybe even their older sister's handbag or auntie's place. What did he care?

"They're a good team," said his questioner. "You been in any of their battles lately?"

"Aye, I'm there all the time," McGraw replied. "Can't let the team down, eh?"

"Naw." The questioner was from someplace out east in Fife. There was no threat from him on some territorial war back in Glasgow but that didn't mean that he didn't know about them.

"How's about the Big BarL or the BarL Bears then?"

"There's only one BarL Team," McGraw answered, not lying for once. "Why bother with the rest? My family go way back with the gangs." He had rolled himself a cigarette and his companion quickly offered him a light from a long silver Ronson that clicked and worked first time. McGraw's eyes caught the lighter. He would have that before long.

"Aye?"

"Billy Fullerton. Know who I mean?"

"The leader of the Billy Boys?"

"The self same man. He was my granny's cousin."

"Fuck sake. Really?"

"I kid you not. Then there was Dandy McKay."

"Who?"

"Just the biggest fuckin' player in Glasgow for years."

"Nah."

"He was a pal o' ma dad's till . . . well . . . when da was still alive." The room around McGraw filled with silence. Even borstal boys were embarrassed by death though some would go on to cause it to arrive early for others and too many would end up dead themselves before long. McGraw looked down at his feet and sad for a few seconds. "We don't like to talk about it much." He was looking up now, a glare on his face. "We're still fuckin' angry about it. Very fuckin' angry. Bastardin' cops. Bastards."

He'd leave the demise of his father hanging in the air, having worked out a long time ago that sometimes an unresolved tale was filled in better and quicker by the listeners and believers than ever he could. It had a further advantage that if any bloke from Glasgow, from Calton, say, knew that his old man had died of cancer rather than on the street, knew that the cops had had sod all to do with it – then McGraw could just say that he hadn't said otherwise.

The easiest targets for this kind of lying patter were the guys who didn't live in Glasgow but that didn't stop McGraw when it came to spinning a good tale. Especially when it came to who had pulled off a certain job.

The newspapers were read every day and tales of robberies circulated almost as much as gang fights. Visitors brought in other stories of jobs done that enhanced the inmates' already comprehensive grasps of raids carried out but not yet solved. All prisons are alive with information – some rumour, some fact, none wasted. Borstals were no different.

Some of these jobs were audacious with shotguns, disguises

and even motors changed to look like cop cars or Customs &
Excise uniforms were worn, especially when it came to hijacking
lorry loads of whisky. McGraw claimed to be associated with the
most daring of the daring.

As if most of the other kids couldn't see through that, he'd add
on details. "They say it was just two large ones that was taken,"
he'd reveal to anyone within earshot. "But Ah can tell you it was
double that." And he'd wink and smile that confident smile.

In the shadows of Barlinnie Prison a bank had been robbed. The
Riddrie branch would become the most robbed bank in Britain one
day but not back then. Then it was the talk of the schemes and the
corridors since whoever had looted the place had not been caught.

"It was pals of mine," McGraw butted into a conversation about
the robbery among a group of guys. He wasn't their pal, not invited,
but that never stopped him.

"You know, Ah think you talk a load of shite," said the biggest.

"Naw, Ah can even tell ye how and how much," he replied.

"Aye?"

"Aye."

"So how the fuck would we know you were right? How the
fuck does anyone?"

"Suit yourself." Uncharacteristically, McGraw had turned to
walk away. Maybe he sensed violence from his accuser and that's
something he never did like facing up to.

"Tell me then," the guy decided to try another tack, "see when
you're with the BarL?"

"Aye."

"You said that you turned up for all their battles?"

"Aye, well if you don't turn up there's no point in being a team
man is there?"

"So, ye'll have been to that epic one with The Gouchos from
Carntyne." The questioner didn't give McGraw time to come back
in. "What dae ye think of the big Campbell then eh? The bold TC
was in mental form that day. Pure mad so he was." He was refer-
ring to TC Campbell, the teenage leader of The Gouchos whose

reputation as a ferocious street fighter was city wide. Since the age of thirteen, TC had chopped and slashed his way through encounter after encounter. He had maimed and scarred more young men than most trained soldiers in times of war. In return his head had been smashed open with a sledgehammer and his guts spilled on to the pavement more than once. He could take and give it. TC was a kid to be feared.

"Well." McGraw drew breath ready to talk of how he had clashed with TC when the man and group moved to the side. There, being led into the Hall, three new inmates were marching beside the screws. Two were tiny, as typical of Glasgow, and looked terrified. The other was tall, athletic, his face scowling, his eyes taking everything in. He looked terrifying. It was TC Campbell.

"Well then you prick, McGraw?"

McGraw slouched off. He had been two seconds away from opening his trap and ending at the sharp end of TC Campbell's wrath. It was something he dreaded and would avoid forever, he promised himself. Years later he would rue eventually breaking that promise to himself. Breaking it time after time.

But in 1967, he had avoided the grief. In 1967 he was counting the days till he left the hellhole of borstal and got back to his life plan – thieving riches.

6

A GOOD NIGHT FOR COPS

The city was getting hot to trot for McGraw. Not the problem of violence and booze as with many young men. His problem was with the cops and it was entirely his own fault. As a robber he was getting too good and too greedy.

They'd worked out that you had to watch a place, watch it for a few days to see the comings and goings of the staff, the watchies, the dogs. See if there was an easy way in and, if not, a safe way in. Always best to hit a place when it was empty, usually at night or if it was shut down at the weekend. There was next to no security and the east end was full of wee businesses with a few quid in some drawer and easily sellable goods for the nabbing. So that's what they did – nabbed the goods.

Often along with his old schoolmates Snaz and Drew Drummond, McGraw would hit a house, a factory or a warehouse and take whatever he could. At £400 or £500 a time the cash was ace for the early 1970s but not big enough to retire or, as McGraw hoped to do, invest in some easy money-spinning lark. So they went on and the cops were on their trail.

After one successful hit on an east end warehouse, the proceeds of money, booze and cigarettes were split up. McGraw stored his spare loot in a hut on an allotment down near the rail track that eventually ran from the east past Blackhill and Royston.

Only a few old codgers worked those allotments and none were too bothered by what their young companion was up to. Besides, they were seldom there after dark – McGraw's favourite time for a visit.

The young robber must have thought he was being smart. After all, the lack of light is the biggest ally of secrecy. Not everyone thought that way.

In a corner of rotting old tenements just across from the allotments, an old man was living out the last of his days in pain and unhappiness. A bad war in France followed by hard work in all weathers as a pee wee man on the railways had ruined his legs and now he couldn't walk without two sticks. Too many smokes and too many chip suppers had blocked his arteries and every short stroll made his face turn purple and the pains thump in his chest. His daughter brought round his shopping, did his housework and a wee boy from down the road fetched his paper, tobacco, milk and bread every day. Apart from them and his wireless he had no company.

It was a hard end to a hard life and he knew it. That didn't mean he was going to let things go.

When he wasn't slumbering in his easy chair next to the fire, he'd make himself a mug of tea and somehow make it to a hard backed chair by the table in front of his window. There he'd sit and watch what little life was left in his little corner of the east end.

Like him, the once thriving, heavily populated area was dying a slow, agonising death. All day he could hear the rumble of big machines and lorries slowly but surely working their way to his home as the slums of the area were razed to the ground. Every week more families collected their belongings together and moved to new places and new hopes in the concrete jungles of Drumchapel, Easterhouse and Castlemilk. He didn't know what he'd do when it came his time. How could he move to another house when he could hardly move across his own floor?

So, every day and night he sat at that window and watched for some life, some movement, some people. When it came he watched it with great interest. It was all he had.

One night, McGraw had gone into his allotment hut and filled a bag with cigarettes and a few bottles of whisky. As he turned to leave the hut his heart leapt – a man was standing at the door watching him. Not just any man but a uniformed copper.

"You'll have a receipt for those goods, I take it," said the cop in a voice singing of the Highlands.

"Aye . . . eh, no." McGraw wasn't ready for this.

"No receipt?" The cop had lifted the tarpaulin covering the rest of McGraw's goods. Sleeves of Senior Service, Woodbine, Embassy and No.6 piled as high as his waist. Next to the fags, cardboard crates of whisky were piled on top of one another. It wasn't the biggest haul in the city but it did need some explaining. "You must have these, eh," the cop went on, "for your shop."

"Shop? Whit . . ."

"'cause that's the only reason I can see for you having all this gear. Must be a good few hundred quids' worth here eh?"

"Aye, a few hundred," McGraw agreed.

"A good memory then?"

"Whit?"

"Well now, you don't have a receipt now do you?"

"Look, Constable . . ."

"McLean. PC McLean to you." The cop towered over McGraw and in that confined space the two were just a couple of feet apart. He smiled down at McGraw who knew well enough never to trust a cop's smile. "And you'll be young Mr McGraw then?"

"How the fuck?" All the time McGraw was trying to edge towards the door and peer out. Cops didn't walk round the streets of Glasgow on their own. Not even the Alsatians went out on their own in that city. He was thinking of making a run for it but not to go cascading into some other rozzer. That was the only excuse they needed to give him a kicking.

"You don't remember me then? That time you and yer pals got done for the warehouse off Alexandria Parade?" McGraw was thinking and remembering but like most other folk the dark uniforms tended to make all cops look the same. It was a habit he would lose but not yet. "Helped get you yer borstal," the policemen offered some clue.

"Aye, aye, Ah'm remembering now." McGraw peeked out the door but all he could see were the shapes of vegetables through the dark night.

"Looking for my mate are ye? Well don't worry, Ah'm here on my tod the night. Just me and you having a wee chat eh?" If he wanted a chat, McGraw would give him a chat. That was one thing he could do par excellence. The pair sparked up cigarettes, eased their arses down on an old bench and blethered.

"Fancy a drink to go with the fag?" McGraw asked lifting one of the bottles of whisky.

"Now then, I don't mind if I do," replied PC McLean and in a jiffy had torn off the cap and glugged a few inches of whisky down his throat. "That's damn fine," he said examining the bottle as carefully as he could in the lack of light. "Damn fine."

"Would ye want some tae take home with you?" McGraw asked sensing he could be walking back to his own bed that night. "On the house, of course."

"From your eh . . . shop . . . like?"

"From my shop, aye. A wee thank you from me to the polis."

"Just as a thank you then?"

"Aye, just a thank you."

"And maybe a wee half bottle for an old man across the way," PC McLean nodded towards the rotting tenements. "A good man that. Keeps his eyes open around here. Told me he thought you were up to badness." The cop roared with laughter and a nervous McGraw joined in.

"No problem," he replied. "Maybe even a bottle and some fags if he's a smoker."

"That's generous of you but he's a pipe man so unless you have some shag there?"

"Naw, just fags."

"Ach well, a bottle of nice whisky will keep him a happy man."

PC McLean left that night with one hundred cigarettes, a bottle of whisky for himself and another bottle for the old watchman. McGraw had done a quick calculation in his head and reckoned it was a small price he was paying not to be arrested. Of course, he moved the rest of his fags and booze that night. He well knew you couldn't trust the cops, especially the bent cops.

But for days after, the episode had caused him food for thought. A few quid in the right hands and he stayed out of jail – a place he hated and, worse, it terrified him. It was well worth it. He was going to take that habit further and no question. But what else could he get from the cops? He was going to find out.

7

A GOOD INVESTMENT

The agonised scream rang out through the factory. It wasn't Drew or Snaz so it had to be McGraw who appeared from his locus holding one arm to his chest. No need to ask what was wrong – as he walked, blood dripped on the ground. They'd have to get help in double quick time.

It was typical of McGraw that in spite of his pain and need to get some help, he insisted that the team carry off most of the goods. There was no point in leaving empty handed, he always said. He thought Snaz and Drew considered him a professional whereas, in reality they were already suspecting something else – money was McGraw's God.

On the way home, Snaz made a suggestion. Why didn't McGraw go back to his house to have his wounds cleaned up? The man was in some pain and didn't argue with the plan. At least in Snaz's house no one was going to ask awkward questions or go to the cops. McGraw was reluctant to walk into the emergency ward of a hospital in case they did just that.

At Snaz's house there was a volunteer to play nurse – his sister Margaret. Soon a basin was filled with boiling water, the Dettol bottle was open and towels and bandages laid out. It only took twenty minutes to tend to McGraw's cut hand and arm but what a twenty minutes. By the end of it he wasn't just patched up – he was in love.

Margaret Adams was small, good looking and feisty. She knew her own mind, talked a lot and carried an air of confidence about her. A year older than McGraw she seemed more experienced, mature and he found that irresistible. The pair became a couple.

For the next year, McGraw worked on the buses officially and unofficially continued robbing – something Margaret was more than aware of and she didn't bat an eye. She was a young woman with ambitions and that needed a man with money. How else was McGraw going to achieve that if not by robbing? Besides it was much preferable to the young men who seemed to want to drink and fight all the time. Her Tam was going places – if she had anything to do with it.

PC McLean had hit pay dirt or at least a small rewarding relationship with McGraw. Every once in a while McGraw would make sure that he got a couple of bottles of whisky, some fags and a few quid. In return he got information.

Sometimes it was just chat and other times gossip. None of that was wasted by the young McGraw. Already he had learned to know as much as possible about everyone. At other times it was a hint that some place's watchman was going on holiday or was off on the sick and they had decided not to replace him meantime. Or where a watchdog had died and there might be two or three days before the owner got a replacement. It was all good stuff and worth every penny for McGraw.

As he drew in more and more money from his evening work, McGraw had started what would be a lifelong habit in giving most of it to Margaret to manage. She was smart that way, making sure none of it was wasted. She added it to savings they accumulated from their jobs – hers in a knitwear factory in the Queenslie estate – as well as some other unofficial earnings.

There was no surprise when almost exactly a year after that night with McGraw's ripped arm, the pair got married and settled into their first flat in Burnet Road, Barlanark. The bride was 19 and the groom 18. Not exactly old but no surprise then in a city like Glasgow.

For the next two years the pattern of their lives was set. Both would work and Tam would rob. At one point he went to graft for one of Margaret's relatives who ran a builders business out by Spateston in Renfrewshire. The awkward journey across town as it was then was compensated for by higher wages.

A few months later McGraw left. He would tell people it was because he was so fed up having to clean the dumper truck he drove that he let it run into a pond one night. All that might well be true but he was also stealing from the place. Copper piping, bathroom suites, roof tiles, brand new timber – anything that anyone wanted. Stealing had become so much of a habit he was ripping off a relative.

PC McLean had bad news for McGraw. There was a divisional crackdown on robberies and his name had come up in briefings a couple of times. Glasgow was about to be a very uncomfortable place for him.

That's when he and Margaret decided to implement their plan of heading to the Big Smoke to make their fortunes. They were doing okay for two young people in Glasgow but imagine how much better they might do in streets they suspected might well be paved with gold.

Like so many Scots before them, they found the move hard to start with. Then came the breaks with both McGraws getting work on the buses. After that Margaret got a job working in the Concorde factory and Tam at an electroplating factory. The increased wages were almost enough to pay for their Wimbledon flat. Plus McGraw hadn't stopped robbing. Something he was to find disappointing.

The familiarity he had with Glasgow might have been dull but it did mean he knew the places to break into. In London, with no local contacts he had to start again and case joints anew each time. Worse, security was better in London and many jobs had to be abandoned because of alarms ringing out. Even when he did get in he'd too often be confronted by a safe.

While his robbing earnings had shrunk McGraw wasn't one to give up. Instead he was fast becoming skilled at dismantling alarm systems and breaking into safes. All good training for the future.

At the electroplating plant, McGraw was promoted to night-shift gaffer. His wages could be enhanced substantially if the shift did more work so he introduced new systems driving the men to much greater productivity. The deal meant he was earning £500 a week and that in 1972. It was a system some of them liked because their bonuses increased too. Yet many hated the break up of their cosy routine whereby dayshifts were expected to do more than nightshift.

One night, McGraw felt a nudge and suddenly he fell into a dipping tank of dangerous chemicals. He was in agony with the flesh of a foot stripped to the bone. After weeks of hospital treatment, he was fit again but out for revenge. He had no idea who had pushed him but he did know who had employed him.

A lawyer promised him a small fortune in compensation for suing the company and he was true to his word. With a fat cheque for many thousands, his savings from his £500 a week job – both fortunes then – in 1974 Margaret decided that she was homesick for Glasgow. The pair upped sticks and headed north. Back to the east end. Back with a vengeance. Now he had enough money to do the place some real damage.

8

NO PLACE LIKE HOME

Glasgow had not stood still. It never does.

Margaret McGraw had headed home from London for many weekends but she was only there to see her family and friends or to go out to a local pub on the Saturday night after a day's shopping in the city centre. Welcome as that was it meant she hadn't a clue as to what was happening on the streets.

Snaz and Drummond were a wee bit different. They had made it down to London for a few months helping McGraw out on some robberies but soon got fed up when the Golden Goose didn't lay her egg for them. They had soon headed back to Glasgow and got on with life as they had before. Back to the thieving in other words.

Yet Snaz and Drummond didn't have McGraw's insatiable appetite for information. They were quite happy planning their own jobs, taking care of themselves. It meant their erstwhile partner was returning to a city that had moved on and he was going to have to get up to date at speed.

An armed mob were tackling every major bank in Scotland and then some without being caught. Rumour had it that the cops called them the XYY Gang after their call out codes. The more dangerous you were, the further through the alphabet they placed you.

The Workers Party of Scotland – a bunch of Maoist revolutionaries – had just been convicted of a similar lark though not on such a grand scale. Their leader, Matthew Lygate, had made some speech from the dock about freedom and capitalism. It fair sent the crooks of Glasgow laughing. Where did he think he was – Cuba?

A new product had hit the streets and was strictly illegal – cannabis. It was popular with the long-haired hippies and increasingly with a whole heap of kids. The mark up wasn't huge unless you dealt on a big scale. Most players just left that to the so-called intelligentsia but some didn't.

A bloke called Archie Steen was just about to be jailed for the execution-style killing of John Stillie and trying to off Walter 'Toe' Elliot – one of the most dangerous men in the city – by shooting at him through his letter box. Word had it that it was all over the sale of dope. Fitness fanatic and hard man Steen wasn't about to spill the truth and Toe Elliot would need months of torture before he'd tell the cops the time of day.

A mad killer dubbed Bible John was still on the loose even though street players had broken their golden rule and were helping the police. The woman-strangler had killed three women, all picked up at the Barrowland Ballroom, and seemed to have disappeared off the face of the earth. Or had he?

Rangers FC had rebuilt the exit where the Ibrox Disaster had happened in 1971 killing sixty-six supporters. It was something at least for a Rangers supporter like McGraw. That was something he'd hide from people later in life but not then. Back then he had no reason to though he didn't have much time to go the matches. Too busy stealing.

James Crosbie, a loner bank robber from Glasgow had been dubbed Britain's Most Wanted when he went on the hoof through Britain. Glasgow faces didn't know that much about Crosbie. He had made his way to London and linked up with some top players. That made him dangerous, so dangerous at one point he would be suspected of killing London cops along with Harry Roberts. It wasn't Crosbie – stealing was his game.

Arthur Thompson was more than ever settled in as top dog. From his house, The Ponderosa, in the north of the city, Thompson's influence reached almost every nook and cranny. Yet he still had a few feuds he couldn't sort out. That was a strange one.

The Welsh family nearby had been fighting him for almost twenty years. Men had been killed, Thompson's mother-in-law blown up in a car bomb, his wife jailed for a night time raid on the Welsh's house yet still the feud went on. If that wasn't bad enough, Thompson was being tackled by new blood.

They called Bobby Dempster 'The Devil' – a blatant name in a city full of murdering chib merchants. He was a big man, strong and happy to show a bit of muscle as required. Stories of him giving groups of hard men a doing were the talk of every pub in the city. Not only was he tough, Dempster was no one's fool either.

He had been watching Thompson and a few of the older faces. Watching how they'd make their money any way they could then invested some into legal business ventures. Some had made it totally legit but it had taken them decades. Dempster wanted that and more and as quickly as possible.

Having set himself up in the Maryhill/Possil side of Glasgow, Dempster had the problem of a bad neighbour. Arthur Thompson owned a garage on Maryhill Road, a carpet warehouse, a few workshops, a wood mill and two pubs. He considered Maryhill as his territory but Dempster disagreed. Result – bloody feud and Thompson learning what many had before him – Bobby Dempster cow-towed to no man. The result was a murderous battle that was raging on with no end in sight.

Other robbers would take little account of all those shenanigans but McGraw immersed himself in it. After all he didn't want to go and rob one of Thompson's pubs now did he? Or new boy Dempster's? That was what he told close allies, of course. Those who knew him tell a different tale. He just loved gossip.

It wasn't just what the Godfather of Glasgow was up to that he wanted to know. Back in his patch in Barlanark he was keenly interested in who was shagging who, which marriages had broken up, whose Uncle Joe had just started a new job, the value of the jackpot at the local Bingo hall and everything else in between.

People who would meet Tam and Margaret McGraw on social occasions at some local club would recount the similarities and the differences between them. They both talked for Scotland – just about different things.

She would blether about the government, some eastern religion, spaceships or the like. He'd blether about whose granny had died, some domestic dispute down the road and who had bought a new car. The same but very different. Most people just wrote them off as a couple of loud-mouthed fools. The same people would live to regret that judgement.

Back in Glasgow from London, the McGraws made a plan. He would start up small businesses with the thousands of pounds they now had behind them. She got a job in WD & HO Wills, the cigarette factory, then based on Alexandra Parade. It was a clean, well-paid job with extras – lorry drivers willing to exchange a load of smokes for a few quid.

Margaret McGraw liked to be out and active, if she could. She had brought a money-making mind to their marriage and it was based on good, old-fashioned principles. Always earn whenever you could. Never waste a penny – thus the long, slow bus journeys from London to Glasgow and not the faster, more expensive train she could well afford. Save, save, save – thus the trips to the shops with the best deals, the clothes bought off the shoplifters and duty free fags and booze whenever possible. The final principle was the one she was most skilled in – invest.

Tam McGraw knew how to steal money. Margaret McGraw knew how to make it grow. What had started as a principle of her looking after all their earnings would become a partnership from hell.

As they settled into their new flat, Margaret went out to work, McGraw hit the streets and the pubs. He had a wad of cash and he was going to use it to make him rich. Hell mend anyone who tried to get in his way.

9

SKINNING THE CAT

McGraw was hot on developing principles too, except he would have struggled with those words. If you have a good, profit making idea why stop it? Improving it is what's required.

Getting back to robbing in Glasgow was like a welcome return home for McGraw but if the city was changing so was he. He was no longer happy at robbing some place that might take him all night but only earn him a couple of hundred pounds. What he needed were bigger, more lucrative targets.

In his first couple of years back, McGraw bought a few taxis and set up a rota of drivers. It had been Margaret's idea after all. She could see that the housing schemes spreading around the edge of the city meant that more people would be using the cabs which up till then had been a privilege of the well off. What they needed was the cheapest cabs possible.

With fuel costing the same for everyone there weren't many areas he could cut back on. But there had to be ways. Surely he could approach the problem differently from other taxi owners?

A few pals were sweet talked into cheap services and repairs, easy for them with their back street workshops that the taxman knew nothing about. Still that wasn't enough.

As with any industry, the drivers took the biggest fall. McGraw would recruit some from the scrap heap. An experienced motor man turned unreliable because of his love affair with booze. Some kid who loved motors – loved them so much he was banned from driving for all their car thefts and speedy chases with the cops.

Illegal, uninsured and with the drivers drawing a fraction of the going rate, McGraw's mini cabs should have been rejected for licences. No problem there, a wee sweetener to PC McLean and some of his mates and they were nodded through. Meeting that rozzer was one of the best events of McGraw's life so far. Having skinned his costs back to the minimum, the taxis were raking in a small fortune.

Now McGraw had more time to concentrate on that good idea that need improving – robbery.

10

BIG BILL'S GANG

"Shotguns?" McGraw was trying to act cool but his red face and dropped jaw told a different tale.

"Aye, shooters," said his companion who had agreed to let him join in a robbery he was planning. "You have a problem wi' that?"

"Naw. Fuck naw," McGraw replied. "Ah was just checking Ah'd heard right."

"It's no fucking sweeties we're nickin' here."

"Ah know, Ah know."

"'N if the cops suss us oot they'll come flying in tooled up." McGraw was imagining some Al Capone style shoot out on the streets – something that Glasgow wasn't entirely unfamiliar with. "Whit we gonnae dae? Just let them take us?"

"Naw. Of course we're no."

"Fuckin' right."

It wasn't that the man was planning a rough and ready robbery. Just the opposite. McGraw had never seen someone so meticulous on planning a raid. Each item of equipment he had to bring was specified – the size and style of his bag, the type of his clothes and spares to change into later were all listed with the warning,

"Any exceptions to this and ye're dumped. Get it?"

"Aye."

"And Ah don't care if it's two minutes before kick off. Forget anything 'n yer chucked. Got it?"

"Aye, got it."

"This has to run like clockwork. Like a military operation. Some of us aren't just working for a few months' rent, right?"

McGraw knew exactly what the man meant. He was Bill Campbell, known as Big Bill, and leader of the UVF in Scotland. Some said he was the leader of the UVF for all overseas. Whether that was true or not McGraw wasn't about to find out. It didn't matter that he kicked with the same foot as Big Bill, the man would tell him nothing about his political life. Told no one.

Through PC McLean and a couple of his other, ever more friendly cops he had found out that certain big raids were happening over Scotland, the Glasgow area in particular. It wasn't that XYY mob but another group and Big Bill's name kept coming up from touts.

The next stage was a wee bit trickier. Through a couple of militants he knew through the Orange Lodge, McGraw asked for a meeting with Big Bill. That had taken two months to set up. Big Bill was important. Who the hell was McGraw? Just a young thief that no one had heard of.

At that meeting, McGraw learned a lesson about preparation. Big Bill knew all about his form, his skills, his family, who he worked with and how much he'd pull in a normal week. He also knew his background and that was important to him. McGraw was a Protestant and a supporter of the Loyalists in Ireland. His best mate and brother-in-law, Snaz Adams, was also a red handed Loyalist often making donations and helping out with the odd stolen car and the like.

Best of all, Big Bill knew that McGraw had been in London and tried to tackle the alarms and the safes. Had he learned much? He hoped so because the places his mob targeted in Scotland were catching up fast with the southerners. Most of all, Big Bill needed an alarm man. Could McGraw cope? Of course he could – or so he said.

At some time in the near future he would get a few hours notice of the job and a meeting place. Could he be ready no matter what day it was? No matter what else was on? Could he guarantee to be stone cold sober and fit? He could? Then he was in.

True to his word, about a week later a strange man tapped

McGraw on the shoulder and gave him the message from Big Bill. Two hours later, dressed in ex-Army fatigue jacket and trousers, wearing big boots, a muffler round his neck and a balaclava in his pocket, McGraw sat in the blacked out back of a van with four men dressed almost identically. He had no idea who they were. Had never seen them before and assumed they were UVF Loyalists from someplace in Scotland or Ireland. He was wrong. The men lived in his own backyard but made a point of not being known, of never being noticed.

As they drove, there was a tense silence from the men with Big Bill rabbiting away. He didn't even tell them where they were going but just reminded them of their individual jobs. As he did so, a wiry man tuned in field radios, giving one to each man and as he did so, gave them false names to use.

"Mickey Mouse."

"Goofy."

"Donald Duck." That night was a Disney theme night.

At the other end of the van a small man was loading sawn off shotguns and handing them out along with a bundle of cartridges. It wasn't the first time McGraw had handled a gun but the first time he had in a situation where they might be used. He sweated and prayed that the cops didn't turn up. Prayed even harder that none of his new colleagues had twitchy fingers.

At the location, the men pulled on their balaclavas and spread out. A ladder was produced and McGraw shimmied up, disconnecting the alarm in about two minutes, a speed he was proud of, especially given his shaking fingers and thumping heart.

Inside the big building he ran with two others – the butchest looking Minnie Mouse and Snow White he ever hoped to see – through long, oil and grease smelling, dark workplaces, up some stairs and into an office. With the curtains pulled a torch was lit and a safe quickly spotted.

"Relax, Goofy," said the guy with the torch. "We can crack that one easily." And they did.

It wasn't till he was back in the van driving at an easy speed towards Glasgow that McGraw recalled that his name for the night had been Goofy.

"Cheeky cunts," he thought, "did they give me that one deliberately?" He soon found out that Goofy was always the name they gave to any new guy – whatever the theme of the night.

At an isolated rubbish dump the men changed into their civvies, dropping their work clothes in a pile. A can of petrol was produced and it was set ablaze as they drove away from the site. Snaking through the south side of Glasgow, now and then the van would stop and a man would get out and leave without as much as a 'cheerio'. Then Goofy's name was called out, his time to depart.

It was the first time he had carried out a job and left the loot with someone else. It wasn't a good feeling. McGraw didn't do trust.

Ten days later a car stopped beside him as he came out of a newsagents and picked up McGraw. After a two minute drive he was dropped off again, this time clutching a cheap nylon holdall.

"Now remember – no fucking spending the loot like you've won the pools." It was a good piece of advice. One that made him safer from the cops. Advice he'd dish out in the future.

Handing over the bundles of used notes to Margaret later that night, McGraw's eyes glittered. He so loved money. Margaret was happy. Everything was good in the world.

"You know, Mags," he said, "I think I've just seen the future."

11

PETERMAN AND THE BOMBER

For the next few years, McGraw was an occasional member of Big Bill's team. Involvement was strictly by invitation only. Aside from Big Bill, the team had no regular members and lacked any routine and even a name.

It was a lucrative business for McGraw and he was learning all the time. On a couple of occasions he had to tackle unusual alarm systems and there was a bit of a sweat on. He always managed it though and had gone out of his way to learn more.

Through his usual chit-chat on the east end streets he had learned of a couple of guys who worked in the alarm business. One specialised in shops in the city centre so was no good to him. The other worked for a firm that covered big premises, even prisons. He would do McGraw nicely. For a few back-handers the guy smuggled McGraw into his work yard late at night and showed him a few tricks. McGraw was getting good at this game.

As for safe breaking, for decades Glasgow had the reputation as a school for safecrackers. Guys like Johnny Ramensky – the tiny man who was freed from jail during the war to work behind Nazi lines – was one of the top teachers. Also Paddy Meehan, a sidekick of Arthur Thompson, who would get jailed wrongly for the killing of Rachel Ross in Ayrshire.

In those days a safecracker in Scotland was called a Peterman. There is a debate about the origins of the word. Some say it's from the French word for explosives. Others that it came from Peterhead

Prison where many captive safecrackers were kept, often in shackles.

The unofficial school had more or less closed down by the late 1970s but that didn't stop McGraw finding a couple of elderly guys willing to show him the ropes. These guys were good, so good they often worked on the big banks and diamond workshops in London. So good no one in the public knew them because they never got caught.

In spite of the best efforts of the two experts, McGraw didn't get that good at safecracking. Too much coolness, thought and precision was required and beyond his capabilities. He just wanted the money and wanted it now. Safecrackers must want to crack the puzzle of the safe and the bigger the challenge the better.

By 1979, the McGraws were well settled. Their legitimate empire had grown under Margaret McGraw's stewardship. They now had a small fleet of taxis working the streets. Added to McGraw's earnings from his own robberies and occasionally with Big Bill, they were ready to expand further. Then came a blow – Big Bill and his mob were making a noise.

The Old Barns pub was a typical Glasgow drinking place and the order of the day in its location on London Road near the Barrowland Ballroom. If you were local you'd also know it was a well known Catholic run bar that attracted a lot of support for the Republican side in Ireland. Not exactly unusual for Glasgow.

It was reasonably busy one night, like any other night, when there was a horrendous boom and the ceiling fell down. Dull eyed boozers shook their heads, laughed, picked lumps of plaster out of their beer and went on drinking. As a terrorist bomb, it wasn't the biggest success.

The cops had arrived on the scene and the Bomb Disposal Squad soon after. A bomb had been exploded all right. A bomb typical of the style used by Loyalists in Ireland.

Security forces feared the day when the Irish Troubles arrived in Glasgow, a teeming city split along the same sectarian divide. Common wisdom had decreed that this wouldn't happen.

Supporters in Glasgow were too useful in making sure that arms, ammo and money got through to the active terrorists in Ireland. Had the Troubles arrived in Glasgow now?

When the UVF claimed responsibility the cops were certain that their city was about to burn in hell.

A short while later, two other bars were hit in the east end, both well-known Republican pubs. Yet the damage was so minimal that they weren't even reported to the police. Was some incompetent madman bombing places and blaming the UVF?

When the Republican supporting Clelland Bar in Hospital Street went up, the cops changed their minds. Whoever had planted that bomb knew what they were doing. But for the grace of some good luck no one was killed but ambulance after ambulance carted seriously injured and broken bodies for emergency medical care.

Across in Belfast, McGurk's Bar went up with a whoosh. Sixteen people died in that explosion and the Security Forces suspected the same team as in Glasgow. This wasn't looking good at all.

Yet the cops had a clue – not from strife torn Northern Ireland spilling with troops and explosive experts, but from Glasgow. Bar staff remembered a guy acting strangely yet not so much for that but because of his weird drink order – a pint of beer and a sherry.

When Forensics found out that the explosives had been packed between a one-armed bandit and a jukebox they also found enough clues to finger their man. It was Big Bill Campbell's mob and the cops were on their tail.

The police were on their way to the east end one night to round up Campbell's team when the radio signalled a major explosion. This time it wasn't a Catholic bar but the Apprentice Boys' Hall in Bridgeton. Was it a reprisal hit by the IRA? No, it was a cockup.

Campbell's mob knew the cops were closing in and decided to hide their stash of explosives. One not-so-bright spark stuck them in the oven at the Apprentice Boys' Hall. Later that night when someone else started to warm up the oven for pies for a social event – the hall went up with a boom.

Big Bill, his brother Colin and the team were quickly rounded up. Bill Campbell got sixteen years and Colin fifteen years. Later Big Bill would be tried and found guilty of the multiple murder at McGurk's Bar in Belfast – a scale of murder that could so easily have happened in Glasgow.

As ordinary members of the public worried and fretted about the details revealed in the trial, McGraw worried about his favourite topics – himself and money. How was he going to replace those earnings? Then one night as he left a pub a stranger stepped out of the darkness.

"How ye doin', Goofy?"

"Whit the fuck?" McGraw thought the serious cops had come for him.

"Dae ye no recognise my face? Nah? My voice?" McGraw was still working out what to do never mind what to say. "Okay how's about the name. Snow White." With a smile the man held out his hand to shake.

Once McGraw had calmed down the man explained his purpose. He, just like McGraw, wasn't political but had been involved in the robberies for a wage. His view was that they had a good formula. One that worked and kept them all out of the pokey. Why waste it?

McGraw couldn't agree more. Game back on. Meantime, McGraw and Margaret were still looking for ways to invest their money. Ways that would bring in big profits. They were about to get an idea from a most unusual source.

12

THE ICEMAN

The Iceman showed McGraw the way though he wasn't even aware of it. Doing favours wasn't in The Iceman's nature.

Frank McPhie was one of the fiercest men in Glasgow. For some years he had been a hitman taking a fee to kill, hurt or maim anyone. Twice he saw off close friends or so street players believed and he didn't correct the rumours. At least they thought they had been close friends but they simply didn't know McPhie well enough.

By the 1970s his reputation on the streets was well established. McPhie didn't work for anyone, only working with them from time to time. Mostly he preferred being on his own since one of him was usually a match for several of the enemy especially when he was tackling innocent people.

For a few years he was picking out farms in the green pastures on Glasgow's borders and making the owners an offer. Pay him a large sum of money or their business would be ruined. Not that he would be doing that himself, of course. Oh no, he could just prevent it from happening. One look at the stranger at their front door told the farmers a different tale. The man was a menace.

They refused, of course. Law abiding people do.

First, a barn would splutter into flames in the middle of the night. Then their tractors ended upside down in some river. If no money was forthcoming still their livestock would be targeted. Wild dogs on the sheep – McPhie liked wild dogs. Cows had their throats slit or acid poured into their drinking water.

No one waited till the next stage – the farmhouse being destroyed – since no one doubted that he would do just that. Most paid up – again and again. They were right first time they met him – Frank McPhie was a menace.

McPhie also wanted money – as much as possible. He took one look around the changing face of Glasgow and sussed out something quickly. The massive new housing schemes might have inside toilets and running water but they lacked a few things. Doctors' surgeries, council offices, banks, DSS outlets and, most important of all, shops.

If the Council didn't build shops for the people McPhie would take the shops to the people. Mobile shops. Ice cream vans. With a bit of reorganisation inside, the vans could hold some bread, milk, more cigarettes, biscuits and other odds and ends. It was an idea whose time had arrived and McPhie was off and running.

With several ice cream vans on the road, McPhie was raking in a lot of money every week and had earned his nickname – The Iceman. Whether that was to do with the ice cream vans or his reputation as a cold killer has now become obscured with time. What is for sure is that Frank McPhie was the one and only Iceman with modern pretenders having tried to steal the name or, more often, been given it by clumsy journalists.

McPhie never cared that much about what most other people thought – unless they were enemies or potential targets. But someone was watching him very closely. Someone McPhie had never heard of. Someone most Glasgow faces wouldn't recognise in the street.

McGraw had big plans.

13

POKEY HATS

"Eight grand."

"Whit?"

"For the van and the round."

"Aye right."

"Cash. Used notes." The man thought for a while looking past McGraw at the kids playing at football on some spare ground nearby. He loved those kids. Loved their cheek. Loved their innocence. It was one of the reasons he had run an ice cream van over so many years.

"Nah."

"Whit? Are you off yer chump?"

"So whit am Ah tae dae for a living after that eh? And how long dae ye think eight thousand will last me and the wife?"

"Look at the age you are," replied McGraw. "Eight grand will last you no problem."

"You cheeky prick. Get the fuck out o' here."

McGraw was having no luck in persuading any of the local drivers to sell him their ice cream vans. No wonder. With a good round they could take in £500 a week if they worked the van for long hours. Good money in anyone's book. Plus half of the owners were getting on a bit. They had afforded the vans in the first place because they had copped a few quid redundancy when their work in the yards, car factory or whatever had closed down. Who would employ them now? But there weren't many people around with eight grand cash. So who would they sell them to?

It just didn't occur to McGraw that a new van cost £12,000. That his £8,000 only amounted to sixteen weeks' profit. Eight grand was the price he had decided on and eight grand they'd accept. Eventually.

Licking his wounds of rejection, McGraw was moaning to Margaret one night.

"The arseholes just can't see sense, Mags. I mean eight grand's a fucking fortune."

"Aye, if you've got nothing." She meant that the ice cream van owners did have something valuable and she couldn't blame them for refusing her husband's magic figure plucked from some place out of his imagination. It wasn't as if that was all they could afford.

"Aye, the daft fuckers." He didn't get her point at all – nothing unusual in that – but she had other ideas.

"How did McPhie get his rounds then?" she asked.

"By making them an offer they couldn't refuse, Ah bet." McGraw formed both his fists into two pistols and pretended to fire at her.

"Well?"

"Aye, well, maybe." McGraw had thought of some brutal coercion long before. His problem with that was he didn't really know these drivers. Didn't know if they'd run right to the cops with his name all over serious charges. Jail time he could do without – especially serious jail time.

"My work's in a bit of bother," Margaret offered.

"Nah. Serious?" He looked worried, once again missing her tone and what she was about to offer.

"They're cutting right back. Might even close doon."

"Aw fuck, just when things were going so well for us tae."

"So, I was wondering if I should go for redundancy." McGraw looked like he had just been punched in the stomach. Redundancy meant unemployment that meant no income and he loved his money. "Get a good few hundred quid," she went on. "Then maybe I could work a bit on the ice cream van."

"Whit fuckin' ice cream van?"

"The one we could rent from Marchetti's." Now McGraw was listening.

Marchetti was a big company based out in Bishopbriggs whose ice cream vans covered patches throughout Glasgow and farther afield. The rental was covered easily by a busy van. "It'd be start," Margaret offered. "Till you find a driver willing to sell to you."

Within a few weeks the McGraws had their first ice cream van on the road, chimes whistling out, kids running to get to the head of the queue. At that time and place it seemed such an innocent thing for them to do. What trouble could there be in selling ice cream? Sooner rather than later, the terrible truth would emerge.

With a couple of young guys helping out, the McGraws' van was on the road for every minute it could. Within days it became clear that they could extend their income by extending their stock. It would be bad business not to. Tea bags, jars of coffee, a few loaves of bread, tubs of margarine, a few bottles of Buckfast under the counter and fiver deals of dope hidden in a sweetie jar.

It was only dope. Everyone smoked dope. Not the hard heroin that was already spreading its grip throughout the city. Besides everyone was doing it. The chip shop near the Garngad. The newsagents in Govan. Every third pub in the city. Why not an ice cream van?

Whatever it was and in spite of his constant denials, McGraw officially became a drug dealer in 1979. Worse was to follow.

14

THE BAR-L AND THE BLUE DOOS

"We're the BarL Team, that's who we fucking are." McGraw was talking too much as usual. "The fucking best." He wasn't far from wrong.

With Big Bill Campbell locked up in jail, the methods he had created went on as per usual. Now all the proceeds went into pockets not collecting cans for the UVF. The take was up, in other words and McGraw loved it.

Early on after the approach by Show White, McGraw had negotiated that a couple of his mates could join in – Snaz and occasionally Drew Drummond. All was fine, especially since the acknowledged leader and organiser was Snow White, a very meticulous man in all his arrangements.

The team continued to tackle a variety of premises including post offices whose security or safes hadn't been improved one bit since Big Bill led them on the raids. As well as the dosh, they'd rip off all the stamps, coupons and postal orders too – worth a couple of grand on some raids. Trouble was that the authorities soon worked out that ploy and would cancel all the postal order numbers as soon as there had been a robbery. No problem, they just sent them across the sea – to Irish Loyalist groups. The slow cops hadn't thought of cancelling the orders in Northern Ireland.

Everything was working out fine with plenty of money and no arrests. The trouble was McGraw wouldn't stop talking.

"Ah'm telling you, we need a name," was one of his typical lines that none of the others could fathom. "How can we be the best if no cunt knows who we are?" Eventually, the others conceded and let him call their group the BarL Team. One up to McGraw but he wanted more than that.

"You're going to have to give us something," said the cop sitting across from McGraw in his Barlanark flat. It was plain-clothes and serious cops McGraw dealt with now. PC McLean had been all right in his day. The pair had moved on from some free fags for a blind eye to tit-bits about what local guy had carried out a burglary to warnings about drug squad raids on ice cream vans.

It was a highly rewarding relationship for both, especially McGraw. The level and amount of information he passed on got to the stage where McLean had to call in CID, all with McGraw's agreement, of course. With them the exchange rate was higher – more lucrative for McGraw and more rewarding for the cops. By this time, he was warning the police of crimes about to be committed, putting them on to folk who were going to be heading to jail. At last, he had found a use for his lifelong habit of talking and wanting to know everything about everyone.

McGraw thought he was smart and his relationship with the cops was strictly secret between his family and them. But then he'd do stupid things like have the cops round to his house or buy them drinks in a bar. After all, didn't all street players want a few cops in their pocket? The people of the east end were becoming suspicious of McGraw and with good reason.

Now the cops wanted something more from him. This was in return for 'losing' the report of his brother William and a range of alleged offences. McGraw had just the very thing to trade.

"You know the BarL Team's robberies?" he asked, knowing fine well he had given the cops the very name of the group. "Frustrate the fuck out of you that you don't get near them? Ah'll give you one."

The following week, having dropped the cash off at a safe place, Snow White stepped out of the van after a raid and headed for home from the city centre. He was going to walk a bit. Do a couple of stops on the underground. Buy a couple of things at a shop at the Barras then catch a bus up the road. It was all perfectly planned out the way he had done so many times before though all by different routes. This time he didn't make it to the underground when the cops arrested him.

At Snow White's house they found enough incriminating evidence under the sink and in a cupboard to find him guilty twice. It was exactly where McGraw said it'd be. He should have known – he planted them after all.

Now the BarL Team had a new leader – at least he thought so – and a new man to split up the loot. Besides, Snow White and his family wouldn't be seeing his cut of that last job. Money, that's what McGraw loved.

To replace Snow White, a new man was drafted in to the BarL Team now and then – TC Campbell. Somehow, TC had survived his years of leading The Gouchos in desperate suicide missions against murderous gangs outnumbering them three to four times. Survived and graduated to adult crime to care for his wife, Liz, and their growing family. A hardman for sure but bright and articulate too. He was just the ticket.

One time the BarL Team raided a very popular social club the night before they were due to bank the week's proceeds. The raid went badly with the safe causing them all sorts of grief. As McGraw turned his attention to the booze and cigarettes, a call came through on the walkie-talkie from one of the lookouts:

"Blue-Doos. Blue-Doos."

It was their code for the cops and the rule was they fled the job as quickly as possible. McGraw was having none of it.

For someone who later claimed wrongly to be the leader of the BarL Team it always seemed to be McGraw who broke their golden rules. Nothing but nothing was going to keep him away from the loot.

That night they had altered their usual procedure slightly. They knew the social club was to produce a lot of goods and as much fags and booze as they could carry. So, they had taken a couple of motors to carry the extra load – including McGraw's estate car.

"C'moan, Goofy, we've got tae get out of here," one of the men shouted.

"Fuck off," McGraw roared in reply, "you go and Ah'll catch you up." As the men traipsed out in double quick time they saw McGraw prise up the metal guard on the public bar and clamber over.

Twenty minutes later the men sat in the east end of Glasgow in their van and waited. They had spotted the cop cars speeding towards the scene as they left in another direction. In the city they were wary that they might have been sprung and expected a cop trap. Two hundred yards down London Road there was the proof – a cop barricade stretching across the road. What the hell would they do?

As they smoked and debated, cop sirens sounded from their rear getting louder and louder. In a flash, McGraw sped past them with two Blue-Doos on his tail. His car skidded first to the left, then the right before smashing into the barricade sending one uniformed cop up into the air then rolling onto its roof sending its load of stolen goods spilling out on to tarmac. Decision made – the van pulled out and headed off to the left. It would be a long way home but safe. The cops would be too busy dealing with McGraw.

The next day, TC Campbell and another member of the BarL Team turned up at McGraw's house. They had to learn what was happening whatever that was.

McGraw sat in an easy chair chain smoking, shoulders stooped and looking worried as hell. He had been charged with a stack of allegations including attempted murder of the copper. He was in big trouble. Around the room Margaret fussed making tea and blethering like there was no tomorrow. Worse than usual. This was one worried woman who knew her man couldn't do jail. Then the phone rang,

"Hello, Jimmy," said Margaret McGraw. "Yes, Jimmy. Aw that's good news, Jimmy, thank you so much for that." Handing the phone to McGraw Margaret prattled to the room, "That's Jimmy."

"No fucking kidding," said TC Campbell.

"He says the problem is solved. No charges against Tam." She was beaming fit to burst.

"That was Jimmy," said McGraw having put down the phone.

"Fuck sake," mumbled TC.

"All the charges have been dropped." McGraw looked like a man who had just got a get out of jail card – and he had.

"So, who the fuck is this Jimmy?" asked TC. "Your lawyer?"

"Naw," replied McGraw too quickly. Then he blushed.

"So who?"

"Just a guy Ah know," stuttered McGraw.

"A guy in a blue uniform by any chance?" asked TC.

"Naw, naw." TC Campbell left twenty minutes later without ever being told who Jimmy was. But he already knew. Jimmy was one of McGraw's contacts in the Serious Crime Squad. Question was, what do you have to do to have an attempted murder on a cop get dropped? TC Campbell and others were about to find out.

15

THRIVING

"You want something big?" McGraw asked the two cops sitting in his motor. "Ah'll give you four right big pricks in one go."

It was 1980 and life had moved on for the McGraws. They had bought a pub, the El Paso, and changed the name to The Caravel. Not that McGraw's name was ever on the licence. It was difficult to achieve that with his criminal record even with backhanders to some Licensing Board members. It was Margaret's name above the door.

As working class pubs went in 1980 it was more drinking den than lounge but it would do. Plus, it was mostly full. Margaret McGraw had scored yet another financial winner. How could a pub lose money in the east end? You'd have to be mentally incompetent or an alcoholic former footballer to do that and, while there were enough of those around running pubs, they were neither.

While Margaret ensured the pub made a lot of money, McGraw treated it like his HQ. The place he liked to be seen. The place he met people, even his police handlers. Local people had him well sussed by then. How did Snow White go down after being so careful? Now and then another of the BarL Team would get caught but never him, Snaz or Drew Drummond.

It wasn't just the robberies that McGraw was up to. He now owned a large group of taxis and they were used to make deliveries of dope when and where they were needed. Not tenner deals but enough to feed the needs of a local dealer. The McGraws could see the money to be made out of hash and weren't about to let that pass. Moreover, smack was now in the city big time, led up by a guy called Jimmy Rea. Heavy addiction, with smackheads needing to score every day, meant that the price was high and the profits obvious. They would watch that market very carefully.

The taxis had other uses like laundering the money lifted from the BarL robberies. And keeping an eye on folk McGraw was interested in, sometimes for the cops. That and a profit. All in all, a good business.

The ice cream business had flourished too. Months after they had rented that Marchetti Brothers van, McGraw was very frustrated. It wasn't that the van wasn't pulling in a profit – it was and handsomely – but the deal of stocking only from Marchettis was costing him money and parking the van at their depot in Bishopbriggs a daily pain.

One day he placed an order for two vans to be paid up over three years never being one to part easily with his dough. That same night four junkies visited certain van owners and told them that they were about to retire – at the end of a shotgun. While McGraw waited for the delivery of his vans, the same junkies set about following the drivers, smashing their windows, giving the owners a good kicking on their way home at night. That worked with one but not the other so McGraw arranged for his ice cream van to be shot at with both barrels of a big shotgun while he was at the wheel. That worked.

Now they could stock up at the nearby Fifti Ices, saving money and time. Now more of the profits were theirs to keep. Yet he wasn't finished yet.

His vans were ordered to stray onto neighbouring runs hitting key places at key times, like a secondary school at lunchtime. Any hassle from the drivers who owned that run was to be reported. When that happened a couple of men were sent out to dissuade the drivers from working at all. The method worked better than he hoped and he was regularly buying out drivers' vans and runs and for much less than the £8,000 he had offered in the beginning.

Add to that a bit of illegal money lending and working a number on ringed cars and the McGraws were doing very well thank you. But he had some business to sort out. Someone was making him very nervous and his time had come.

"Ah want you to set up a job for me," he told Frank McPhie, The Iceman. "I want three men escaped from Barlinnie Jail." He could tell by the look on McPhie's face that he didn't fancy that much. McPhie was probably wondering who this guy McGraw was. Where had he sprung from? "It's all right. *You* don't have to do it. I know who I want to take on the job."

"Who the fuck's that then?"

"TC Campbell."

"How's that?"

"He can handle that kind of game and he's pals with the family of a couple of the guys."

It all sounded reasonable but it was a lie. What McGraw meant was that TC's time had come for a long jail stretch.

16

BREAKOUT FROM BAR-L

The clunk of keys rattled through the night silence. The man gripped them tight, muffling any noise. They were almost at the door, so near, too near to be caught now.

Out in the dark they sprinted on tiptoe, one by one, till all were against the wall pushed back, far into the darkness. They were working the plan. Who could see them here? They prayed to any and every God that they were right.

One checked his watch, guarding the luminous glow with one hand. Across the way a door opened and two male voices could be heard chatting. All leaned hard into the wall, deeper into the shadow and held their breaths.

"Celtic the best team in Scotland? Now you are talking shite."

"Of course they are, man. Ye think the Gers are gonnae get in their way?"

"Naw, oor team is shite. Doon the Lodge not a fucking soul talks about fitba these days. Not fuckin' one."

"So who then?"

"The sheep shaggers." The man strained out loud followed by the banging of metal drums one against the other. "The Dons. The fucking Aberdeen, man."

"Now you are talking shite." A door banged and the voices disappeared. Checking his watch again, a rope fell right beside him followed by one shrill, light whistle. They knew the score now. Had rehearsed it so often it would stick in their minds forever. A quick scramble up that rope, down the other side and they'd be free. FREE.

A long pint of draft beer. In bed, naked with a woman. A long lie in and a proper fry up. Real fags. A bet on at the bookies and watching the race on the telly. No Barlinnie bully, Orange Lodge, thick-necked prick in a uniform bawling at you and ordering you what to do. No watching your back for the quick blade merchants earning a tenner in a crowded corridor.

FREE.

Up they went one by one and down again just as easily.

"Hello there, boys," said the tall man with long hair, dark eyes and a beard. "I was just passing and thought I'd look you up." The shotgun in his hand told otherwise. Throwing on the coats and hats he had brought them they traipsed off one by one heading for the car with its dim sidelights on. The driver sat with a fag in his mouth and sawn off shotgun across his lap. He said nothing, just peering out the window looking for the first sign of trouble. All ensconced, he eased the car into first and rolled quietly away.

FREE.

The first two of the escapees were brothers – John and Jim Steele. They were robbers – armed if necessary – and well known in the east end of the city. Their father, Andy Steele, was an infamous robber in the post-war years, the days when crooks applied a lot of imagination and initiative to their ploys. They had a young brother, Joe, who was rated by no one at that time for being too young and too inexperienced. But in later years it was Joe the world would come to know.

The third party was one Archie Steen, the same Archie Steen who was jailed in 1975 for the execution-style murder of John Stillie and attempting to kill Walter 'Toe' Elliot.

As soon as the cops heard the names they knew where to look – Glasgow's east end – and they knew who to go to, as well.

"Ah told you Ah'd give you four big ones," said McGraw to

his police handlers. "Now give me a week and Ah'll get them for ye."

"Good one, Tam," nodded Jimmy from the Serious Crime Squad. "But what do you want for them?"

"Want? Me?" McGraw sounded outraged, hurt. "Let's just say Ah want some credit. You know, in the future." As well as TC Campbell locked up out of the way, his trap shut, his suspicions silenced, McGraw was thinking to himself. That and a favour in return from the cops. A double earner – just the kind he liked.

One week later three men sat having a quiet chat and a pint in the Busby Hotel in the southside of Glasgow. It was a welcoming hotel, quiet and right on the outskirts of the city. As close to the countryside as you could get without actually leaving the town.

Bar staff thought the men polite, courteous and generous with their tanner tips. They had all arrived separately within ten minutes of each other and could come back any time they wanted. It looked like they were waiting for someone and that someone was late. Then the bar door burst in.

"POLICE," went up the roar. "ARMED POLICE. Put your hands on your head and lie on the floor. NOW." Dark uniforms carrying rifles and pistols swarmed into the bar. One of the three men looked like he was about to take them on, put up a fight, then changed his mind and slowly slid to the ground. With armed cops standing over the captives, their mates searched the toilets – both ladies and gents – behind the bar and then the kitchen and the rest of the hotel. Only a blind man wouldn't notice how disappointed they were when an hour later they left with the three men only.

"He wisna there? Fuck sakes. Ye weren't too early were you?" McGraw wasn't happy. He had nothing against the Steele brothers and Archie Steen – hadn't he allowed them a wee bit of freedom – it was TC Campbell he had planned to set up. TC Campbell he had inveigled into the meeting with the three.

"We were there all fucking day, watching from across the way and on every road to the place." The cop might be a double dealer with robbers like McGraw but he wasn't about to take any criticism of his work, especially not from rats like McGraw. "We even waited an extra twenty minutes. No fucking show."

"Fuck."

"Aye, fuck right enough, Tam."

"But ye'll still get him for it. Right?"

McGraw went on to explain his rationale. That everyone knew that TC was pally with John and Jim's father, Andy. That he liked their mother, Maggie, and had bailed her out a few times when young Joe had left her so short she couldn't afford her light or her rent. Everyone knew that.

They also knew TC hated hard drugs. That some dull eyed pub dwellers had Archie Steen down as an anti-drug avenger. That his targets, Stillie and Toe Elliot, were well reputed to be getting into smack early on. Planning to take over from Jim Rea. Everyone knew that.

"Anyway, it was fucking him," he ended in exasperation. "I should fucking know. I arranged for him to do the bastarding job though he doesn't know that."

TC Campbell was arrested and charged with the break out. A break out from any jail by the inmates themselves is serious. Masterminding the escape from the outside, getting keys and ropes then turning up hefting shotguns was much more serious. In the old days men convicted of that would have been sent to penal servitude. Australia maybe, to die in some snake-infested swamp. In 1980 they would just jail him for a long, long time during which the screws would treat him like dirt, would grind him under their boots and brutality.

At the High Court, TC Campbell pled not guilty. He wasn't there. He had an alibi. There was no evidence. No forensics. The Steeles and Steen were saying sod all. No one had actually seen him. A couple of screws had spotted a dark outline that could've been him but hadn't actually clocked him.

The cops and Crown were under pressure. They couldn't let anyone orchestrate an armed break out from the BarL jail. No one. They had to hurt someone badly and they didn't care if it was the guilty person or not. It was the message to be sent out that was the most important thing. The message was all. They knew TC was a bad one. Had been all his adult life. Whether it was him or not they just wanted him off the street. He'd do them nicely, thank you.

TC won his case and walked free.

Out in the east end TC's family and supporters gathered together for a wee celebratory party. In walked McGraw and Margaret full of cheer and congratulations. McGraw smiled and laughed all night, even buying some drinks. At one time he got up to sing a song. Everyone could see how happy he was that TC was free. And that was the point.

Inside McGraw was fuming. He wasn't finished with TC yet. Not finished at all.

17

COPS AND FISTICUFFS

The BarL Team continued as usual, escaping the arm of the law apart from occasional arrests of individual members, often as they went home from some raid. But no one arrested squawked to the cops or grassed on their mates so it was business as usual.

That included the occasional involvement of TC Campbell. No one knew that McGraw had tried to set TC up, especially Campbell himself. When McGraw started dropping him from the line-ups on robberies, others objected. After all he was a hard man with a cool head and sealed lips – perfect for the jobs. McGraw was over-ruled – belying his later claims to lead the team – and TC was in.

One day TC was in McGraw's house when the phone rang.

"FUCK SAKE," said McGraw returning the phone to its cradle. "That was Jimmy warning me that the Scottish Crime Squad are heading my way fast. The bastards are going to lift me."

"What for?" someone asked.

"For any-fucking-thing." The other men got up, ready to leave and fast. "Where yese going? Stay here. Be ma witnesses." They shook their heads and were off towards the door. "Come oan, ye cunts. The place is spotless. Cleaner than ma dick. They'll find nothin'."

"Aye they will," said TC. "They'll find whatever they're bringing with them to plant on ye and they're no about tae find me."

With McGraw still shouting the odds, TC and the other men headed out and off. While the others ran for cover as far away as they could, TC stood at a nearby corner, close enough to watch. He knew Jimmy worked for the Serious Crime Squad based in the west of Scotland but the Scottish Crime Squad had a national remit. The pair sometimes didn't see eye-to-eye and this seemed like one of those times.

Four unmarked cars came into the street at speed. Big men in dark suits piled out and into McGraw's house, not waiting for him to open the door. TC could hear shouting from the inside. McGraw shouting,

"Phone the Serious mob. They'll tell yese. Ah'm no tae be touched." Outside a cop with a plastic bag full of some powder went round McGraw's car trying to prise off a hubcap. They weren't listening. They were setting McGraw up with drugs.

The cop had just planted the goods when suits came bundling out the door. McGraw was shouting and bawling as he was led away by his arms. The closer he got to the motor the more he leaned back like some young kid refusing to go to the dentist's. Behind him Margaret was screaming at all the neighbours who had come out to see what the fuss was about,

"They're lifting Tam for nuttin. Pure fucking nuttin." Even from a distance TC knew that some of the neighbours would be struggling to hide their mirth. Tam McGraw arrested? That suited them just dandy.

Four other cars sped into the street. TC wondered if McGraw had put a call out to some of his workers and minders. Offered them big bucks to come rescue him. Almost right. It was the Serious Crime Squad led by the bold Jimmy.

Almost instantly Jimmy and the head honcho of the Scottish Crime mob started rowing.

"He's our man," shouted Jimmy. "We'll fucking take him."

"No according to ma warrant," growled the other bloke.

"You know what ye're doing here?" Jimmy demanded. "You are jeopardising a good contact."

"A fucking grass you mean and you let him off with too fucking much."

"He's our fucking man."

Jimmy had managed to wrestle hold of one of McGraw's arms

– the Scottish Crime Squad the other. The two detectives started to yank and pull – tug of war with McGraw as the rope. For some reason he didn't look too happy about that.

Who landed the first punch TC couldn't tell. Like any battle it seemed as if suddenly the sides went for each other. Cop versus cop. They were punching, kicking and head butting each other all over the place. In the middle stood McGraw, his jaw hanging open, a free man whose legs simply didn't work.

His neighbours didn't have the same problem. If there was polis punching to be done in their street they were going to give it a go. They all piled in, some pulling out fence posts, others fetching baseball bats or brush handles from their houses. It was a rammy big time between Scotland's most elite detective squads with the punters punching any man in a suit.

As suddenly as it had started it stopped. Jimmy and the Serious mob had won the day. They bundled McGraw into one of their motors and roared out of the street. As cavalry went, McGraw couldn't have hoped for better.

TC Campbell was laughing fit to pee himself. Cops having a public punch up – who would have thought – but there was a serious side to the half hour of fun. Suspicious as he might have been that McGraw was a grass, he now knew it as fact. As he strolled home he made himself a bet that McGraw would be charged with nothing. That the drugs planted in his car would be removed by the cops to wait for some similar dirty job in the future. The next day he won his bet.

As McGraw had been driven away in the cop car, he had sat and fumed. Out loud about the Scottish Crime Squad coming after him but inwardly about a piece of outstanding business. He had spotted TC Campbell watching the melee and listening to the raised voices of him and the cops. The man had seen and heard everything. Everyone knew that TC hated grasses and would spread the word about him around the city. If McGraw left it at that he was finished. He was going to have to do something about TC. Something extreme.

"I'm going to get you, Campbell," McGraw promised himself.

18

BUSINESS METHODS

Life just got better and better for McGraw – or so he thought.

Over the first couple of years of the 1980s he expanded his few taxis into Mac Cars, one of the biggest minicab firms in Glasgow. The method of expansion wasn't that deployed by your average businessman, unless average means violent.

A bit of blood and guts was very persuasive and cheap. He had learned this from his time in taking over the ice cream runs from a few old codgers or isolated young guys. Especially, if you used hired help who were short of a few bob for a debt to him on the moneylending front or to some dealer for their drugs. Employing such folk was to be a habit for the rest of his life. Sometimes it worked well and other times it would go disastrously wrong.

Small five-man cab firms were given offers they couldn't refuse.

The window came smashing in, shaking the cab controller out of her wits. It took her long seconds to realise she was okay but the building wasn't. The missile wasn't a boulder or a brick. It was a Molotov Cocktail and the dry wooden floor of the hut was already alight.

The fire ran in a line between her and the only door. Soon that wee hut would become her fiery coffin. Choking from the acid smoke that suddenly filled the place she radioed out to her boss. Her uncle and boss.

"Ah fuckin' told yese to listen to them," she half screamed, half sobbed into the mic. "These bastards aren't joking."

She was right. For weeks they had been visiting that place

making their threats. Car tyres had been slashed, windows smashed and her uncle had his face badly cracked on his way home one night. He had gone to the cops but nothing had happened. Not a thing. That seemed to be the way these days when you complained about McGraw. Still he wouldn't listen. Still he held out.

"Get out o' there, Shona. Get fuckin' out now." Her uncle had already turned his car around and was heading to the control office breaking the speed limits and crashing through red lights. The fare he had been on his way to pick up wasn't on his mind at all. What's a three quid hire into the city centre when your business has been torched and your favourite niece is still in there playing with fire?

When he arrived Shona was standing back from the burning hut. Her head bowed, her smoke blackened face lightened by two lines of tears running down her cheeks.

"They were in earlier tonight," she said so quietly he could hardly hear her, "looking for you." He put his arm round her but he couldn't, simply couldn't take his eyes from his life's work burning to the ground. "Ah said you had a night off. They didn't believe me. One," she sobbed, "one touched me here," she put a hand to her breasts, "and licked me with his tongue. His filthy tongue all the way up my face."

"Cunts." His voice broke with anger. "Filthy cunts."

"They hadnae left five minutes when this happened." Behind them the siren of a fire engine grew louder and louder. As it sped into the street they moved slowly back to give the officers the room to do their work. He knew it was too late now. Knew he couldn't afford to replace the radio. To buy a new place. Or even rent. "Promise me something." She turned and looked down at her wee uncle.

"Anything."

"Promise me you'll chuck this in."

"Oh aye, hen. Ah'm finished with this game."

Three weeks later she was signing on as unemployed and he found himself driving his car for Mac Cars like so many before and after him. He hated what he was doing but he needed a wage. Doesn't everyone?

Along with the expansion of Mac Cars, McGraw had continued to bully and brutalise people out of their ice cream runs. His tactics now included drivers who would simply move in on lucrative territories because they had no place else to go.

"Take over the round and make it pay and ye've got a job," McGraw would tell them. "No profit, no wages. Got it?" Most got it.

They'd pull up beside other vans and open for sales. Sweetie hungry kids wouldn't care to stand in a queue for the old van that they had been going to for years. Fag starved mothers went to the quickest place for ten Embassy Regal or two singles and two matches. Hungover fathers just wanted Irn Bru. Did it matter who they bought it from?

The established round owners were far from happy. Rows happened, fistfights broke out and the young drivers McGraw hired won more often than not. Sometimes the vans would find themselves nose to tail as they rushed to some key spot at some key time. First there got most of the trade so a race was on. Races that too often concluded with one van being shunted off the road by another.

Glasgow is a hard city full of hard men and women. Even ordinary men and women fighting for their livelihoods. When those intimidations didn't work, one day they'd find themselves serving a queue of punters when a car would drive up and out rushed masked men with baseball bats in their mitts. The customers scattered as the men set about the van and driver with the bats.

If that didn't persuade the round owner, a lone man with a shotgun would see to their van.

Complaints to the cops were useless. Most of this action was happening in the east end – the very place where every rozzer knew that McGraw was useful to them. Knew that if they messed with that man the Serious Crime Squad would be at their door and they could kiss their careers goodbye. He was never charged.

Some or all of that panoply of approaches worked with most drivers and as they moved on, McGraw's crew moved in and he got richer every week. None of that put McGraw off wanting more dosh still. That meant the robberies went on and he had to expand his businesses as fast as he could – under Margaret's guidance, of course. Then he got some news that would change his tack and, accidentally, open a door to see to TC Campbell.

19

NASTY MEN AND NINETY NINES

"This is serious, Tam," said one of McGraw's regular police contacts.

"Listen to him, Tam. He's telling ye how it is," said the other cop. The pair always worked as a double act and seemed to have only one case on their books – handling McGraw. They were such frequent visitors to McGraw's house and his pub, The Caravel, that locals had given them various nicknames – The Dicks, Willie and Wanker, Curly and Cockeye amongst others. We'll use one of the more polite ones – Laurel and Hardy, otherwise known as The Comedians after a TV show that had been very popular and very funny. They were a local joke in other words.

The pair had been blatant in their association with McGraw. There would be many days and nights they'd simply stand in The Caravel drinking beers and shorts all on the house. They'd get drunk and lippy with the locals, talking about who they could get done and what they could set up. Maybe they thought they were on safe ground in McGraw's pub but all they had done was upset the locals.

"The heavies from Northern Ireland are on your case," said Laurel.

"Whit the fucking terrorists?" asked McGraw.

"Naw, worse. It's the fucking security forces pissed off that somebody's sending a stack of postal orders to Loyalist groups. Thousands of pounds' worth every week."

"You can see their point, Tam," added Hardy trying to be reasonable. McGraw just looked at him as if he had dropped a loud smelly fart.

"They reckoned Strathclyde Polis were doing fuck all to stop them so they're here now."

"Out to get ye."

"Out to get the BarL Team."

"You're gonnae have to cool it for a bit. If these pricks catch ye they'll fucking shoot ye. It's a war they're fighting."

"One more thing, Tam," said Laurel. "They're saying that some of the postal orders are being cashed for the IRA. How the fuck did that happen? Are you playing both sides across there?"

"Me? No way, man. For fuck's sake – you know whose side Ah'm on. We're all on the same side." It was a dig at a Glasgow police tradition of only hiring Protestants. A dig that wasn't far from the truth even in 1984.

"You fucking sure?"

"Certain."

McGraw prayed that this news didn't slip out to people like Snaz. He had been made an honorary commander of the UDA for his fundraising. He'd go mental if he discovered McGraw had been greasing the palms of the other side. Pure mental.

Much as McGraw loved money he got the cops' point. What good is being rich if he was dead? The BarL Team were going to have to cease business for a while. But that didn't mean that he was going to stop making money. He would use the time to examine other markets he had been thinking about. Like smack. That had to be a good earner. Also, expand his legitimate enterprises. It was high time his ice cream vans took over more of the city.

When McGraw was explaining the situation to Drew Drummond and Snaz, they understood entirely but neither wanted to sit and do nothing. Drew was keen to get into pubs and clubs. For Snaz on the other hand it was ice cream vans. He wanted one that was top of the range.

"A Boxer, you mean. They are fucking classy," said McGraw.

"Cost you £15K to £20K though." That would do him fine but he wanted help in securing a round that would bring in the money and large. "I think I have the very place for ye," said McGraw.

Garthamlock as an area was a big earner for ice cream vans but was already well provided. The main seller was run by a popular and respected local woman, Agnes Lafferty née Campbell, the very sister of one TC Campbell. Agnes worked with the local community groups and had been determined to provide a quality, low cost service to the people. She only ever got a van after a local community group failed to get a licence to run one – a failure that had more to do with a couple of brown envelopes stashed with cash that McGraw had slipped to some of the key people.

As such Agnes' van wasn't related to the Marchetti Brothers who charged a fortune for their goods. Hers stocked up from any cash and carry or direct from the manufacturer where the prices were best and passed most of that saving on to her paying customers. Flogging Mars Bars at 15p rather than 22p was an approach that was attractive to folks mostly dependent on welfare benefits. Especially when the same mark down was applied to everything else she sold.

In the area Agnes' main competition came from Penny Mitchell whose family ran Marchettis. Old Penny didn't like Agnes' work at all so Marchettis moved in six vans to try and crowd her out. They failed.

Next they went to the cops with an allegation – Agnes Lafferty was selling stolen goods. She had to be to sell at those low prices. When the cops pounced on her – they knew whose sister she was – Agnes calmly showed them all the receipts and the prices marked by the manufacturers.

As a long term strategy, the Marchettis left one extra van on the area with the task of hassling Agnes Lafferty. The round was worth a lot of money and well worth that extra expense. This van was driven by Andrew 'Fat Boy' Doyle, entirely the wrong young man for the job.

Doyle was a big guy but a bit of a gentle giant. He was eighteen years old, affable, hard working but rather than hassle Agnes he'd stop his van alongside hers and have a wee blether. The Marchetti crew was furious.

One man had seen all this aggro and decided there was room to nudge the others out. McGraw would have that Garthamlock round whatever it took.

McGraw's drivers were given the line, "Get into Garthamlock and push that fat bastard out." He was a young guy, no fighter and on his own. What was he going to do? Accept all their hassle for the measly wage that Marchetti would be paying him? No chance.

Every chance. Doyle might have been easy going but he was moral. He had been given a job and he'd do that job no matter what anyone else did or said.

Though Andrew Doyle didn't sell many 99s it worked well enough for him to be asked by Marchettis to cover Ruchazie, another lucrative round and the area he lived in. Locals were more likely to buy from a popular local man. There would be independent competitors, he was warned, but if he could make the round pay well, it was his.

Ruchazie brought all of the old tricks back from that other mob. They blocked him while one of their vans sold to the punters. They shouted at him. Jumped on him at night after he'd parked his van, kicked seven shades out of him. Sent men with baseball bats after him and his van. Everything. One night McGraw slipped a local guy a tenner to sneak into the Marchetti parking area and shoot up Doyle's motor. He did. Or he thought he had but ice cream vans all looked the same. He blasted the wrong van.

The next day Doyle found himself entering Ruchazie. As he did so, a group of two Boxer ice cream vans were heading towards him blocking the road. They were bigger, brighter, faster and much, much newer than his old motor. No problem with that.

Doyle hit the accelerator and headed straight towards them, a wide grin splitting his face. He didn't know who these guys were and he didn't much care. He'd taken enough rap from other drivers trying to bully him. Only feet away, the two Boxer vans veered off the road. The tyres of one caught in a ditch and it was sent spilling on to its side.

It might be brand new but now it was badly bashed and was going to cost a small fortune to fix. The next day up in C Hall in Barlinnie, Snaz Adams was going to get some bad news. He was being held pending some ice cream war charges from Castlemilk but now he had more to worry about. His brand new van was all bashed to hell.

Enough was enough. That night McGraw called one of his taxi drivers and asked him to take him for a drive.

"We're going for a wee visit up the road to Ruchazie," he said. "Somebody is about to get a wake up call."

20

A JUNKY PROMISE

"You boys want a lift?" The taxi had pulled over as the two young men had waved at it. The driver was Chris, a young local guy they both knew and hoped he'd give them a freebie ride to their home patch. Trouble was there was a punter in the cab.

"How ye doing, lads?" asked the older passenger – a guy with a familiar face in his early thirties.

"Aye fine," one had mumbled.

"Jump in, we'll give you a lift." Not a paying passenger then. He had a face they recognised all right, a face they should know but they were heroin addicts and had been chasing the smack for two or three years. That's why they were there, on Bankend Street in Ruchazie, scoring some heroin off a dealer. Heroin they couldn't wait to get pumped into their veins when they got home. Heroin ruled their lives. How would they know the name of that familiar face? "You guys fancy earning a few quid?" the familiar face asked. "Young guys are always short of a bit of readies, eh?"

"Aye," they mumbled, not lying. They had to steal to get the ten pounds each for the deals they had just scored and tomorrow would be more of the same old same old.

"There's a wee job that needs doing," said Chris as he steered the car through the Glasgow streets. Outside on the pavement young kids were larking about hours after they should have been in bed. Two drunks were standing holding on to each other with one arm, waving the others in the air as if they were about to fight. They'd be talking football, though. Three young women in

72

full make up and skirts not reaching much of their thighs strode down the road heading for the nearest bar to catch a couple of rounds and maybe pull some boys. "Just a wee torch job on a door. Fuck all really." Chris wasn't underplaying the task. Setting front doors alight had become almost routine as a warning to people all over Glasgow. So routine most of the big petrol companies had banned the sale of petrol in cans. No matter your motor might have run out and you were stranded – a ban was a ban. No one ever got hurt. Well, hardly ever.

"Twenty quid," said the familiar face. "Between the pair of yese like." The offered wages weren't an accident. Chris had spotted the two young men earlier as he had driven into Bankend Street. He was on the lookout for someone who might be up to torching a door and he knew that pair. Had told the familiar face they were junkies probably out to score some smack. Familiar face had looked into the heroin business. He knew that a tenner was the standard deal. So there he was offering their next score for a job that would take ten minutes.

"Aye," mumbled one of the junkies, "that sounds good."

"Ye'll do it then?" asked Chris.

"Sure, aye," they both nodded.

"Pick you up back here at midnight then right?"

"Aye, aye."

Outside on the pavement the two young men stopped for a chat.

"What you think?" asked one.

"Ah think Ah'm for my bedroom to pump this lot into my body."

"Naaaaw." His mate sounded scunnered like he had bothered to tell him something so obvious. Across the way, a group of teenage boys strolled, their clothes all tight denims, baggy t-shirts and dark blouson jackets all of different colours but a uniform all the same. Then there was a meat cleaver carried by one and a long, old-fashioned bayonet by another. He prayed they were going to some battle and not looking for two weak junkies to torment.

They might be much younger but team handed they were killers. He watched them carefully as he went on, "About the job? Are you up for it?"

"Aye right."

"Ye're no doing it?"

"No fucking chance. Ah'm a junky no a jakie."

"Aye, Ah know. At fucking midnight, man, Ah'll be fucking zombified to a soundtrack of Talking Heads." The pair of them nodded and threw weak smiles. The teenage team had passed them now and were turning a corner out of sight. That didn't mean the two were safe. These teenagers liked to play tricks.

"Who was that other cunt in the motor, by the way?"

"Him? Ah couldnae get his name tae start with but now Ah have. That's McGraw. Every fucker knows him."

"Aye, a fucking gangster but."

"Aye, even though the cunt dresses like some fucking down and out."

"Aye, the scruffy fuck eh?" And the young men laughed at McGraw. "And a polis grass."

"Fucking too true." He spat on the ground in disgust. In the distance they heard the roar of boys' voices, angry and aggressive, heading into some bloody battle. There would be some poor bastard about to get hurt. They didn't care. At least it wasn't them.

"A killer?"

"Whit?

"Does he murder fuckers?

"Ah don't think so. Ah cannae think of any."

The night was yet young.

"The little bastards," growled McGraw as the car waited at the meeting spot at midnight and the two young junkies didn't show.

"Well, I warned you they were smackheads," said Chris reasonably. "Probably too stoned up tae care or remember."

"Fucking drugs, man, who'd do them eh? Just a bloody waste."

"Aye and the pricks that deal them eh."

"Lowest of the low, Ah'd say."

"Aye."

"Ah'd shoot the cunts." McGraw was sounding disgusted and venomous like he meant every word. Like he had done before about heavy drugs. Like he would do again even as his troops were selling smack on the streets.

"Where do you want to go now then?" Chris asked. "Just chuck it for the night?"

"Not a chance," McGraw rolled down the car window and spat on the pavement, dipped his hand in his pocket and pulled out his fags and lighter. He smoked a lot but tension and anger made him smoke more. "The job has to be done tonight," he said still raging inside. "Let's head back towards The Caravel. Pick up some boys tae do it for us." Chris sighed with relief. He didn't mind driving men to do this kind of torching job but he wasn't sure of ever doing it himself. Fire was dangerous, was what he thought. Too dangerous. "The arseholes will be well asleep by the time we get back," added McGraw as Chris steered the car towards The Caravel. "But no for long eh," he cackled at his own joke spewing fag smoke into the air. "No for fucking long."

21

THE FIRE

"Sorry, I can't sell you that," said the teenage girl working in the petrol station.

"Whaaat?" The young man eyed her belligerently like she had just insulted him.

"It's a company policy," she blushed. After all it was around 1am in Ruchazie, one of the roughest areas of the east end. God knows who she might be dealing with or what he might do next.

"How no?"

"I don't know," she lied. "It's just a company rule." Her boss, a young businesslike man, had just moved up beside her, wary that she was about to get grief.

"What's going on?" he asked so she explained that all she was doing was keeping the company rules, something that he himself had drummed into her a few months ago and regularly since. It was all about the number of front doors that were getting torched, they both knew that, and that the company had been asked by the cops to impose the ban telling them to phone them if a genuine breakdown case came in to buy a can of fuel. They would sort it out. An old Escort Popular car sat and waited for the young man. Inside were two other young men and an older guy in his thirties. The garage boss cast his eye over them and recognised the older one. Everyone in the east end of Glasgow knew that face. It was McGraw.

"I did right didn't I?" the girl asked.

"Aye, but this time it's okay."

"What?"

"Just sell them the can of petrol but," he said without explanation. She did as her boss told her in spite of being intrigued as to why. He was her boss after all. What harm could there be? She would soon learn.

"Right, ye know what to do?" McGraw, the man paying the pipers, asked.

"Aye, of course, it's no the first time." So, he knew. They had torched a couple of other doors for him and did okay. Created a right blaze. Almost killed the poor sods he was leaning on. Risky but it did the trick, all right, and that's all he cared about.

"Go on then and hurry the fuck up."

At the top of the stairs the men found the right door. These bloody flats in Bankend Street all looked the same. But they got it all right, the one where the Doyles lived. It had to be this one. But there were two doors right next to each other. Which was the right one?

"Fuck it," one whispered. "Let's do one and get the fuck out of here. It's too fucking dodgy hanging around with this." He lifted the can of petrol.

"Nah. Let's do both."

The gallon of petrol was poured over the doors, its acid smell filling the air. One match struck, lit, dropped and they went up with a whoosh. The men were out of there and fast.

Down on the street they ran to the Escort as quickly and quietly as they could. Chris, the driver, reversed it away and stopped, the engine still running. These had been his orders. McGraw wanted to make sure the flames were starting. Wanted no mistakes. Chris didn't like this bit. What if the cops came by on some late night patrol? What if some nosy old neighbour spotted them and made a call? What if . . .

"What the fuck?" Flames were licking through the roof of the modern tenement. That wasn't meant to happen. It was only the door that was meant to go up. "Get the fuck out of here," McGraw ordered. Chris didn't hesitate. Reversing at speed he turned fast and skidded round the L-bend that made up Bankend Street and right into the side of another car. "Keep moving," screamed McGraw, the boss. But there was no life in the motor. It had stalled. Or Chris was just too nervous on the gas pedal and flooded it. They had picked up an old car just for this job, now they were paying the price. Worse, the driver of the other car was coming to get them. They were out of the Escort and on their toes with him not far behind.

Up closes, over fences and walls, through back closes the men ran in four different directions. The pursuer tried hard but he was nowhere near them. He'd had a great night out with his mate and their girlfriends. A great night that didn't leave him much energy for a mental case hunt through Ruchazie. Making his way back to Bankend Street he spotted him. The older guy with the familiar face had doubled back, got in the car and was driving away fast.

"Ye fucking bastard," he roared as the car sped past him. "Ah fucking know you. Ah'll fucking get yese." He swore that he would. Not only did he recognise McGraw, he knew one of the younger blokes signed on at the DSS on the same day as him. "Ah'll fucking get yese all right." Then he heard a crackle and a snap. Looking up he saw it. The roof of the flat ablaze and flames flickering behind the windows. He knew the family who lived in there. That was the Doyle place. There were stacks of them and a wee baby. "Get tae a phone, and get the fire brigade," he roared at his mate as he dashed towards the flat entrance. Fighting the smoke that ripped his lungs and blinded his eyes he made it to six feet from the door. It was blazing and farting in the fire, the yellow and blue tongues of fire flickering out at him, trying to lick him in. He couldn't get near.

On the other side of the door the Doyle family had wakened to a ceiling and walls of fire. Fear and panic gripping their guts they fought to the door only to be beaten back by the heat. Christine got her eighteen-month-old son, Mark, on the floor where he could breathe and lay over him, protecting him from the white hot cinders and falling timbers that were thumping hard and hot on her naked back. It would cost her her life. James Doyle senior got to a window and forced it open, the searing heat of the glass and wood stripping the skin from his hands. As the window fell open the flames inside flurried up, moving stronger and stronger. After several long minutes fire engines screamed into the street, ladders were raised, hoses started spraying water and a rescue party was sent up. It was too late for Christine and Anthony. It was soon going to be too late for four others including Andrew Doyle.

On 16 April 1984 a fire was started in Bankend Street. It was going to burn for years.

McGraw ordered that fire to be lit, many people knew that. But who would pay the price? And why?

22

SLEEPLESS NIGHTS
AND WATCHFUL DAYS

McGraw couldn't sleep. It was a recent habit of his to sit up at night worrying about some deal, fretting over some ploy and if he wasn't careful it was going to become a habit for life. That night, more than most, he had a lot to worry about.

That door was torched too much. What the hell could've made it go up like that? After he had retrieved the Escort from Bankend Street, with that other driver shaking his fist at him, he had driven home fast, stopping only to pick up Chris. He couldn't see the other two. They'd be all right. He'd have to see them later but now, early that morning, he had something else to do. Something he always did and that morning it was more important than ever.

"You all right, Tam?" asked another man in the shop seeing his face gone chalk white.

"Eh? Aye, Ah'm just feeling a bit hungover, know."

"Aw aye, Ah know all right," the bloke laughed and went on to buy his fags, rolls and a bottle of Irn Bru. McGraw wasn't hungover, he was petrified.

He had just read the *Daily Record* and it was full of one story – the terrible fire that had killed two people with a baby dying later and three others in a serious state. He hadn't ordered a murder. He'd ordered a warning. That was all. Just a warning but three people had already died and maybe more to come. If he was caught he'd spend his life in jail. Not just life the way the courts meant it but real life, his total life till he died.

McGraw hated jail. The places frightened him, removed those bits of power and protection he had in the outside world and made him vulnerable. Anybody with a jail-made blade could take him out especially if he got done for killing several folk including that baby. Cons hate child killers. For the rest of his life? He'd have to stop that and stop that now.

Out in the street in Ruchazie a car horn went beep-beep-beep. Then beep-beep-beep. The young junky from the night before had just wakened, had his morning hit and was pulling himself together.

"Go see who the noisy bugger is eh?" ordered his father. "Tell him tae shut it or Ah'll shut it for him."

Out on the street, Chris the taxi driver was sitting in his cab, his hand on the horn. When he spotted the junky he rolled down his window.

"See last night, wee man? You didn't see us right? We weren't here. You don't know us and we don't know you, right?"

"Right," his voice croaked into action.

"It better be right mind," Chris warned. "Certain people know about you. Will come looking for ye."

"It's no problem. I saw SFA."

"Right," and with that he drove off, his orders from McGraw duly carried out. The other junky had already had the same warning. Those two better keep their traps shut.

Wandering back into the living room and pouring himself a cup of tea, the young junky puzzled over what Chris was fussing about.

"Would you look at that," spat his father. "There are some right animals about." He threw across the *Daily Record*. The front page answered his question. Terrible fire in Bankend Street. Three dead. Three others fighting for life. The junky came out in a sweat. He was leaving Glasgow that day. That very day and he might never come back.

"Ah've got the word on that fire for ye," said McGraw to Laurel later that day.

"Good man."

"Ye know TC Campbell bought an ice cream van two years ago?"

"Aye."

"And his sister runs one?"

"So far ye're telling us nothing at all. Get to the point eh."

"That Agnes caused grief for the Marchettis in Garthamlock and the boy given the job of keeping her under control was . . ." McGraw stopped speaking and took his time picking up his fag. Inside he was queasy, sick, terrified but outside he was doing a good job of looking and sounding cool – so he thought.

"Want help with that?" Hardy stretched out his hand, flicking his lighter into action. McGraw was shaking all over the place. The man could be a bit paranoid but today he was a total mess. The two cops wondered what had upset him. For a man who set hard men on innocent folk to terrorise them it had to be something really bad.

"Andrew Doyle."

"Fuck sake."

"Fuck sake right enough," McGraw went on, "and there's more. TC's close to his family, especially Agnes. Didn't like Doyle's attitude. Was out to get him. And . . ."

"When TC gets on your case you're in big trouble," Hardy finished the sentence spot on.

"We'll get on to him fast," said Laurel and the two cops rose to leave. "It's high time we jailed that bastard again."

23

AT ALL COSTS

They drowned and died as they lay in hospital beds – terrible, agonising, slow deaths.

The three Doyle men were so badly burned in their house fire that they needed the heaviest duty painkillers the hospital could give them. As well as dulling some of the pain, the drugs reduced their lungs' ability to work, to clear out the fluids that gathered there. Slowly the fluid built up till they could breathe no more, drowning in their own fluids.

It was now six deaths – the biggest single murder in modern times.

People and the newspapers were raging. It was number one item in the news, on the TV with regular radio updates. Politicians spoke out in disgust. Holy men raged in churches. Columnists argued that when they were caught the death penalty should return – just for them. Someone had killed six innocent people by the stroke of one match and that someone must be caught. If the police had felt under pressure before, this time they were in danger of being buried.

"Get a result, any fucking result," senior officers raged at the investigating team. "How many troops do ye need? Fine, we'll draft every man and woman in from every division."

Strathclyde Police had been created nine years before to make one of the biggest police forces in the world. Now the crime rate in Ayr, and Motherwell, Airdrie and Greenock or even the other badlands of Glasgow would be ignored. Catching the Doyles' killer was all they had to do. But they knew who they were out to get.

"You weren't meant to sell them petrol in a can," the CID man said looking down at the young girl.

"Ah know," she replied feeling scared, nervous.

"So why did ye?" the other detective demanded.

"Ah told ye. My boss said I should."

"We'll be seeing him later."

"Well, he's no here," she said in a quiet voice.

"When's he on then?"

"He's no on. He's not here. I think he left."

"What?" The cops eyed each other. This was happening too often in the Doyle murder investigation. "Where did he go to?"

She shrugged and replied, "No one knows. He just seems to have left."

"But he was here that night?"

"Aye."

"And now he's no."

"Naw."

"So it's just your word then eh."

"Aye, but Ah'm trying to help," she almost bleated, interpreting their tone as accusing her of something. Something she hadn't done. "Ah'd do anything to help catch that murderer. Anything." Like most of the rest of the caring world she was angry and horrified by the murder of the Doyle family. She had contacted the cops to tell them about the men buying a gallon can of petrol that night so close to Bankend Street. Now they seemed to be giving her a bad time. She had told them about the Escort, the bit of its registration number she could recall and the boss getting her to break company rules when he saw who was there. "He recognised the older guy I think," she added. "He looked kind of familiar."

"Would this be him?" One cop showed her a photograph. A mugshot taken from a police file. She held the picture in both hands and looked at it intently.

"That's Mr Campbell." There was shock in her voice.

"Aye, Thomas Campbell. Some folk know him as TC," one cop replied.

"How do ye know him?" the other detective asked, suspicion dripping through his voice. People around here didn't like the police. She might be sweet, almost innocent looking, and seemed helpful but had she been set up?

"My sister babysits for him and his wife sometimes. She stays up the same close. He's a nice man. Pays her a bit extra."

"So, was it him?"

"Him?" Shock shook her tones. "Naw, no way was it him."

"Are ye sure?"

"Positive. I recognised the face of the older guy but I didn't know him. If it was Mr Campbell I would've said hello."

"So could you describe this Mystery Man then?"

"Aye, I think so. Kind of tall, skinny, with fairish hair. Might've been dyed though. Awfy scruffy dressed. Like he was broke."

"Right, but you're sure it wasn't Campbell?" She looked down at the picture of TC Campbell with his dark hair, dark eyes, straight back and knew he wore fashionable gear. Casual but smart was how he dressed. What part of her description did the cop not get?

"Ah'm sure."

"Right but we'll need ye to think about it for a couple of days and we'll come back."

"Fine but maybe you could bring other pictures, you know. Of guys that look like the one I saw."

"Aye, maybe."

Two days later they came back all right and carried a picture. The same picture of TC Campbell. One week later the same. A few days later the same. It was like they were shouting at her THIS IS THE MAN. More and more she felt as if she and the cops were on different sides while all she wanted to do was help catch the Doyles' killer. She might be young, they might scare her but she knew what and who she saw and it wasn't TC Campbell. She kept telling them that and they kept coming back till her head was spinning.

"Right round the corner from the fire," the driver told the police. "They were in a hurry. Like they were running away from something. Took that corner like banshees and straight into the side of my motor." The detective eyed the man suspiciously. He was local, his car wasn't worth much and he might well be working a scam for some insurance claim.

"And you say you recognised two of the men."

"Aye, one from the dole when Ah'm signing on. Don't know his name like but if you come with me next time Ah'll point him out to you."

"Good," the cop said with no enthusiasm. "And the older guy, this'll be him eh?" He showed him a picture, the same mugshot of TC Campbell he'd shown the young woman.

"Him, naw. It was McGraw. Tam McGraw I keep telling yese."

"It was very late, right?"

"Aye, about two in the morning."

"Dark eh?"

"Aye, dark as fucking night." The driver wondered if the cop was trying to be sarcastic or something.

"And the lights in Bankend Street aren't that good eh? Bit hard to see Ah'd say."

"Naw, naw. Where they skelped my motor was right under a street lamp. I saw them aw right. As clear as day."

"Could ye look at the picture again, please."

"What for? Ah've told ye it was not him." He spoke the last four words slowly.

"Just the same." The cop pushed the picture forward.

"It's time you pricks got a grip," the man stormed. "What's all this with this other bloke? Don't ye want tae catch the killers? Like you're taking the piss or something." He stood up and was heading out of the interview room.

"Don't you want to report the damage to your car?"

"Ma motor? Nah, it isn't worth that much. Ah'll get a mate to fix it." He was up and off. The cops wouldn't be going back to him that often. Wouldn't be going to the dole with him. He was an angry man who couldn't be persuaded. No point in wasting their time.

As Strathclyde cops swarmed all over the east end of Glasgow, TC Campbell got on with his life. They hadn't been near him – not yet – but an old pal was about to set him right.

The man turned up out of the blue. He lived down in Greenock, miles from Glasgow on the Firth of Clyde. Not a huge distance away but far enough to see itself as a different community for most things including crime. Except this time.

"They just picked me up, Tommy. You know how it is. Could've been for a few things." TC nodded his head. He knew the guy's form from when they met in jail. He had been doing a ten stretch for gang rioting, the other bloke less for an armed robbery. "At first it seemed that way then they started talking about Glasgow. Like the last time I'd been here and so on." Tommy dragged deep on his roll up, listening and being patient, knowing the guy would reach his point in good time. Outside on the street an ice cream van's familiar chimes twinkled through the air. "Then they asked when I'd last seen you. Ah told them. Then they said that we could come to an arrangement, them and me. That if I could tell them about you and the Doyle murders this other matter would get dropped." The guy was heading to court soon on another robbery charge and was looking at years in the jail if found guilty. "They wanted me to set you up, Tommy. Ah told them to fuck off."

He was the first to visit TC Campbell but he wasn't the last. Most were friendly, warning TC that the cops were out to get them, others seemed friendly but were on someone else's side. McGraw was going to see to that.

A guy called Jimmy paid him a visit with a very generous offer. A bag of powder, pure heroin he said, worth three grand but TC's for a mere £600. Then as much more of that as he wanted, all at the same price. The deal refused, Jimmy was kindly but firmly shown the door.

From a side bedroom TC watched him through binoculars. As he walked into an industrial estate, a car pulled up. Inside were three members of the Serious Crime Squad, all familiar faces to anyone who knew McGraw. There was a brief conversation, the bag of powder handed over then the car pulled away. Seconds later a different car pulled in full of the hulking breadths of four top UDA supporters. Jimmy got in and the car drove off. Now TC knew they really were out to take him off the streets.

One guy came into his house a few days later to tell him, "There's only one name the cops are saying in the east end right now – TC Campbell. They're going to get you for those murders, Tommy, one way or another. Take my advice – disappear."

Tommy Campbell didn't disappear. He knew the cops had an old score to settle with him. That small matter of the Steeles' and Archie Steen's break out from Barlinnie that they still believed he was guilty of whatever the High Court said. Glasgow cops had long, bitter memories but the murder of six innocent people? Him?

The next day TC Campbell was arrested and charged with the murders. While he argued his case, outraged they could even have suspected him of such an atrocity, out in familiar territory someone else was getting bad news.

"It's one thing charging and arresting him, Tam, it's another making it stick." The detective Laurel was looking at McGraw square on. That look he used when he was going to be doing some straight talking. "That set-up with the smack was a good try but it didn't work. So hard luck," he continued. "We're going tae need some more assistance than that. We have to. It's not us in charge of this, Tam. It's Charlie Craig passing it on to Goldilocks."

"Goldilocks?"

"Aye, DS Norrie Walker. Flavour of the month in the CID. He's been told to get a conviction or he'll be back in uniform." McGraw dragged on his cigarette and threw Laurel a sour look. He didn't like the sound of this. "More help from someone we trust."

"That's you, Tam," said Hardy. "You're going to have to go to jail."

24

WHO YOU KNOW

The air in the exercise yard was cold and still. It was as if the weather felt the pain and the sadness of the men who walked step by slow step, their hearts heavy with their grief. After all, they were the most hated men in the country.

TC Campbell wasn't alone. It seemed that the cops had pulled in a small army of suspects, including his brother-in-law, Shadda, his nephew Thomas and down in the women's jail, his sister Agnes. That last one hurt him bad. Of all the people who wouldn't be involved in crime, Agnes was top of his list. Surely they all couldn't, wouldn't have been there that night torching one wee door. It was as if the cops had cast a wide net and pulled in everyone who knew anyone who had any connection with one man – TC Campbell.

What the hell were the police up to? No one knew.

"Nah, we'll be okay," offered one. "We didn't do it right but the bastards have to show that they're doing something to solve the killings. Anything."

"You think that's good enough?" asked TC. "Trust in the Scottish justice system?" His voice was rising, sounding angry, frustrated. "Are you off yer nut?"

"Tommy is absolutely right." It was the guy walking behind them – McGraw – like them remanded on charges to do with the Doyles' deaths. "If we don't work together and try and make sense of all this – well, we're fucked." There were some in that group – Shadda Lafferty, TC's brother-in-law, who didn't like McGraw.

Tamby Gray, who hated him. And others like Gary Moore who didn't rate him one way or another. But why should they bother about that now? McGraw, like them, was arrested for the most heinous murders and, like them, was saying he was innocent. If they could be lifted for something they didn't do, then why not McGraw too?

"What are they saying to you?" one asked McGraw. It was the question he was waiting for. He kicked a stone at his feet, then turned and faced the guy. Three others stood around listening. "They claim that I would've wanted Andrew Doyle dead. Claimed that I was trying to muscle in on his territory and chose him as a weak link." He scooped a packet of cigarettes out of his pocket and offered them around the group. They all took one. A real fag in jail is worth a fortune and a welcome break from the endless roll ups they all smoked. But they knew McGraw was worth a good few quid with his ice cream vans, taxis and whatever else.

"Bastards are saying that to me as well," offered Shadda Lafferty. "Because he hassled Agnes in Garthamlock they claim I was out to get him." The others nodded, listening intently.

"They want me to own up on driving the motor that night," said Gary Moore, a well-known car freak, driver and thief. "That night I was a lot of things. Stoned out of my skull. On a wee job to do with kitchen units and that. And with a new piece of skirt."

"So what's new, you dirty bastard," the men all laughed knowing that Gary was almost as keen on women as he was on motors. Almost.

So the conversations went on and on over days. The men would get pulled away separately for interview by the cops and return to their cells many hours later, worn out, exhausted and very angry. They needed to talk then, get the whole nonsense off their chest. They couldn't trust anyone else – not even other prisoners. BarL is full of people who'd sell their grannies for a tenner. Imagine the temptation of making up some story about the men accused of the Doyle murders. With each other they were all safe, or so they thought.

A few weeks into their remand, McGraw was driven out of the jail for interview by the cops, not at the usual Baird Street where everyone else was interviewed but Orkney Street in Govan. An old-style police station built round a central square that allowed prisoners to be dropped off or picked up away from the public's gaze.

In a private room, DS Norrie Walker was waiting for him along with his boss, Charlie Craig, and a young woman with a thick writing pad and a bundle of pencils.

"This is our memory," said Craig nodding at the young woman. "But don't worry, all the papers will be destroyed as soon as we're done with them." The room smelled mouldy and reeked of old tobacco smoke that had collected there over many years. McGraw decided to add to it and lit up his own fag.

"Do well," said Walker, "and we'll give you half an hour alone with Margaret." McGraw's eyes lit up at that.

"You promise?" he asked.

"We want line and verse of what each of them are saying, especially Campbell. Give us that and we'll send a motor for your wife."

McGraw didn't need to be asked twice. He started to speak, making innocent comments seem sinister and adding many things on straight from his imagination. Everything he said was cosseted by what he knew about each and every one of his fellow accused. Listening to street gossip and story telling was proving useful still. Especially about TC Campbell. He wasn't going to let him walk back out again.

By the time McGraw had finished he had given the cops enough information to have every accused, apart from Agnes, charged with all sorts of crimes from stoning ice cream vans, beating up Andrew Doyle to paying other mobs to do exactly the same thing. He knew he was on easy ground. The Marchetti crew had been boasting about how they had gone to the newspapers with their version of events. The tales they told added up to the same answer – Ice Cream Wars. Whenever these guys went to trial there would be anger in

91

the hearts of almost everyone in that courtroom. Fighting wars over ice cream vans was an outrage. It was wee kids who queued up for cones, wasn't it. They'd hang the accused out to dry.

"Very good, Tam," said Norrie Walker. "Very full. But there's just one thing missing."

"What's that?" McGraw was angry. He could talk and talk but even his throat was sore from the hours of giving them the low down. What else could they expect?

"The murders." Walker spoke quietly, holding McGraw's eyes in a steady stare. "We need to get one or more of them on murder."

"What ye want me to do about it?" McGraw demanded. "Beat the fuckers into a confession?"

"If necessary." And Walker left the room.

McGraw sat there stunned and angry. How much did they expect of him? Then again if Campbell did go down for the Doyle murders he'd be away for decades. Maybe he'd die in jail. Then the idea hit him.

"NEED TO SPEAK TO WALKER AGAIN," he bawled at the cop standing outside the door of his room. "It's urgent. I know the very man he wants."

A few days later, the men charged with the Doyle offences had something new to talk about. McGraw had been taken away for a police interview the day before and never returned. Released by the Procurator Fiscal, the screws had said. All charges dropped. Maybe that's what you get for having a few quid to throw at lawyers, some wondered. But there was more. There were new guys on the charges.

Young Joe Steele had been arrested. No surprise there for TC Campbell. TC didn't know Joe that well and what he knew he didn't like. But he knew Joe's mother and father and they were okay. As for his older brothers, John and Jim, well he had been tried for allegedly breaking them out of Barlinnie. Yet Joe was the least of their concerns.

"Seems like there's another guy arrested," said one. "Somebody called John Campbell. No relation of yours, Tommy?"

"Nah," he replied, "unless ma Da had been getting around a bit more than we thought." The men laughed. Yet none of them knew this John Campbell so worried not at all about what he might be charged with, how he was in the pot. "Oh aye and some young guy called Billy Love." They looked at each other and shrugged their shoulders. A couple had heard of Billy Love but still that didn't help them much. They wouldn't have long to wait.

"Are you Tommy Campbell?" the young guy asked the next day.

"Aye, that's me," said Tommy bracing himself for an attack. The newspapers had been full of the Doyle murders and those arrested. The Ice Cream Wars stories raged and then there were the deaths of those poor folk and that wee baby. TC knew that most folk would see them as being guilty already and more than one con would want to hurt them. No attack came.

"How do ye do?" he said. "Ah'm John Campbell. One of your co-accused." John Campbell had just been arrested and had no copies of the charges. When TC gave him a look at his copy the young guy laughed out loud. "There's no problem with this lot," he said. "Ah know exactly where Ah was on every date."

"Aye, but so do the rest of us, man," said TC.

"Maybe but Ah'm safe as houses," John Campbell went on. "Ah was in the clink. Banged up along with Billy Love. Their own records will prove Ah'm no their man."

"Is that what happened to Billy Love then?" someone asked.

"What ye mean?"

"Well he's a free man. Word is he's done a deal."

"Billy? Ha," John Campbell laughed. "He'll have done some deal all right. He's got a wee habit ye know. But he'll be sound. Turn round and bite the bastarding cops. You'll see."

In the kitchen of his flat in Barlanark, McGraw was sitting at a table in front of a steaming plate of his favourite meal – mince and mashed tatties.

"Ah fucking hate that place, Mags," he said of prison. "Hate it worse every time."

"Ah know, Tam, but why did the boys have ye in there anyway?" she replied.

"The Doyle deaths aren't really their shout, ye know. Too serious." How much more serious can you get than the Serious Crime Squad, some eavesdroppers might wonder. "And between you and me, Ah wanted to help anyway. Ah mean, Mags, that poor wee baby eh?" She nodded her agreement.

"Is there any word about the case? Ye know. Are things moving on?"

"They're moving on all right," he nodded as he ate and spoke. "Just between you and me eh, seems somebody heard them talking about the fire. Said it was only meant to be a frightener." McGraw winked at his wife.

"Fuck sake," she sighed in disbelief.

"Aye, as good as a confession." He chewed and nodded. "They are well fucked now."

25

COPS OR CONS

McGraw was finished with the Doyle trial as a suspect but he wasn't finished with the trial. That would be too much like trust.

First stop he went round to the guys who had lit the fire that night.

"I think it's best if you two lived some place out of Glasgow," he said. "There's no point in making it easy for the cops eh? Fuck knows who spotted you that night." That didn't please the two guys that much. Glasgow was where the big money could be made. "Look, I'll make it worth your while." McGraw handed them two bankrolls of money. More money than they had ever seen before, never mind owned.

"That's good," said one of the men, "but what about the future?"

"What about the fucking future?" McGraw asked.

"Well, this will help us but you don't think it'll keep us forever eh?" They wanted an annual payment but their negotiating position was weak. What were they going to do? Go to the cops and put themselves in for multiple murder?

"We've taken a bit of advice," said the other.

"You've fucking what?"

"Don't worry. He's no going to blab."

"But we thought we should," said the other.

"Who the fuck from?" McGraw demanded. The two men looked at each other.

"Frank McPhie," one replied. McGraw's face went ashen. McPhie was a serious player who would drop him with a bullet or even shop him to the cops in a blink. Worse, he had been known to do some work for Arthur Thompson, The Godfather. There was a man McGraw did not want to cross. "You know, The Iceman."

"Ah fucking know who McPhie is," McGraw snarled.

That day the payment was increased and the agreement struck that a similar payment would be made every year. One of the men moved to Lanarkshire near Hamilton. The other headed east, to Fife. McGraw had paid for their silence and silence is what he got. McPhie was their insurance and got a few quid every year for his trouble. It was an arrangement that suited them well till many years later when someone would upset the apple cart big time.

Some of the accused men's families got a visit from McGraw and a few quid too. Nothing much. Just enough to make them see him in a good light and, of course, to blether and help him find out the inside story of what was going on. There was no way he wanted this trial business to come exploding back in his face.

Then he called on Liz Campbell, TC's wife, to see if there was any way he could help with her ice cream van. Maybe get some of his guys to load it up for her. Do some visits to the cash and carry. Orders went out to his men to leave Liz and Agnes Lafferty's territories alone – for the moment. Meantime, three of his vans quietly slipped into territories that formerly belonged to some of the other accused. No point in wasting the chance to make some cash.

All the time he was meeting with police handlers. Most of it was business as usual. Could they get some charge dropped against a particular guy? In return, did they know who was doing all the housebreakings in Cambuslang? He did. So they swapped.

All the time the Doyle trial was right there on the table. He was feeding the police with every piece of information he could to help their case, all the time making sure he knew what was going on. Making sure the heat didn't turn on him.

The trial was a long, drawn out affair with a cast of hundreds. At times the cases of the accused seemed strong, that conviction was highly unlikely if not impossible. All peppered with scenes of humour and humanity.

A man we call the Silver Fox proved reluctant to give evidence though officially blamed poor health. When eventually dragged into court he started by answering a few questions then clutched at his chest, falling to his knees. The place went into meltdown with a nurse rushing in and starting to save his life. That's when she realised the old sod was faking it.

A young woman sashayed, dressed coyly enough, but every heterosexual man's eyes turned to follow her progress. She had the fullest bosom and a figure to kill for. She was Jackie, Joe Steele's lover and his alibi for a couple of things. It was something that Joe hadn't been too keen to use on the grounds that his wife wouldn't be too pleased. But this was as important as it gets. The lawyers slowed their pace right down in asking her questions. Cross-examination took an age. Even the judge didn't seem to mind and chatted to her a wee bit. Yet she stuck to her story all the time. Joe couldn't have done some of the things the cops claimed. She knew since they had been in bed together.

One old woman gave evidence related to mobbing and rioting, a charge most of them faced. She remembered the night, 15 April 1984, and the time well – the comedian Tommy Cooper had just died on live TV. It was far from his best gag.

Forensics were produced. Like half a thumbprint from high up on the inside passenger window of some car. TC Campbell's thumbprint in a car he had never seen.

Then an A-to-Z of Glasgow with a nice clear blue mark on Bankend Street was produced with the police claiming they found it at TC Campbell's. Like a local man would need to mark a map to make sure he knew where he was going? To make sure he found his way to a street he could see from his own home?

There was that jacket found by the police in the car not on the first search or even the second, third or fourth. Months after the motor had been left lying in a police car pound a novice cop was ordered to search it again: "Particularly the back seat." Sure enough he found a jacket. A jacket that belonged to Shadda Lafferty, so the cops claimed.

From the witness box, Shadda was asked to try on that jacket by his defence QC. He did and the court erupted in laughter. Not the biggest of men, the sleeves were about a foot too long and the hem trailed on the ground.

"Ah'm an alky no a fucking clown," Shadda announced. Point made.

Two witnesses – a man and woman – were brought into court under a heavy police guard. It seems they had been under police protection for a couple of months, being key prosecution witnesses. Someone had slipped the wink that they were the most reluctant prosecution witnesses ever. They didn't help the prosecution at all, instead spoke out about being there against their will. When defence QCs got into the game the witnesses claimed they had left the so-called safe house three times and three times they had been caught and forced back by the cops. That morning they had refused to leave for court so a team of police had manhandled them out of the house and into waiting cars and at the court they had been thrown into cells.

"Were you forced to leave in a hurry?" asked one QC.

"Aye, look." The man held up a foot, a naked foot. They had taken him so fast they didn't stop for footwear or a jacket.

One by one the accused were released with no charges to account for or found guilty of some lesser crime and dismissed from the trial. The wigs even conceded that TC wasn't there on Bankend Street that night but that didn't mean he hadn't caused the murder to happen. It didn't mean that at all and in Scotland it carried the same weight as if he had lit the blaze.

Then came the cop evidence:

"The Fire at Fat Boy's was only meant to be a frightener that went too far." That's what they claimed TC said to them when arrested. One after another quoted exactly those words. A free confession apparently, and from a man who had been at odds with the cops almost all his days. A guy who was so particular about telling the police nothing that he had even made up another language and taught all his associates. This same man had just offered that confession. Well, the cops said so.

Finally, there was the main man, Billy Love. The man who McGraw had suggested to the cops. The man who McGraw had visited by some of his boys to be sure that Billy would play along. Love's choices were stark. A beating every chance they got from McGraw's heavies and a stiff period in jail from the cops for outstanding charges – or sing the song that would jail TC Campbell for the rest of his life. He chose to sing.

In the witness stand at the High Court, Billy Love looked and sounded nervous, terrified even. For a career criminal used to robbing houses and shooting up ice cream vans, he made for a bad liar.

He told his tale of being in the Netherfield Bar and hearing TC, Tamby, Joe Steele and others in conversation over a drink. There he overheard them talking about, "The Fire at Fat Boy's was only meant to be a frightener that went too far." Exactly the words being quoted by the cops.

Cross-examination was fierce.

What date was that?

Are you sure?

What pub?

And where?

Can you ID TC Campbell?

Of course he could. Everyone in Scotland could from the newspapers alone.

Was he sure it was him?

Is he sure it was the others?

When in doubt Billy Love just said that it could've been that date or could've been the other. Some thought he might as well have said that he just didn't know.

At the back of the court, McGraw's spies sat and they weren't happy. Not happy at all. It didn't seem to them that Love had nailed TC. Didn't seem like it all.

Summing up to the jury before they made their decision, the judge gave them a frank warning.

They might choose to believe that all the cops were lying bullies. Good men who had served without incident in their careers. That was the only way to find TC and Joe not guilty. Blame all those cops for lying. Would the jury really want to do that?

TC Campbell and Joe Steele were found guilty and jailed for life for the murders of the six Doyles. Overnight, on the streets of Glasgow they became the most hated men.

Overnight, McGraw came a man who was now planning to take over the whole of the city. Who was going to stop him?

26

LICENSED TO DEAL

Murder was always a Glasgow theme. Always had been. All that changed were some of the reasons for killing and there was a new one in town – heroin.

The heroin market had been active in Glasgow forever. For many decades it was just the arty-farty intelligentsia that used the deadly powder. Then that began to spread, slowly at first, and a few men took control. Guys who could deal to the scruffy west end set who thought they were artists experimenting in life as well as to those ordinary souls who had fallen foul of the drug. Either way they made a good deal of money.

One of the main Glasgow traffickers was a guy called Jimmy Rea. Rea would run his big Volvo down to Liverpool, London or across to Amsterdam to pick up his supplies. Better still, he'd get a colleague, Dahwal Haq Quereshi, a Pakistani civil servant in the Ministry of Agriculture, to buy it out there and carry it back on a flight. As much as £1,000,000 worth in his suitcase. The cops and Customs hadn't awakened to drugs trafficking then. There were no sniffer dogs on the borders. No spot checks of cars on the road. No drugs units or sod all. Rea would store his gear in a scrapyard in Airdrie then dish it out via a widening range of small time dealers.

If there's a good profit to be made, others will always want their share. Jimmy Rea's time was about to end.

Rea had got into some company he thought was good for him. Arthur 'Fatboy' Thompson was the son of Arthur Thompson, The

Godfather after all. The trouble was that The Godfather knew nothing about Fatboy's games.

Fatboy had been set up with a garage in Maryhill Road with the idea that he could learn a trick of business or two. He did that okay but it bored him.

The garage was a front for many things, including Fatboy's love of guns and bullets. In the 1980s he could buy the parts from iron-mongers and put together his own collection of powerful pistols and the occasional rifle. Where better to store them than a locker at that garage. After all, his old man was well in with the cops having traded them information for a blind eye for years.

Fatboy wanted to be a real gangster and he knew what they dealt in – heroin.

Linking in and working for other drug dealers, Fatboy decided to sort them out. One guy got set up with a steering wheel column full of smack and an anonymous call to the cops. Another, Ted Hughes, was about to go on a journey and wasn't coming back. Having bought a big black Merc from Fatboy he set off to collect some smack from down south. His car had only made it half way home when the cop cars appeared, courtesy of a call from Fatboy.

A call to the cops then Customs is all it took to get Jimmy Rea – with the details of his storage, routes and dealers, of course. There were very few people who knew all the details of what Rea had been up to and Fatboy was one. In case he decided to squeal in jail – where he was sent for twelve years along with a lot of his cohorts – he was sent a little warning and his family sent bullets through their letterboxes. Rea kept quiet. He was the first major dealer to be jailed in Scotland. He wouldn't be the last.

A few years before, in 1982, Walter 'Toe' Elliot showed his hand. Known as the Little General from his days leading the infamous Calton Tongs gang, Toe Elliot was small, impeccably dressed and often wore a long coat to conceal his pair of sawn off shotguns. When Archie Steen had been done for attempting to murder Eliot it was rumoured that it had been about drug deals. Now the rumour mongers claimed they were right.

Along with hardman Ronnie Neeson, Elliot was trading in heroin. He was upset that one of his dealers, Robert Kane, was cheating him. Warning him several times and crushing his hand with a baseball bat had no effect at all. So Elliot and Neeson cornered Kane in a house in Maryhill, beat him viciously and stabbed him to death.

Toe Elliot was one of the few Glasgow faces who could stand up to Arthur Thompson. Yet Elliot wouldn't be breathing free air for many years to come.

Now Fatboy thought he was Mr Big in charge of Glasgow's heroin. But someone was watching close by. McGraw had ambitions.

It was now common knowledge in the east end that McGraw's relationship with the cops was more than paying a couple of bent ones to help him out. He paid for nothing, except with information and only when they paid him back.

"Cops in his pocket?" one street player said. "Nah, they both have each other by the balls. It's some kind of sick dance where no one can let go. Innocent people will pay the price."

It was around then that McGraw was given the name The Licensee, as in licensed to commit crime. Not wanting to leave him on his own, Margaret was soon given her nickname based on her love of gold and her habit of wearing every single piece she had all at once. The Jeweller was born.

Laurel and Hardy were well known as McGraw's cops. So well known that when they hung out at The Caravel getting drunk and bolshie on the house, people began to complain to their top brass. On more than one occasion they were hauled in for "discipline". In reality they were told to be more careful, more cautious, as if the damage could be undone.

On one occasion a great show was made of suspending Laurel and Hardy from duty for a few days. On their first day back, there was their car outside McGraw's flat in Barlanark, like they didn't care who saw them. A group of young guys didn't like this one bit and decided to teach them a lesson.

When the cops emerged two hours later there was their unmarked car on its roof on the ground, spinning slowly round and round. Their report to their superiors would have made for fun reading yet the incident didn't result in them being taken off the street. They had been ordered to tackle a new problem, a major issue that was about to set Glasgow on fire. Heroin was the target and McGraw was their man.

"It's easy, Tam," said Laurel. "You get your first load of smack for free. Maybe another couple of loads. You get some boys dealing and you tell us about the big guys you meet."

"Free?" That was a word McGraw loved. "How much is it worth?" The two cops looked at each other and shrugged. It was the mid-1980s and they hadn't the knowledge of trade value versus street value. They didn't have the knowledge of purity or of anything very much. All they knew was that drug dealers made a lot of cash, it was illegal and there were some big names they wanted to hook.

"A good few thousand at least," said Hardy.

"Aye, at least," Laurel supported. "The mark up is huge and you're getting the gear for free but."

"An all Ah've got to do is tell you about some guys. Just any guys." McGraw wasn't finished. This offer seemed too good to be true. With him looking at the heroin market for a while, now he was being given free smack and police protection. That just sounded too good.

"Aye, as long as they're involved in the drugs though," Laurel sounded a bit hesitant.

"But there's some we want you to watch out for, in particular," added Hardy.

"Right." McGraw knew there was going to be a catch.

"Well, one in particular."

"Gonnae spit it out," McGraw demanded.

"Arthur Thompson."

"ARE YOU OFF YER FUCKING CHUMPS?" McGraw roared his response. "Fuck with Thompson? Do you think Ah'm suicidal?"

"Naw, naw. No old Thompson." Laurel had his hands up, open palmed in front of him signalling for McGraw to calm down. "Young Thompson. Fatboy."

McGraw was nodding at the comment, "Why the fuck did ye no say so in the first place?" Young Thompson was a different beast all together. He looked a bit like his Da in the face but there the similarity ended. He was a fat chump who couldn't survive without his old man's reputation and the young guys he hired to protect him. Lately he had hired two new boys – Paul Ferris and a Tam Bagan. They were handy right enough. Very handy with reputations that grew every day. He wouldn't want to mess with those two.

"Another thing, Tam," said Laurel as if reading his mind. "We're no looking to lift Fatboy. We just want ye to keep an eye on him. We want to be sure he doesn't dig in too deep. Get too big." McGraw was nodding his head. This was a strange one all right. Free smack from the cops to infiltrate the world of drug dealers, make a fortune, not get arrested but to keep his eye on Fatboy. Very bloody strange.

"Are we on, Tam?"

"Aye, we're on." Hardy opened a big sports bag he'd brought in with him with the word Head emblazoned on the side. There wasn't any sports gear in there, just a big bag of smack. "Here's your gear, Tam." The drugs were stuffed back in the bag, zipped up and passed to McGraw. Within minutes of them leaving, that smack would be out of his house. He was going to have it dumped on an old couple he sometimes used for taking care of stuff. For a handful of notes a week, they would stow the bag nice and safe in some cupboard and look after it for as long as he wanted. For that they didn't open the bag or their lips.

"You all right with that stuff, Tam?" Laurel asked nodding at the Head bag. "Know how to handle it?" McGraw threw him a sour look.

"Safe as houses with me. Safe as fucking houses."

Junkies in Glasgow were soon to find out different.

27

THE DEAL

Every inch of that way is stained with blood. Or so it seems to those who know the east of Glasgow.

Blackhill to Barlanark isn't far no matter how you travel. On a street map of Glasgow they are practically next door to each other. Straight along past Barlinnie Prison. Through Riddrie and on to Glasgow Road. Out east through Ruchazie, Garthamlock, outskirting Easterhouse and turn right before you get near to Baillieston. Saying it is easy, it slips off the tongue but we're in badlands. Areas potted with hell, the hell humans create.

McGraw had to do that journey in reverse. Not alone, of course. His car was driven by a young minder carrying a shooter in the back waistband of his trousers. By his side an older face, someone used to violence in Belfast and Glasgow, with a shotgun under his seat, the butt leaning on his foot ready for a quick lift. They were ready all right.

No junkies in the party that day. Those wrecks were okay for sending out on a task. Maybe some old guy to be scared. Some money-owing kid slashed. A woman's house wrecked. A taxi to be torched. Most junkies could do all that and would do it cheap but not that day. No risks were to be taken that day.

The destination was in Blackhill at the Provanmill Inn. It was Arthur Thompson Senior's HQ and a hundred yards from his house, The Ponderosa. He had built his home out of a council house till its gaudiness and no-taste splendour became infamous all over the city. Now, at the other end of a short row of council houses, he had built a home for Fatboy.

"One big bomb is all it would take," some of his enemies would muse. "WHAM. Two Thompsons for the price of one." They were right but no one would try it. What if old Thompson survived? His revenge didn't bear thinking about.

The meeting was on a day The Godfather wouldn't be there. That didn't worry McGraw. He'd met the man before if only briefly. But now he was meeting Fatboy and, though he claimed differently, the young Thompson didn't want his father around.

McGraw had sent an old ally to get the message to Fatboy. Jonah McKenzie, known as Blind Jonah having lost the sight in one eye in a battle, had been a good help to McGraw. One time a bunch of young east end Turks were intent on giving McGraw a beating. Jonah had dived in saving the day and McGraw almost singlehanded. He had taken a right hammering even though he won. Other men would have rewarded Blind Jonah. McGraw simply took a lesson from it and never again went out alone.

Jonah was one of those Glasgow boys who grew up in the gang system then wanted to progress in the only way he could in the only thing he was good at – crime. He had hung out in places where the faces were more organised, more intent on making money and offered his skills as a fighter. They were gratefully accepted.

Fatboy Thompson had a problem. Paul Ferris, his main equaliser, was in jail. Fatboy had given him the task of recovering £50,000 that some team had cheated him out of. For months Ferris had been on their trail picking them off one-by-one outside clubs like Panama Jax in the early hours of the morning. Ferris hadn't got the money but he did have a warrant for his arrest for fourteen attempted murders.

Hiding out in Arthur Thompson Senior's house down in Rothesay on the Isle of Bute, it took the Serious Crime Squad only a few hours to find and arrest him. While there, the cops claimed they found some smack on Ferris and a dealer's delivery list among other things. He was denying any involvement in drugs, claiming a set up, but what the future held for him at trial was anyone's guess. With Ferris in jail, even with Tam Bagan still there, Fatboy needed more manpower. Blind Jonah would do nicely.

The meeting in Provanmill Inn didn't look like a meeting. It was two men having a quiet drink and a blether. More experienced men would've held it elsewhere, in some place where privacy was guaranteed. Fatboy wasn't like most men. He liked to be seen as important.

McGraw wasn't like most men either. His tooled up driver was still at the wheel of the car, its engine idling gently. The older man went into the pub separate from McGraw. Standing at the bar he slowly sipped a half pint of export, his raggedy coat concealing the shape and weight of his sawn off shotgun.

"It's great quality," said McGraw.

"It better be," said Fatboy looking straight at him, trying to look hard.

"Ah'll tell you what," McGraw went on, "as a mark of trust Ah'll give you the first lot for free." There was that word again. "If you're satisfied with it, we do business. Deal?" Fatboy looked at him trying hard to think of a question that would make life difficult for McGraw. The pair knew of each other but didn't know each other. It was his duty to stamp his authority on this meet, to remind McGraw he was The Godfather's son. Over in the corner two drunks started to raise their voices at each other.

"Elvis Presley? Are you totally mental?"

"Ah'm fucking telling yese, Elvis is the man."

"Aye the man in the can – big fat fucker in a white romper suit."

"Romper suit? Ya cheeky bastard. That's a cat suit."

"Some podgy fucking pussy then . . ."

People around them simply ignored the pair as if they were so used to them arguing they didn't hear them anymore.

"Free?" asked Fatboy.

"Free," confirmed McGraw. Fatboy had asked Blind Jonah all

about McGraw before the meeting. The worst thing the man could say about him was that he was mean and a penny pincher. Now he was offering him valuable goods at no charge. Too good to be true?

"Deal." Fatboy held out his hand to shake and soon McGraw was ordering them two more drinks.

"Just to seal the transaction eh," he said.

"They'll be on the house," Fatboy said nodding to the barman.

"Here's to a prosperous partnership," said McGraw raising his glass of vodka and lemonade.

"Partnership?" asked Fatboy, nursing his beer.

"Aye, partnership."

"Listen, Ah'm no partner to nobody. Ah'm The Godfather's son."

Having made arrangements for a handover of the goods, a week's grace then for them to meet again, the pair had never mentioned the word heroin. Yet heroin was what they were talking about. McGraw was going to give Fatboy some of the deal his cops had passed to him. A sweetener. An enticement. Then he'd get into the real business. Fatboy's business.

As he left the pub, McGraw noticed that the two arguing drunks had made up. With one arm wrapped round each other, they quietly sang a half decent rendition of 'Wise Men Say'. Thompson's HQ or no, it was just another Glasgow pub.

McGraw got back into his car with his men and headed towards home.

"He is some arsehole that one," he offered. The men turned and looked at him. "Know what he calls his father?"

"Da?" someone tried.

"Nuh. The fucking Godfather. Like he's in some Hollywood film."

"Arsehole," the two men agreed.

"That one needs a seeing to right enough," thought McGraw as the car slowly drove him back to the east end, "and I'm the man to see to it."

28

THE DYING STREETS

Over the next few days the heroin was passed from McGraw's men to Fatboy's crew – Blind Jonah to be precise. Back at his flat, Jonah cut and mixed the gear and wrapped it into tenner bundles. He was under strict instructions to sell that separately from the rest of their heroin and only to well-known guys who knew their smack. Then he had to ask the punters how the heroin was. Fatboy didn't have a chemist to test the gear – he had public feedback.

A few days later McGraw got the call from Fatboy wanting another meeting. At that Fatboy said the gear was alright. Just alright. And, yes, he'd buy some but only if the price was right. McGraw said he'd see what he could do. Both were lying.

Blind Jonah had had a habit for years and he knew his gear. He kept a score of McGraw's smack and shot it up the night after he'd flogged the rest. It was the best hit he'd ever had bar none.

"That stuff was pure and high quality," he later told Fatboy. "Man, I cut it and cut it again and still it gave the most beautiful hit." Fatboy's eyes had turned beadier buried in his flabby cheeks and he even put down a Mars Bar halfway through a mouthful.

"Worth buying some then?" he asked.

"Fuck aye. As much as ye can get."

"Ah will but Ah've a better idea," Fatboy said. "Ah'm gonnae find out who that McGraw cunt bought that from."

A couple of days later McGraw had a chat with Laurel and Hardy.

"Ah'm right in there with Fatboy," he declared. "He's going to be no problem." The cops looked and listened, waited for him to go on. "We're going into partnership," he said. "One thing though, I need more of that smack. Seems his customers like it."

"Did you sell him all of it?" Hardy asked.

"Naw, just gave him a wee bit as a taster. My guys sold the rest themselves."

"Where?"

"What?"

"Where did your guys sell the heroin?"

"There's nothing to worry about," McGraw insisted. "They spread that around a bit. Some in the east end. A bit in Possil. Quite a bit in the Gorbals."

"Fuck." Both cops spat the word out at the same time.

"What's up?"

"How did ye sell it?" one asked.

"To make some cash of course," McGraw replied looking at him as if he had two skulls and both were thick.

"Nah, no how as in why but how as in fucking HOW." It was Laurel and McGraw was trying to remember if he had ever raised his voice at him before. He reckoned not.

"Just bundled it up in wee wraps. You know, tenner wraps and flogged it."

"You didn't cut it?" asked Laurel.

"Cut it? What the fuck's that?" McGraw didn't know what he meant or even what his guys had done with the heroin. He'd had it passed from one of his men to another well away from him. Dealing in smack carried a ten to twelve year sentence in jail and he wasn't going to risk that.

These were guys who he usually dealt with. Men who'd run some stolen money through the taxis and a couple of shops for him. Guys who'd arrange for some mouthy kid to get slashed. Blokes who knew all about that so they had to know about heroin. Didn't they?

"SHITE." This time it was Hardy doing the shouting. "Do you no read the papers, Tam?"

"Ye know Ah do."

"About junkies being found dead?"

"But they're junkies. Junkies fucking die."

Hardy ignored him and went on, "Dying all over the city but particularly the east end, fucking Possil and bastarding Govan where they go to the Gorbals to buy their smack." The penny was dropping for McGraw. His ignorance and that of his men meant they had sold pure heroin to junkies so used to their gear being cut more times than a sliced loaf.

Every shooting gallery, every derelict close, every sunlight-free car park stairwell was producing bodies of young men and women killed by pure heroin. The cops had put reports out on the deaths but not why they had died. Pure heroin was rare in Glasgow at that time and Strathclyde, like most large police forces, had a policy of one hand not knowing what the other was up to most of the time. They had to – there were too many bent coppers around. Too many willing to sell some snippet to the gangsters or, at the very least, to some journalist for a small brown envelope.

The only place they knew it was found was in their pound of confiscated goods. Had someone stolen some? Had some colleagues gone native? Till they found out that answer they were going to stay schtum. No bad thing anyway warning junkies and young kids that heroin kills. That would do just by itself.

Down at a flat in Charing Cross Road, Soho, London, Arthur Thompson Senior was having a meeting. One of those meetings he doesn't want anyone else to know about. One of those meetings he had to attend because he was ordered to. That place in Charing Cross Road was the secret HQ of a group from MI5 intent on smashing organised crime in London and elsewhere. At that time they were particularly interested in Ireland.

"We said that you could do some drugs," said the tall man in the black suit, white shirt and dark tie. "That was SOME drugs."

"Aye, and that's what I have been doing," replied Thompson. "A wee bit of dope and that's it." If Thompson admitted it, he hated how these toffy-spoken, Oxbridge-trained, ex-Army freaks ordered him about. Hated how they had sussed a few of his ploys and threatened to reveal them to the Loyalists and the Kray twin supporters unless he did what they said. But he loved how in return for his information he was allowed to commit some very lucrative criminal enterprises.

"Your son seems to have different ideas."

"Young Arthur?"

"Yes. Young Arthur is keeping bad company and getting carried away. Thinks he is some character from *Godfather III*."

"Ach, he's just young." Thompson knew what his oldest son was and what he wasn't capable of. At least he was a world better than his youngest boy, Billy, who was proving to be useless at almost everything.

"Is that your answer?"

Thompson nodded with a look that threw hate across the room.

"Well." He held on to the last letters for an age. "You'll have to help us more with Ireland. Seems the Loyalist groups are getting frisky. Some tapes would be helpful." Thompson had informed on the London gangs, helped the spooks take out more than one Glasgow player, a handful of Scousers and at least three Geordies. He'd given them names, addresses and pack drills for several of the Irish mob. Now they wanted tapes. "For our continuing co-operation." Old Thompson nodded, got up and slowly left the room. He knew what they wanted and, after all, what choice did he have? It would be his son or the tapes. It would have to be the tapes.

Two minutes after Thompson had cleared the building, the MI5 man was on the phone to a top Glasgow cop.

"A problem at this end," he said. "We'll need your help to bring someone in. Your man McGraw will be useful in this."

29

DONE AND LAID OUT TO DRY

"Keep going." The car was slowing down. "Naw, keep fucking going." Fatboy was in a panic and insistent.

"What's up?" asked Tam Bagan as he moved down a gear and speeded away.

"We're being followed," squeaked Fatboy. "Bloody car full of cops behind us." It was the middle of the evening, dark and there were a few cars moving through Blackhill and following them up towards the park at Hogganfield Loch. At the junction, Bagan stopped and indicated left. "Where the fuck ye going?" demanded Fatboy.

"Ah'm checking out if anyone's following us?"

"Nah, head for the motorway," rumbled Fatboy. "RIGHT. Turn right." Bagan ignored him and turned left. He was fed up with Fatboy's constant paranoia. Always seeing some drama and danger where there wasn't any. Bagan just wanted to confirm they weren't being followed, drop Fatboy off and get on home. It had been a long day.

"It'll be easier this way," Bagan reassured him, pulling out left at the junction and heading left, on to the old road to Stirling, up past what used to be massive rhubarb fields. It was a road that brought back bad memories. When he first worked for the Thompsons him and Ferris had to babysit Fatboy all the time and Fatboy wanted to go shooting. He'd order them out into this countryside, on the small and quiet lanes, and standing up through the sunroof of the car would blast at every road sign and tree he could see. It ended the night his waist size got too big and he stuck in the damned sunroof space.

Yet Fatboy could be really mental for a man with no street cred. He had been known to shoot at passing cars on the motorway and once blasted a magnum round through the back of one car, through the seats and wounded the driver in the back. Why? Just for a laugh.

Then there were the personal grudges. For some reason he took it bad against John 'The Irishman' Friel, trying to set him up with a rogue machine gun and bullets in the boot of his car. When that didn't stick he got one of the family's men to steal a lorry and drive it straight through the front window of a restaurant Friel was eating at. The idea was for Fatboy to come out blasting off a machine gun. Trouble was one of his father's London mates was having dinner at that time. A quiet word in his ear and Fatboy was out of there.

It wasn't that he was tough. He simply believed that as The Godfather's son no one would touch him. That didn't stop him being paranoid.

"It's the big black motor," said Fatboy. "Is it following us?"

"It's coming this way."

"Told ye. Didn't I just tell ye? Bloody cops."

"Relax," said Bagan. "They might be citizens who live out this way."

"Aye right," said Fatboy who always chose to believe the worst when it came to his personal security. The pair travelled at the legal speed out towards Stirling, and then turned left again on a wee back road that would eventually take them to Stepps. The trouble was that the road had high hedges, grass and trees at both sides and turned this way and that. The only way to suss if they were being followed was to drive the few miles to the end and sit and wait to see what car, if any, emerged.

Bagan understood why Fatboy was more paranoid than usual. Fatboy had been doing big business on the heroin front. Or at least Blind Jonah had on his behalf. Fatboy didn't touch the gear.

Would never carry it and only visited Jonah's flat where all the cutting happened to dish out orders and make sure his worker wasn't consuming their product. The smack feeding the habits of the north and north east of the city now came from Fatboy's stock and it was a market that was expanding every day. The cops had to have noticed something.

Bagan was far from happy with Fatboy's dealing with McGraw, a man he preferred to call The Licensee. Since the time he shot down two men in Easterhouse – a time he was just a kid really – Bagan had heard that McGraw could not be trusted.

Up in Easterhouse the place was too big, the people too many and the teams too fierce and all too close to Barlanark. McGraw made a point of taking the cocky ones out either by the straightforward brutality of men he hired or by a quiet word in some cop's ear.

Good men's bodies had been ruined forever, sometimes so badly they had to leave the city to be safe. Honest men lay rotting in prison cells, jailed for something they didn't do. All on The Licensee's word. He did not trust that man.

Now Fatboy was in cahoots with him over smack. The pair set up their delivery runs together and had divided the city with McGraw having a free hand in the east end proper. It was going to come to grief for Fatboy, Bagan could see that.

At the end of the short country road, Bagan drove out and pulled into a lay-by forty yards away. They sat and waited for a full five minutes before Bagan pulled out.

"Where ye going, man?" demanded Fatboy.

"Taking you home."

"Nah, give it another five minutes just to be sure."

"Fuck off," Bagan replied. "I could crawl that road twice in five minutes. It's safe. Absolutely safe." On he drove till he dropped Fatboy off at his place.

"Outside The Ponderosa, Tam," he ordered. "Ah'm going to have a confab with The Godfather for a wee while."

A few minutes later, Bagan's car was stopped by the cops. They searched his car and grilled him – not about the heroin that Fatboy feared but about guns. There was no mistake in that. Tam Bagan was known to be a shooter, was well established in Thompson Senior's employ and was also known to be one of the coolest, calmest gunmen in the city. Calmer and more ruthless than even Ferris. But Bagan wasn't stupid or careless. The cops found nothing and he told them less. A few evenings later, Fatboy was driving home from Jonah's flat when the cops gave chase. He put his foot down and headed through the winding, narrow streets of Blackhill. He knew those streets intimately but so did the cops.

When they finally stopped and arrested him he was charged with dealing in drugs and throwing tenner bags of smack out of his car window as he drove.

In the search of his room they found a porn magazine in a waste paper bin. Nothing unusual in that. Yet at Blind Jonah's flat they found a corner of one of the pages that had been used to wrap up some smack. Too neat and tidy, street players thought, but neat enough. Fatboy, Blind Jonah and possibly Bagan were going down.

Shortly after Fatboy's arrest, McGraw had a visit – from Arthur Thompson, his father. The old man already suspected that McGraw was involved in Fatboy's dealing and had a proposition for him. Take the rap or at least give evidence and get him off. It was the least he could do. For his troubles? Twenty grand, cash in hand delivered anywhere he wanted. It wasn't like McGraw to turn away from so much money but this time he did. He knew all about Thompson's reputation for being mean and not paying debts. Apart from that, why would he want to help Fatboy when he had gone to considerable lengths to get the man in trouble? It was no deal.

The phone rang in McGraw's home minutes after the trial had ended.

"Task done," said the familiar voice at the other end of the line.

"Was everything and everybody where I said they'd be?" McGraw asked.

"Inch perfect," came the reply.

"Will I be seeing the Fatboy for a while?"

"Not unless you fancy some prison visiting over the next few years," came the laughing reply. "Maybe as much as eleven. The territory is now yours," added the cop. "You've just won a gold watch."

McGraw was going to take a lot more than that if he could. He was going to take everything.

30

UP AND OUT?

The McGraws were happy. Business was going well so they could now move upwards to a fancy mansion in Mount Vernon as they had always dreamed.

The house at Carrick Drive was bought in double quick time. That type of move is easy when you have pots of gold lying about. The streets where he used to hang about as a kid hoping for some rich brat to steal from were now his. He belonged there. But moving was going to take longer. Much longer.

Some say it was all about the McGraws taking their time to get things right in their new home. Sure enough, some of the rooms were changed, carpets laid, the garden done and so on. Yet those on the inside say there was more to it than that.

If McGraw had robbed the houses and children in those streets so might someone else. When you were involved in organised crime, as he was up to his neck, there were others to watch out for – those you had harmed and those paid to harm you.

Mount Vernon might be less than two miles from where he lived and four social classes up but it was also a short journey into isolation. Down in Barlanark he had his safety devices. Men who lived nearby. Cops who would watch his house at night. Around him would be his taxis, ice cream vans, The Caravel bar and so on. Mount Vernon would have him, Margaret and their son William – named after his father's brother but known as Winkie by everyone – that's all. Just the McGraws.

McGraw decided he needed some security. An alarm system

would do but he wanted something special. In the 1980s and the days before our streets were littered with CCTV cameras and our banks wired to the moon, he got hold of an alarm expert and went to town. Over the next few years, CCTV was installed covering every angle round the house. The garden, front and rear, was strewn with trip lights that would brighten the whole street in the middle of the night. Sensors were laid in the driveway to set off the CCTV cameras in the garden when even a small bird landed never mind a car or a human being. With a fat brown envelope to two councillors, permission was given to dig up the public road in front of his house and lay even more sensors fitted to cameras on lampposts and hedge posts.

All very thorough and dramatic and even better that some of the gear had been redirected from a planned security upgrade at Barlinnie Prison. "Better" for McGraw meant "cheaper". McGraw had enough security there to protect the Queen. Still he wasn't for moving in.

For years McGraw would stay on in his pokey council flat in Barlanark in spite of having an expensive, well equipped, totally secure home just up the road. In spite of his wife and son moving up there. In spite of his family and friends scratching their skulls and asking him why. In spite of it costing him a fortune.

Paranoia was settling in to McGraw. Always an anxious man, with every successful move he made, every extra quid in his kitty, every new business bought he slept less and less, worrying more and more. The rot was beginning to take over.

In jail Blind Jonah wasn't a happy man. He knew that Fatboy and his father were looking for someone to blame for him being caught. It didn't help when Fatboy went down for ten years, Jonah for much less and Bagan for eight. He was The Godfather's son. They weren't meant to do this to him. Fatboy was fuming up in Peterhead Prison, ranting and cursing at everyone and everything. Someone had put him in and someone would pay.

The drugs bust was a set up, for sure. Fatboy never carried smack. A gun, aye, but never drugs. He expected other people to take those risks. One night Jonah got chatting to another prisoner. "That magazine done for him," he explained. "Ma house was like a fucking bakery – covered in powder. A link between Fatboy's place and my place was all they needed."

"How the fuck did that happen but?" the other con asked.

"Think we used porn to wrap up our smack all the time eh? Charge the junkies an extra quid for a look at some fanny?" Blind Jonah could be a funny man but he could also be sarcastic. Lodged in between he had a short fuse that you prayed never went off in your company. "Think Fatboy bothered his arse with my kind of porn magazines? He had fucking videos that would make you bleed from yer eyes."

"So whit then? Magic?" The other con didn't know it but he was one place away from a Blind Jonah kicking.

"Magic? Aye that'll be it." Blind Jonah had gone quiet, looking at the man contemplating re-jigging his face permanently. "Black fucking magic. That's what. Some cunt put that magazine in Fatboy's room and wrapped some smack in a page."

"Who? The cops?" Jonah had gone quiet, like he was thinking hard because he was. He was trying to remember through all the fug of the smack he'd taken. "Nah, Big Man. Worse than that." He was up and heading out of the cell.

"Where are youse off to?"

"Got a call to make."

"Who the fuck to in such a hurry?"

Jonah stopped in his tracks. "You know, you can be a right cheeky prick sometimes." Then he was off. The phone call was too important to delay. With a bit of luck Jonah would forget the guy ever spoke. Forget that feeling he had right there of shoving the man's head up his arse. With some luck.

Out in the hall Jonah joined the queue for the phone feeling the change in his pocket, counting it by touch, hoping it was enough. The man on the phone was standing huddled over it, one hand covering where his mouth was pressed into the mouthpiece, facing away from the queue, his body bent into the wall. He didn't want anyone to hear what he was saying. He was failing.

"But, Jean. It's a hellish thing to hear when you're in jail . . . Ah know, Ah know . . . 'Course Ah didn't believe it . . . Then you missed a couple of visits . . . Ill is she. Ma wee darling . . . Then him eh . . . Could ye no ask ma mother to babysit? Or your sister? . . . Jean, he's a junky. Yer no daft enough to go with a fucking smackhead are ye? . . . It's only six years, hen. No long really . . . Jean, tell me yer no fucking him . . . Jean? . . . Jean, YA CUNT . . . Fucking hang up on me eh?"

He started battering the handset against the wall, tears streaming down his red face, a ball of wet foam dripping from the corner of his mouth. Two screws who had been chatting a good bit down the hall were on him double quick. He stuck the nut into one of them before they got him under control. Still screaming and swearing he was being half pulled, half dragged away, down the hall where they'd turn sharp left, through three sets of doors, down a flight of stairs and sling him in a dark, cold solitary cell for enough days or weeks to wear him out.

"Know that arsehole's name?" the guy behind him in the queue asked Jonah.

"Naw."

"John. Fucking John." The guy was laughing out loud but Blind Jonah wasn't getting it. "He doesn't get Dear John letters. Just hears Dear John gossip. That wife of his must have shagged everybody with a cock in Drumchapel and he's only been inside a year."

Jonah didn't laugh. He just made a decision.

"Ah can't talk on this phone," he said ten minutes later when he had reached the front of the queue. "Too many listening lugs. You'll come and see me? Good."

McGraw was in big trouble. A top man was going to be after his blood.

31

THE MEET

Heads turned and looked up as one man walked slowly into The Caravel bar a few days later. He wasn't that tall but was broad-chested, fierce-faced and had a confidence that only came with the capacity to inflict extreme violence in those badlands. Arthur Thompson Senior had arrived.

When McGraw saw him he almost lost it right there on the floor. Thompson just didn't turn up one night for a friendly drink.

"Word?" Thompson said to McGraw motioning to the side.

"Aye, of course, what do ye want to drink?" As a barman fetched them drinks they took a seat and people nearby moved farther away. A few old timers downed their booze and headed out the door. If there was going to be trouble they didn't want to catch a stray bullet.

"Ah've been speaking to a bird in a cage," started Thompson. "Seems Ah need to speak to you about some paperwork that got moved around." Maybe fear was sharpening his brain but McGraw sussed immediately what Thompson meant.

"You mean a wee blind bird and a fanny magazine?" Thompson stayed silent but the look in his eyes told McGraw he was right. "Maybe the blind budgie is blaming me before he gets nabbed as a grass." Across the bar, McGraw noticed a stranger who had walked in three feet after Thompson. He looked like a Manson – maybe Billy – loyal associates of the man. Thompson had come with a gunman. Trouble could be on his agenda right there in that pub.

"Maybe. But when he tells me that your men were the only outsiders in that flat, it needs some explanation." The look in his eye spelled out what would happen to McGraw if the explanation wasn't adequate. Thompson was furious with everyone who had anything to do with Fatboy. His son wasn't meant to be in jail, full stop.

"Of course, my men were in that place," he was spluttering, the hint of a stutter coming through in his voice. He knew when he set up Fatboy for the cops that this conversation might happen. He was ready for it. Yet still he was terrified of old Thompson. Every man in his right mind would be. "Young Arthur and I had a business going there. Some of my goods was coming through that place. Ah had to be sure they were being handled right." Thompson thought about what he was saying and had to accept that he'd do the same. Send round some safe hands to oversee the business. "Besides, if one of my boys went native how the fuck would they get that magazine into Fatboy's place?" There McGraw had a point but still it wasn't good enough.

"Ah know about you, McGraw, you and yer polis pals. All ye had to do was slip them the pages."

"Oh aye? And for that they'd let me off dealing in . . ." Suddenly McGraw realised his voice was getting too high pitched and lowered it to a mere suggestion of a whisper. ". . . smack? Aye right."

Thompson thought about his own deal with the cops and security forces, a deal they offered to him to trade in drugs safely as long as he kept passing them information. He even recalled being shocked by their suggestion – not that he'd show that to them – but who was this McGraw? Just a wee man who passed some uniforms a few sleeves of fags and case of whisky now and then. He was small change that McGraw.

"Maybe no," Thompson replied though if McGraw thought that indicated some trust in him he was off his head. McGraw knew better but he had another line to give old Thompson.

"Then maybe Ah should tell ye something Ah've just found out?"

Thompson nodded.

"That Bagan was pulled in by the cops just a wee while before your boy got lifted." McGraw had known since the day after that had happened months before and let that thought hang in the air. That suspicion. Thompson didn't know this and it bothered him. Bagan was a loose cannon. Brought up by members of his own family but he wasn't family. He was three times as bright and twice as vicious as young Arthur and he knew it. That boy Bagan might have got to thinking that he was the new man to take over from Thompson. Maybe tried to butter that process by getting his son the jail. Maybe.

"And Bagan had been in both the blind guy's flat and my Arthur's place eh? Could've taken the magazine from one and dumped it in the other? Is that your point?"

"Aye. Why would I want your boy jailed?" McGraw lowered his voice to a coarse whisper. "We were making a lot of money."

"In that dirty fucking business."

The shrug had left McGraw's shoulders before he realised it. "Ah know what ye mean. But it's the modern way." Another shrug, apologetic this time. "In fact Ah was about to visit young Arthur this week. Make him an offer to take care of his business while he was away. Ah know you wouldn't . . ."

"NUH."

"So Ah thought my boys could and Arthur would earn some money while he's banged up."

"And what would you get out of it?" Thompson trusted no one, particularly over cash.

"A percentage. Just a few quid a week." It sounded like a reasonable idea to Arthur Thompson. No one would lose and if McGraw didn't do that then some other bastard would slip in and take over the trade.

"You see young Arthur about that."

Slowly, Arthur Thompson got to his feet and headed towards the door. As he moved across the room, here and there men held out their hands for a shake, offered him a drink, clapped him on the back. Brief encounters that would earn them brownie points in pubs for the rest of their lives. As Thompson got close to the door, his minder followed, casting his eyes this way and that over the pub crowd. Trusting no one. The way he was paid to do.

McGraw had pulled off his sting. So what if The Godfather shot Bagan and Blind Jonah? What did he care? With Fatboy out of his way, he was going to take over his territory and get rich. Richer than anyone could imagine since the Fatboy wouldn't see a penny.

Who could stop him now?

32

THE GLASGOW TWO

"To him and only him, right." McGraw had passed a package to one of his taxi drivers who would earn his fares differently that day.

One journey to Edinburgh, get there early, a cup of tea and a burger in a café and then another cup of tea with the man he was meeting. They'd know each other since the driver would be reading or at least pretending to read *No Mean City* while his company would be carrying *The Papers of Tony Veitch*. All very spy thriller it seemed with a literary taste of Glasgow's streets all the way through yet there was nothing fancy about it. Both books were popular among ordinary folk and stood out more than a copy of some newspaper. The two men had never met before and would never meet again if McGraw had anything to do with it.

After the tea and a chat, when they stood up to leave, the other man would lift the zipped nylon bag the driver had planted under the table. End of job.

What was in the bag? The driver didn't know and didn't care. A full day's shift pay for three hours' work was his type of deal.

Would it have made any difference if he had known? That it was an annual payment to one of the killers of the Doyle family? That it was silence money?

What if he had known that a colleague of his would make a similar trip in two days' time to a place in East Kilbride and deliver another package?

The sods had been negotiating an increase in their payments and McGraw knew whose fault it was. That man again.

Since the minute he was convicted, TC Campbell had created hell. For a short while he stacked all his energy into lodging his appeal. It wasn't easy since he was denied Legal Aid and he was skint. With no other viable choice he decided to present his own appeal. It was either that or surrender to jail and TC Campbell never surrendered.

When he discovered that Peterhead and Perth jails didn't have that many legal books and those they did have had more pages torn out than left in (the classy paper made for good joint skins), he raised a fuss, writing to everyone in power and appealing to organisations that might help. The result was that every jail in Scotland had to be furnished with legal texts. It was a bloody nose for the politicians and grey suited civil servants by a man who was convicted of the most evil murders in Scotland till that time. They didn't like it.

Campbell lost that appeal in double quick time, so he tested if the sword was mightier than the pen. One night he and others broke out of the dungeons of Peterhead's solitary confinement block and took over the jail, keys and all. They could have taken a bus, opened the gates and driven away but TC wasn't for running. Innocence is what he wanted. He'd stay and fight for that.

The next morning they gave themselves up – point made. Within twenty-four hours he was rushed to hospital so badly mangled by the screws' fists and boots he was declared dead. They had mashed his face, broken an arm and a leg, splintered his back-bone and more. But he wasn't dead.

As TC Campbell set about suing the Secretary of State word spread among the cons. Not the old time boys who knew their men. They always knew Campbell was innocent. But the rogues, the short sentence boys, the robbers and the rioters.

TC Campbell is innocent, was the word.

Slowly, the inmates of Scotland's jails started to raise mayhem but it soon picked up speed. Jails were wrecked, men sat on rooftops for days, buildings torched, screws were taken hostage. Even down in the dark dungeons of the digger, weak, half-blind men created hell.

Banners were strung from the jail walls:

FREE THE GLASGOW TWO

Even trouble merchants like Sammy 'The Bear' Ralston and the bold Jaimba McLean would create hell to kick back at the staff. Up on the roof of Barlinnie they scrambled to sit and freeze out their negotiation but not without strung together sheets and a pot of black paint. The TV cameras would be watching so let them watch this: FREE THE GLASGOW TWO.

The riots were for TC Campbell and Joe Steele. The riots were for the innocent. The unjust were fighting for justice.

Every time a banner went up and was splashed across the newspapers and the TV news, McGraw could feel his charges going up from the two who lit that fire. Every bloody time and it was all that TC Campbell's fault.

Even though he was thrown into the worst cells, the ones with no glass, no sink, no toilet, no electricity, only a concrete bed and he refused to work, refused to eat jail food claiming the status of a remand prisoner therefore innocent, now and then some prisoner would approach TC Campbell and ask,

"Tommy, we know you didn't do it so who did kill the Doyles?"

Campbell would look at the man with his dark eyes, the look that didn't give his feelings away, and think over what he had read from the legal papers of the case that he had managed to wrangle off the Crown. He had read parts of the tale he had never read before. Crucial aspects the jury weren't told. Screeds of evidence that were useful to his defence and Joe's yet their lawyers were kept in the dark. Evidence that would've said don't blame Campbell, blame him. HIM.

"You want to know who killed the Doyles?" he asked the con. "How the fuck should Ah know? Ah wasn't there."

Another con was about to leave another jail. A younger guy whose old man had been a good friend to Campbell. A guy who was fast making a name for himself for all the wrong reasons.

He had just been involved in a riot in Shotts Prison, wrecking millions of pounds worth of new development. For once the riot wasn't dedicated to The Glasgow Two. It was a fight against the cruel treatment of prisoners by the screws so why lie?

They had taken an officer hostage, keeping him for three days. He made sure the man was kept safe. He went on to negotiate an end to the riot including statements read out on Radio Clyde. A signed statement from the hostage about how well he was looked after. An end to one riot that didn't end with the cons forced to run the gauntlet of truncheon blows on their skulls and power hoses on their bodies. A peaceful end that saw no retribution by riot staff raiding some poor sod's cell in the middle of the night to torture him alone before they moved on to their next target

It was a victory praised among his own kind. A tactic that hinted of a brain and fluency as well as well as his proven capacity for violence. A brain that would lead him soon to have doubts over Arthur Thompson and very soon lead to the trail of HIM.

The pair of them didn't know it then but an alliance was about to be struck. Paul Ferris was free and trouble was coming McGraw's way.

33

DAMP SQUIBS AND
PHANTOM BOMBS

"Ah've been talking to some of my pet poodles," said McGraw, the confidence of his mood written all over his face. "They've got interesting news for you."

Arthur Thompson sat at his old battered desk and glowered at the man. He hadn't sought this meeting. He was working at the sawmill, one of several he owned. Lately he had struck a deal with a well-known Bridgeton man about the waste from old derelict houses in Glasgow and it was bringing in a lot of extra wood. He had to make sure his men were processing it as quickly as possible to bring in his cash. He could get a good few quid from that quality of wood especially since he had forced the other guy to remove the nails and clean it all up before passing it to him. What the guy wouldn't be seeing was any payment. This lark was pure profit, just the way Thompson liked it. He'd no time for messing about with arseholes like McGraw.

"You mean the polis, aye?" Thompson confirmed.

"Aye, my lap dogs," smiled McGraw. "Ah give them a few quid now and then and they do me favours." He explained his relationship with the police like some old time gangster might talk about bribing some cops. Gangsters have always wanted to own a cop or two except that's not how it was with McGraw. He gave the police a lot more than a few quid and got a lot more back. "That business with young Arthur has been bothering me," he went on. "It was definitely Bagan and the cop in charge of the case."

"The arresting officer?" asked Thompson.

"That's the one. They did some deal saving Bagan a good few years in jail and in return . . ."

"He got young Arthur."

McGraw nodded back at Thompson as he spoke the words.

"I see the cunt's getting out soon."

"Aye, so what?" asked Thompson.

"Maybe you should set something up for him." Thompson was already ahead of him on that score. He was already planning a wee hit job with the gun to be planted in Bagan's house. "If I were you," McGraw started and decided to brazen the even fiercer scowl from Thompson, a man who took advice from no one, "Ah'd bomb the fucker. Just a thought."

McGraw stood up and headed for the door. He looked calm enough but inside his heart was thumping fit to burst through his chest. Scared of Thompson? Bloody terrified. That's why he wanted to be seen by him as being of some help. Why he had made the whole story up about Bagan and the cop. If Bagan ended up back in jail or dead what did he care? His so-called drug dealing partner Fatboy would see it as a favour and McGraw would claim the credit. With the Thompsons that was bound to be worth some business, some money.

Arthur Thompson sat and mused over what McGraw had said. He still didn't like the man, he despised him, but his idea might have its strong points. Bombs weren't new in Glasgow after all. Wasn't his own mother-in-law killed in his car when the Welshes planted a bomb under it? Didn't Big Bill Campbell's UVF crew try and bomb pubs in Glasgow?

Life had become a wee bit complicated for Thompson. Ferris had got out of jail and wasn't himself. Before, if he asked Ferris to do one thing or a hundred, he'd get it done in double quick time. Now he was taking his time. He'd even refused to slash that young boxer, Gary Jacobs, on the simple basis that he didn't like the guy who asked him to do it. No matter that the guy was a good pal of Thompson.

He hadn't said anything but Thomson thought he might have suspicions about how he got arrested. On the run from the cops for the attempted murders and hiding out at the Thompson house on the Isle of Bute, armed cops were at his door in hours. Only four people knew about his retreat to that refuge – Ferris, his girl-friend Anne Marie McCafferty, young Arty and him. Who did he think belled the cops?

That bloody smack the cops claimed to have found on him. He played them back at their own game and got a specialist in from some university who proved that the wee bag of smack couldn't have been in his pocket. So he went down for a couple of other things, but not the twelve years that they had hoped. But how did the cops know he was there on Bute?

Young Arthur had made it too neat when he called the police. He should've left it a day or two. Ferris wasn't going anywhere. But no, no the stupid young bastard just loved playing at gang-sters and couldn't wait. Who did Ferris suspect now then? Young Arthur? Him? No one else for sure.

If Ferris broke away it could be big trouble for Thompson and he knew that. Worse, what if he and Bagan teamed up when the latter got out of jail? Those two would make some team.

What better way than to get Bagan sent back to jail in double quick time? Who else would they blame for killing the cop? A bit of evidence planted here and there and a word in the right ear – that should see to him.

Who better to carry out the deed? He knew the very man.

"A bomb?" Ferris wasn't often lost for words but this was one of those rare times.

"Aye," one man said but both nodded. They were two of Thompson's old warhorses. The guys who had run with him over the years. Ever careful, he had sent them to speak to Ferris, to get him to do the job. "We don't want any mistakes. The bastard could dodge a bullet."

"But a bomb?"

"It's no fucking problem," one replied, angry at Ferris'

questioning that Thompson had warned him of. "We know people. Safe as fuck."

"Why a bomb though?" Ferris got the point of taking out a cop who had set Fatboy up. That rationale he could understand but ever since his last arrest he was quietly suspicious of anything the Thompsons said or suggested. As far as Arthur Senior went that meant Ferris was doubting the word of someone he had previously believed to be a top man.

"Think of the attention it would get. Every bastarding bent cop would get the message loud and clear." That was something else Ferris was in favour of. "Especially when we pass an anonymous message to the press." The man wasn't lying. Thompson had every intention of passing that message to the media. The question is who would it finger? Bagan? Ferris? Both? "It'd be a lot simpler. Believe me. Ah know how we can get that man."

Thompson's men went on to explain that on certain days the cop in question drove into the city centre for a personal meeting. They hinted that it was of a sexual nature but didn't spell that out. He always parked his car up one of three lanes. Quiet lanes with no one around. All that Paul Ferris had to do was plant the bomb, retire a distance and wait for the explosion when the cop returned to the motor.

"The city centre? Is that no always packed with people? Are we not likely to get other casualties?" asked Ferris.

"Can't rule that out entirely but it's no likely down the lanes he parks in. Are you worried about the bomb?"

"Aye, who wouldn't be?"

"Well, don't. Thompson knows men that could fix us up one in a blink. Dead safe to handle. Dead reliable." He wasn't lying about the contacts. Arthur Thompson had been secretly dealing in firearms and ammo with the Loyalist groups in Ireland for years. If they couldn't build him a bomb, who could?

Ferris went off to think about the bombing, perplexed at how events were turning out. He had chosen a life of crime to make money and now here he was being asked to be a bomber. He didn't mind the violence but he did mind if some innocent party got jailed and he wasn't too sure about Thompson blaming the cop. Not too sure at all.

Tam Bagan was just out of jail and wasn't in a good mood. Bagan felt let down by the Thompsons when he went down. He did know that Fatboy kept ranting to every inmate who'd listen, blaming everyone for him ending up in jail, making a hit list he was going to get his father to sort out – permanently. Some days at the top of that list would be Bagan.

Ferris didn't know if Bagan played any part in Fatboy being jailed. If he didn't know he'd hold his peace, keep watching, keep learning till he worked out the truth. That was all, keeping an open mind. It strained their relationship.

In such a short while so much had changed for Ferris and Bagan. They had gone from the top two equalisers for the so-called Godfather to isolated individuals not even sure about each other.

Ferris decided against the bomb and decided he was leaving Thompson. As of that day he was out on his own for better or worse.

He had a living to make though and a lot of ways to make it. As a base he didn't move far. Just a couple of miles to the east. Near Garthamlock, Ruchazie, Baillieston and Barlanark. Tam Bagan was out on his own too and followed Ferris east. Both slap bang into the territory of McGraw.

"The revolt of the mice," Thompson would laugh out loud in pubs, playing down the two young men who had made the most feared duo in the city.

A few weeks later a young hooded man ran into the office of Arthur Thompson's sawmill with a revolver. From a few feet away he fired. The damp bullet hit the deck. Moving a bit closer he fired again. The slug dipped as it travelled, hitting Thompson in the groin. Some damp ammo saved his life.

Instead of bleeding to death on the floor, Thompson drove himself to the Royal Infirmary and got urgent medical help. He had slipped with his drill and the bit had entered his body, he told the doctor. With the bullet removed the young medic presented it back to him saying in a sarcastic voice, "You might want your drill bit back."

"It was they pricks – Bagan and Ferris," said the youngest Thompson boy, Billy, in the visiting area of Peterhead Prison.

"Maybe," Fatboy Thompson replied between slurps of Coke and big mouthfuls of chocolate, "but I think different."

"How?"

"Never mind what you think of they bastards. They are lethal. They would've blown his head off and shoved a knife up his arse for good luck."

"Who then?"

"That fucking snake McGraw."

Trouble was about to erupt in the east end and McGraw was in the hot seat.

34

OUTED AND DAMNED

"Tam, you better get down here fast," said the familiar voice on the phone.

"Why the fuck?" McGraw yawned. It was four in the morning and he'd only just managed to get to sleep ten minutes before.

"Yer pub's on fire."

McGraw didn't hesitate. He was dressed, packing a gun in his waistband, in his motor and driving fast through the scheme, not caring about being out on his own in the dark – for once.

At least he wasn't on his own. In the back seat was Zoltan, his Rottweiler. Zoltan was bad tempered, would bite anything, ate too much and farted with every second step but McGraw doted on him and he on McGraw. There were those who thought that McGraw now preferred Zoltan to his own son, Winkie, especially since the young man had taken to heroin and been thrown out of the family home. But that morning, Zoltan provided another use. If anyone tried to jump McGraw they'd have to fight a lion first.

Manny McDonnell was the bearer of bad news. Irish, he had landed in Glasgow a couple of years before and had quickly impressed that he could handle himself. McGraw had plans for Ireland. Plans and ideas that would make him money. Manny would be useful to him, or so he thought.

Standing outside The Caravel, the smell of acrid smoke burned his nose. The roof had been torched but only by an amateur. A section of the roof had been badly singed while two holes had burned right through but not fiercely enough to cause major damage inside. A few chairs and a table were written off and smoke clarted the walls. It was annoying. Very annoying. McGraw could see it was going to cost him money and inconvenience. Someone was going to pay for it.

Outside, dawn was breaking. A dull, bluish grey light was rising slowly above the city, bringing out shapes and forms that were so familiar. Coming towards them, two young boys were heading to work in early morning milk rounds, bent over into their walk, dragging quick puffs from their fags.

"HA! Fucking look at that," said one laughing.

"He'll be fucking furious that prick."

"Aye, but it's true but."

One of the boys looked up and spotted McGraw and Manny, nudged his mate and they speeded up their walk passing the men fast.

"What the fuck were they arseholes laughing at?" asked McGraw. He and Manny walked down near the spot. There on the road in bold white, huge painted letters was:

McCRAW IS A GRASS

McGraw went mental. It might almost be 1990 but being a grass was still the worst thing that could be said about you on the streets. That had to go and go fast.

He didn't notice the misspelling of his name. Others did and some liked it so much they took to calling him The Craw as well as The Licensee. McGraw was fast becoming a man with too many names.

McGraw called a builder friend, Trevor Lawson, and asked him to fix it. Lawson was really just a knockdown man rather than a builder but he knew people. A couple of his guys set to work with a special paint solution. No joy. Whatever paint had been used wasn't for shifting easily.

Three weeks and a different attempt every day eventually blurred most of the letters but left a big white stain. By that time the words and the laughs were well embedded in locals' minds. All they had to do was look at that white mess for the memory to flood back.

In the middle of all this some local young guys decided to take it a stage further. Late one night they made a raid on the local cop shop. The next morning, there it was. A big, blue Police Station sign right above McGraw's door with the light working too, thanks to some batteries and wire. He really had been sussed and everyone in the east end was laughing at him.

McGraw wanted the culprit caught. Word was spread around the scene that there was few quid in it for anyone with any information. He didn't have to wait long. Up in Blackhill, young Billy Thompson was hanging around with his mates every night, buzzed up on glue, drunk on cider or totally stoned on dope and smack. Billy just talked and talked and from day one had been boasting that it was him who had torched The Caravel.

Billy listened to everything his big brother Fatboy said. When Fatboy started to complain that he wasn't getting any cash for his drug territory from McGraw as agreed he soon blamed McGraw for grassing him up to the cops, for him being in jail.

Fatboy's father listened and nodded. He'd wait his time to sort that one out. Billy was no bright bulb. He had to do something right away.

McGraw couldn't hurt Billy. That would bring the force of his father down on him. But he could demand the one thing that was due – financial compensation for the damage to his pub.

McGraw was renowned as one of the meanest men in the east end but there was another man who beat him hands down – Arthur Thompson.

From early in his career Thompson had earned some of his reputation by the ferocity he used when men owed him money. Crucifixions and being buried alive in the concrete stanchions of the Kingston Bridge were just two of his methods. There were many more and occasionally he'd use them against folk who claimed that he had a debt to them.

McGraw and Thompson were about to go head-to-head.

The power of Arthur Thompson was undisputed. With only a few thorns in his side he had ruled the Glasgow streets for almost thirty years. The question was, had McGraw grown strong enough to take him on?

"Gangs? That's something for the kids," many an old time Glasgow face will say. They weren't members of gangs. Didn't work for anyone. Didn't have some undying allegiance to some leader. But that doesn't mean to say they weren't organised.

Over the years McGraw had gathered around him well-known faces who would do a job of work for him – for money, of course, only for money. He liked to present himself as the leader but that's not how it was. It rarely is.

His associates included Snaz, his brother-in-law, of course. Two men who had met at school were still working, robbing and getting rich together just the way they had always planned.

Snaz was a hard man and well respected in the east end. Even those who despised McGraw would spare good thoughts for Snaz. It was like the old adage – you can choose your friends but not your relatives. Those who didn't understand why Snaz worked for McGraw blamed his sister, Margaret, The Jeweller, for marrying McGraw. They forgot that the two men had been pals since boyhood and had a deep friendship.

Snaz was a strict supporter of the Loyalists in Ireland and, as such, had a lot of pull among their supporters in Glasgow. Very soon that would become even more important to McGraw.

Then there was Manny McDonnell. He had arrived from Ireland with one tale – that he had been active in the politics but had grown weary of it all. A Catholic, he was a supporter of the Republican movement and an active terrorist for the IRA. But money had gone missing from funds and some blamed McDonnell. They weren't just going to leave it at that.

Some in the east end who knew about McGraw's support for the Loyalist groups thought it strange that he and McDonnell were associates. But McGraw thought his leanings towards that side were secret. Thought that he could play both sides of the sectarian divide. He didn't know it at that time but he was trying the same ploy adopted by Arthur Thompson for years.

In future years, McGraw had plans to develop in Ireland. McDonnell might be useful to him in that – if he survived long enough.

There was Drew Drummond, of course, now running clubs and pubs in the city as he had planned after the BarL Team had stopped their robbing. To the outside world, Drummond was a straight-forward entrepreneur and businessman. In the east end he was a pal of McGraw's and that carried other responsibilities.

There was Trevor Lawson, the young builder. A straightforward man, he had got caught up with McGraw in a few illegal larks. Buying up stolen goods at a knockdown price, employing guys without the taxman knowing – that kind of stuff – but it was enough to compromise him. McGraw knew that he could ask Lawson to do a variety of things and they would get done – either that or some cops would be told of his past.

Then there was another brother-in-law, John Healy. Based in the southside of Glasgow in Thornliebank, Healy was known to be one of the fiercest players in the city. Around 1990 he was still young but McGraw recognised his talent and his steel. He was one for the future as well as being family.

George McCormack was officially a taxi driver. Called Crater Face because of a badly pock marked face, unofficially he was up for anything else that needed doing. A safe pair of hands for McGraw. He had another asset – a promising young cousin.

Billy McPhee was tall, strong and cared for no one – ideal attrib-utes if McGraw needed someone knifed. He had been a football casual, supporting Rangers, and specialised in taking a Stanley knife down the faces of injured enemy lying on the ground. Casuals didn't like that kind of easy blood – they preferred the guys who showed bravado and led the charge – but McGraw could use the man and would.

A pair of roofers, Gordon Ross and Chic Glackin, were also hanging around. The pair were greater associates of a man McGraw was friendly with, Bobby Glover, and he was getting into cahoots with Paul Ferris. But Ross and Glackin didn't work for anyone.

They were hardmen who wanted to make some money. Wanted it so bad they had just been jailed for three years for trafficking hash from Amsterdam. Caught, yes, but they had tried out a few ideas that McGraw liked, ideas he reckoned they could improve on.

There was his wife, Margaret, The Jeweller. As always she looked after the money and the businesses and looked after them well. If any crooked plan came up that would cost a few quid to set up, McGraw had to get the dosh from her. In spite of his money, he went about dressed as scruffily as he had when he was a bus conductor. Money was for growing not spending.

James 'Mudsie' Mullen and his brother Patrick agreed. They were businessmen. Shady, maybe, but businessmen all the same, particularly Mudsie. They had set about building up an empire of trading outlets and would expand into Ireland soon enough.

Last but far from least, was Joe Hanlon, known as Bananas for as long as anyone could recall. No one can remember precisely why he got that nickname but they all knew that Joe was one of the best streetfighters Glasgow had ever produced. Joe was the bouncer on the door of The Caravel – not the easiest or safest of jobs – but he was also much more than that. Whenever McGraw wanted to feel safe, he got Joe to tag along with him. If he ever needed some hard team sorted out he'd just send in Joe. No team, just Joe.

Add to that the scores of junkies he could hire for a tenner, taxi drivers who would do small jobs or happily launder his stolen money, ice cream van drivers who distributed bundles of drugs and his cop contacts who bailed him out scot-free all the time, it made for some collection of manpower.

Yet, was it enough to put him on a level Arthur Thompson would respect? He would soon find out.

35

MEETINGS FROM HELL

"Ah've always tried to do the right thing by you." McGraw's voice was high, almost squealing, but he didn't notice.

"Aye." Thompson's voice didn't waver, nor did his gaze. He didn't rate the man and that was that.

"Did Ah no tell ye about Bagan and the cops? Did Ah no?"

"Did ye?" Thompson was in usual talkative mood, as in not saying much. Speaking, never mind wittering away like a banshee like this guy, was a sign of weakness as far as he was concerned.

"Ye know Ah did. But what Billy did to my place isn't on. Can you no see that?"

"So you're no a fucking grass then?"

"Course Ah'm no a fucking grass but that's no my point. It's the damage to the pub. Cost me a lot of money so it did." They were standing in the storage area in a separate room at the back of the bar. Crates and barrels lay here and there in no particular order, boxes of crisps and nuts were piled up on the other, the sink was manky, cobwebs hung from every corner and the floor hadn't seen a brush in a long time. Thompson wondered about McGraw's high standards and how a wee fire was going to cost him that much.

"Probably done you a fucking favour," he said looking around.

It had taken McGraw two months to arrange this meeting with Thompson simply refusing to speak to anyone he sent or reply to any message. Eventually, the only place he was willing to meet was at The Caravel and in the backroom. He'd come in by the back fire escape and would leave that way too. No way did Thompson want to advertise talking with someone like McGraw. McGraw, on the other hand, let it be known that Thompson was coming to his place, to sort out that problem – a bit of boasting that was going to lead to serious trouble.

The meeting had lasted thirty minutes with McGraw doing all the pleading and demanding, Thompson hardly bothering to reply. Suddenly, Thompson agreed a price of compensation for the damage to the pub without conceding any guilt on Billy's behalf and began to take his leave.

"It was good that we talked, Arthur," said McGraw following him out. Thompson looked round the waste ground car park before he left the shelter of the building. He might have been carrying his Beretta but he was on his own. Better safe than sorry all the time and he just didn't trust McGraw. "Good too that we agreed a figure. Excellent." Thompson had already decided he wasn't going to pay McGraw a penny. He had just agreed to get out of his company, to get away from him. "And Ah'm sure we can do business in the future, you know," McGraw went on, "that bene-fits both of us . . ." On and on he went and Thompson wondered if he was ever going to shut up. Then there was the screech of car tyres.

Across the waste ground coming at speed was a car driven by Tam Bagan with a bunch of his crew inside. It slid to a halt lying straight across the front of Thompson's motor. If he wanted to leave in a hurry he'd have to reverse in an area pitted with deep potholes and scarred with shards of glass and rusty metal spikes. First, he'd have to make it into his car.

Bagan was out and at Thompson in a flash. He had to thank McGraw for the warning that he would find Thompson right there on that day and he had a few issues with his former boss. His fat son was still ranting in the jails blaming him for his prison time and putting his name on some hit list he was forever reading out.

"Ah'm going to get ma Da to sort this lot," he'd boast. "The Godfather will kill them all starting with Bagan . . ."

All that was getting on Tam Bagan's nerves never mind that Fatboy and his father owed him money he was never going to see. He had nothing to do with Fatboy getting the jail. That was his own stupid fault and his father said nothing, just let him rant on. Well, the old bastard was going to pay the price. Or was he?

As the two teams faced each other, Thompson reckoned he was a dead man and lost the plot. Pulling his Beretta from his jacket he pistol-whipped, butted and kicked Bagan, knocking him to the ground. Standing there above him, he aimed the pistol at Bagan's face. That's when family proved valuable.

A cousin of Bagan's was in his company and went for Thompson. As the old gangster turned on everyone else, training his gun on them, Bagan jumped from the ground and battered him again and again. Now it was reverse roles with Bagan standing over Thompson, his gun aimed at the middle of his face.

"Who's the big man now, arsehole, eh? No big down there waiting to kiss goodbye to your shitty life," roared Bagan.

Beside him McGraw started hollering, "NO HERE, TAM. DON'T SHOOT HIM HERE."

Terrified by the sudden attack he suddenly realised that if Thompson got shot dead there, Bagan and his mates would be out of there in a flash but where could he go with his pub only yards away? Nowhere. The murder squad would be there in a jiff asking all sorts of questions. Not even his cops could get him free of this one. At the very least he'd be forced to tell them who the killer was. Tell them in court, the way you're not meant to, the way that would bring Bagan's friends and family down on him with a vengeance.

McGraw wasn't shouting to save Thompson's life. He was pleading for his own.

Bagan's cousin and another mate put hands on his shoulders and a quiet nod. He wasn't long out of jail – what did he want to go back for?

The fury still welling inside him, Bagan thrashed Thompson once across the face with the gun. Getting back inside his car,

Bagan watched as his team turned on the old gangster's motor, kicking in the lights.

"Drive home in that, you prick," they said before getting into Bagan's motor and driving off.

McGraw helped Thompson to his feet, only to be shrugged off by the older man. With a glower, Thompson got in his car and revved up the engine. Then he seemed to remember something. Through his broken window he spat a large gob of blood onto the ground.

"Meant to tell you," he said to McGraw. "Young Arthur has a new pal in the jail." He stopped and spat more blood out, wiping the crimson smear from his face with the back of his hand. "Frank McPhie." He looked at McGraw and gave the closest he could to a smile. A kind of crooked grin. Shoving the car into gear he took off, heading home without saying another word. No 'thanks for saving my life'. Nothing. Just that The Iceman was the Fatboy's minder in jail. The Iceman who McGraw feared. The same Iceman who knew all about the Doyles and who every year got a cut of large payments he made to the two fire lighters. The two killers. That Iceman.

Back in The Caravel, McGraw needed a very large, strong drink. His hands were shaking, his voice almost gone but inside he was fuming. Terrified and fuming.

"We're going to need some men," he said to a close ally.

"What for?"

"Ah've just met two pricks whose time has come."

36

BUMP IN THE NIGHT

It was a dark night and late. Two men had taken a drive into the scheme to say hello to some old pals. They were driving out now, heading to other affairs. Then they saw him.

Arthur Thompson had been to the Provanmill Inn, his well-known HQ. He'd had a few drinks, was in a cheerful mood and heading off home to The Ponderosa where his wife, Rita, would be waiting.

"There's that old bastard," said one.

"On his fucking own."

"Want to see a good trick?"

The car hit him full on, sending him spinning and landing with a crunch on the road. Yards away the car stopped, its brakes screeching the tyres against the road. The driver looked over his shoulder, watching the man on the road. He moved. Struggled for a while then slowly edged up till he was leaning on an elbow.

"Fuck that."

The car reversed over the man. Stopped then drove over him again. Now he was still. The pair got out of the car. One scanning the area for nosy neighbours who might be watching, the other heading to the man on the road.

"Thought you might, you arsehole."

His hand was inside his jacket, resting on the butt of his gun. Pulling away his hand and lifting the gun, the man felt the finely balanced weight of the pistol in his gloved mitt. A Beretta as usual. Classy. Going to the front of his own car he shot a bullet though the bodywork.

"What the fuck you doing?" his mate demanded.

"Evidence. Just evidence in case that old cunt survives or someone has spotted us through their net curtains. In case we need a reason." The other guy laughed. His pal thought of everything.

Placing the gun by the man's side the pair dashed into their motor and off. They'd take care of that car soon but now they were heading for the city centre. Some place busy. Some place they'd be known. An alibi place.

Behind them the man on the ground stirred. His body felt wrecked and wracked in pain. He knew who had run over him. He'd spotted the bastards seconds before the car had hit. He knew their game and he was going to ruin it.

It took him long seconds to raise himself on to one elbow. It felt like his legs were broken, his insides wrenched apart.

It took longer seconds for his hand to find his gun. One long deep breath, his arm slowly back then he threw the pistol with all his might.

Ten yards away, on some long grass-covered waste ground, the gun landed with a dull thump. Back on the road, the man collapsed. Acid spew swelled into his mouth.

"Fuck," he groaned then passed out.

Minutes later he would come round, confronted by a friendly face. But it was different, too different from anyone he knew. What was it? Aye, the dark glasses. Who wears dark glasses at night in a Glasgow scheme?

"Arthur? It's all right." The voice sounded familiar. "It's me. Blind Jonah. Ah'll make sure you're fine."

"Arthur Thompson going to die? That's a shame." It was McGraw blethering out loud with a wide smile in The Caravel the next morning. "Shows you what happens to cunts when they mess with me, eh?" A wee nod and a wise wink. No more to be said.

McGraw was taking the credit. McGraw was lying again. It was a lie that was going to haunt him very soon.

37

GOOD BUSINESS, BAD BUSINESS

McGraw thought nothing of it. Why should he? It was just another two east end boys starting up wee businesses, trying to make a few quid.

Bobby Glover was a main man. Anyone who knew him knew that and that included Paul Ferris. After Ferris' split from Thompson the pair met up as Ferris met with a lot of east end faces. He had a living to earn and that would take new contacts. Bobby Glover was the one who impressed him straightaway.

Money, as legitimate as possible, was Bobby's aim. What other reason was there to get into crime? It was exactly Ferris' aim too. Why risk jail or even death if you aren't out to make a few quid? What's the point?

While other players were content to make their way outwith the law, these two always wanted a legitimate life, if they could. Besides, some businesses were so lucrative they were almost theft but theft they wouldn't get jailed for.

The pair of them had a lot in common. Both had sons almost the same age. Both were committed to their kids. Neither wanted their boys to follow the same crooked businesses as them. There was only one way to make sure of that – go legit.

Ferris had various wee larks going like selling second hand cars but wanted something better. The older Glover had gone further, owning The Cottage Bar, a few ice cream vans and some taxis. It looked like Glover had made it and had it easy but he wasn't where he wanted to be yet and it wasn't always like that.

To those and such as those he didn't mind admitting that in his early days his loving wife, Eileen, had supported them through her well honed skills as a shoplifter. Flogging the gear round the east end brought her into contact with a lot of people – including the McGraws who they considered to be friends. But Bobby Glover never quite trusted McGraw. Didn't trust him at all.

Glover was old school, believing that being a grass was the lowest of the low, hurting women or kids was punishable in the most extreme ways and men should work to protect the frail and elderly who lived on their streets. He knew McGraw broke all those rules and that made him someone Bobby Glover couldn't trust.

Ferris and Glover bought into a small company, Cottage Conservatories, that installed double glazing.

Business was going well. But they had another idea of installing new kitchens by replacing the worktops and fronts on the existing structures creating an entire new look but at a fraction of the price of getting a brand new kitchen. It was popular with the punters.

An old pal of Ferris approached them. Tam Bagan didn't want to be a criminal all his life either. Worse, his wife had started dipping into drugs and that was becoming a bigger and bigger problem for him. What he needed was a good way of earning a living that didn't keep him out all night, that didn't run the constant risk of jail. A legal life. Unlike the other pair, he had a role model to base his aims on – Arthur Thompson.

Bagan and his siblings were raised by a relative of Thompson's. Though not blood related he might as well have been a nephew of the man they called The Godfather and bright enough to learn from him.

Being a tough guy was no problem. Tam Bagan was seen as one of the hardest young men in Glasgow from a very early age long before he worked for Thompson. At only twenty-one, two young Easterhouse guys thought they'd double deal him and almost died as a result, pumped full of bullets from his gun. No one messed with Bagan.

But he also watched and could see that Arthur Thompson wasn't all about crime and corruption. Could tell that he seemed to spend most of his life dealing with businesses often run for him by others but his nevertheless. What the young Bagan wouldn't have known was that most of these were stolen, the owners coerced to work Thompson's way and hand over most of their takings every week. They were legal, that's all he knew.

Bagan had a brain so Glover and Ferris allowed him in on their business ventures. The three young men were pleased by their deal and looked forward to getting rich fast. Meantime they had other business to be taking care of.

Armed robberies were happening throughout Scotland and the cops were nowhere near catching the team. Banks and security vans were being taken out almost at will. Occasionally a post office would get done but only one of the bigger ones with a stash of cash out the back. That crew were so good that the cops suspected the BarL Team were back at work. McGraw knew different.

For a few years he had been setting up robberies but strictly for others to do the dangerous work. It was a common ploy in the crime world where senior, experienced robbers would do the planning, advise the team leader then sit back and wait for a successful heist when he'd receive a large cut of the takings. A lot of dosh for little risk.

Yet McGraw knew that the jobs he set up weren't matching someone else's work. He and his police partners suspected another team – Ferris, Glover, Bagan and Joe Hanlon, McGraw's young minder. Suspecting is as far as they ever got.

McGraw didn't like that much. He thought he was due a cut at least but the four men wouldn't tell him anything and he knew if he pressed they'd stick his cut up his rear end – a bullet not a pile of banknotes.

That was a minor irritation for McGraw since he was busy enough. On that score he was using Bagan more and more. As in that incident with Arthur Thompson, Bagan was the type of guy McGraw liked to have around him – tough as nails. He was also bright and maybe the kind of guy McGraw wanted to draw into his business. Maybe he could make money out of Bagan?

One day McGraw asked Bagan to go along with him on a wee errand.

"Just dropping something off," he said. "No problem."

They stopped the car outside a pub and McGraw pulled a wad of notes from his pocket and carefully counted out £1,400 which he then stuffed in an envelope. Two minutes later they were standing chatting to a man Bagan recognised. He was a cop and he got the envelope.

Bagan later asked McGraw what he was up to.

"Just paying my way," he replied. "That's how you have to work these days. You have to deal with the cops. Call it an insurance policy."

"What?"

"Well it is when you have this." From inside his scruffy jacket McGraw pulled a tape recorder that was still on. One that had taped the cop talking about the money and so on. "Think he'll ever put me in now?" But even that didn't make McGraw happy for long. "Ah remember when it used to be a crate of fucking whisky," he moaned.

Bagan hadn't been there by accident. McGraw wanted to draw him in, to show him how powerful he was.

Another time shortly after that, McGraw was furious. Some drug dealer had been straying into his territory and selling quality gear cheap. McGraw was going to get him or at least watch others do the dirty.

He called up Bagan, Glover and Hanlon and asked them for a hand. What he meant was that they should hurt these men badly while he watched from safety. Maybe he'd brave coming in after the event and causing them some damage when there was no risk to himself.

They cornered the guys in a street in the east end but they fled fast in their motor. McGraw and the others took after them. There followed a car chase at over 100mph. McGraw's car kept ramming the other one, trying to force it off the road and someone in their car was firing a pistol at them. The chase went all the way to Coatbridge but hadn't gone unnoticed. Someone had belled the cops.

All six men were lifted and locked up in the cells. Bagan, Glover and Hanlon reckoned they were in big trouble. Carrying guns and attempted murder at least. A few hours later the four were released and never heard of the charges again. The other two went down big time for drug dealing. McGraw's cops had worked their magic again. No one was complaining – that night at least.

Bagan was being drawn in, shown McGraw's secrets. There was nothing wrong with what he was being shown. It seemed McGraw was simply bribing some cops large for favours. They were useful favours as in getting charges dropped or maybe locating a target. Just get a cop to pull his details out of the National Police Computer.

The loose association of some of the most feared gangsters in the country worked in relative peace and harmony with each other in Glasgow's east end. Yet McGraw couldn't let old sores heal. They had to be scratched. He had one man in his sights, a man who owed him large. He was going after the runt.

38

THE RUNT RUNS

"Who's about who needs a few quid?" McGraw was asking around his associates. "Ah need big guys who look good in uniform."

The last bit flummoxed folk. What sort of uniforms had McGraw in mind?

"Ah bet it's polis uniforms," one guy offered one night.

"Aye, the fucking pervo's about to admit they give him a hard on," some other guy said.

"Can't be getting enough these days," offered another.

"Eh?"

"Working so much with the plainclothes mob."

"Ha. Needs some cunts to dress up eh."

They weren't far from the truth.

McGraw was owed money and it was burning a hole in what he had for a soul. With other men he'd just send some heavies round to sort it or kill them. Maybe both. But you didn't do that with The Godfather. With Arthur Thompson.

Thompson hadn't paid a bean for the fire damage Billy Thompson had caused The Caravel. That irked McGraw. Money was everything.

He didn't consider that he had paid Fatboy zilch for his drugs territory since he had been jailed. That he was making tens of thousands of pounds a week out of a guy he had helped the cops set up and jail. When it came to money the only word McGraw understood was more.

The idea had come from an unexpected source. In prison, Fatboy was still ranting. For a while he had moved away from his hit list to another theme – killing Paul Ferris in a most creative way.

A bullet in the head was too good for him. He'd be kidnapped, rolled up in a carpet and taken to Fatboy's house. Down in the basement he'd be injected with smack contaminated with HIV, Hep. C and every other disease known to man for one simple reason – he'd use hypos that had come straight from the handbags of the cheapest street whores well on their way to death.

Being fed only a wee bit of water Ferris would die a slow, painful death and Fatboy would watch, tormenting him all the way. Perfect for agonising revenge. Only one problem – Fatboy announced to the world that was exactly what he was going to do.

Beside him, The Iceman must have rolled his eyes and wondered what he had got himself into. All right, no one had actually tried to harm Fatboy – his father's reputation made sure of that. So, The Iceman's job was easy if it wasn't for all that shite the Fatboy talked. Maybe it was time to resign?

Ferris just laughed at the tales.

McGraw had another idea. Maybe it was time to copy?

Billy Thompson, just like his big brother, was a creature of habit. Not a great idea for a street player since it gave your enemies an idea of where you'd be and when. But he was The Godfather's son. What did he have to fear from anyone?

Most days he was hitting The Anvil pub a stone's throw away from Barlinnie Prison and a short walk from his house. It was just another Riddrie pub with a few old boys taking their time over their one pint of heavy. He would be a sitting duck.

A couple of guys would go in wearing cop uniforms that he'd borrow from some of his pet polis. They'd need to know the routine so they could copy the cops in arresting Billy, put handcuffs on him and get him out of there. In the back of a Transit made up to look like a police meat wagon, they'd roll him in a carpet. That's when the penny would drop. Billy would have listened to Fatboy's tales till it made him sick. He'd know all about his big brother's plans for Ferris including that carpet.

After that they'd take him to some empty flat, one of the many that McGraw now owned (The Jeweller saw to that). Tie him to a chair, muffled, and threaten to inject him with a nasty looking hypo. It wouldn't be full of dodgy smack though, it'd just look the part. That's when they'd get him to phone his father – all tearful and terrified – and beg him to pay a ransom. Fifty grand ought to be enough, McGraw reckoned, though the figure dwarfed the deal with Thompson on the pub damage.

All that McGraw needed was three or four capable guys, none of whom Billy recognised. Who was around?

Big Gordon Ross was just out of jail for his drug trafficking as was his pal Chic Glackin. Both were short of cash and keen to earn. Then there was Billy McPhee. He was okay in knifing some-body when McGraw asked and always held his tongue so maybe it was time to test him out further. Best of all Billy Thompson wouldn't know any of them.

"Billy Thompson." Billy turned round the drink half way to his mouth. "I have a warrant for your arrest for possession of drugs. Please come with us." Everyone bar smacked-up Billy had turned and stared as soon as the two cops entered the pub. Now no one was taking their eyes off the scene.

"Do ye fuck," squealed Billy, all the time wondering if they did. He'd had a smack problem since his teens and it was getting worse and worse. Maybe one night he'd got searched and charged? How was he supposed to recall? But he wasn't going to go easy.

The big handsome cop cuffed one of Billy's wrists and then cuffed him to himself. "Ah said NOOOOO," screamed Billy. "Yer no taking me."

The two cops managed to manhandle Billy outside even though he was kicking, holding back, pulling to the side. The bar customers followed them.

"They're no real polis," Billy screamed showing a lot more insight in that second than he did most of his life. "They're fucking taking me HOSTAGE."

Slowly, the 'cops' realised that the pub had been packed. That it was filled with men wearing half a uniform, a bit like cop uniforms, like off duty cops. Prison warden uniforms. It was payday at Barlinnie and the staff were having a few drinks.

McGraw had planned a great deal spot on but not the day of the kidnap. To make matters worse there was something he didn't know. Arthur Thompson had been supplementing the wages of some Barlinnie screws for years. After all Barlinnie was where his men would tend to go if lifted. It was also where his enemies were held captive. Help or hurt, either way it was worth the money and meant he had many pals who happened to work in that jail.

As one 'cop' opened the back doors of the van, some of the off duty screws grabbed Billy. Tug of war on. The Transit driver sat and revved the engine. Should he get out and help? Too late. The cuffs burst and Billy fell into the arms of his helpers.

The 'cops' were in the van and out of there in a flash. As they sped away, angry screws chased them waving their fists and shouting abuse. What the kidnappers thought would be a good laugh turned out to be one of the most embarrassing incidents of their lives.

Back outside the pub, off duty screws were helping Billy to his feet.

"Are you okay, son?" asked one. Skinny Billy looked at him, his eyes large, popping out his skull, his face death white, then he took to his heels and ran.

"What the fuck?" asked one of the men.

"Think that Billy's no just weak up top," said someone tapping the side of their head and looking down at the ground. There was a large puddle of steaming fluid.

"He's pished himself."

"Fucking runt."

A few days later in the Provanmill Inn, Arthur Thompson sat at his usual gunslinger's position at the end of the bar and dealt with an unwelcome guest.

"Ah heard about your boy's trouble," said McGraw. "The other day in Riddrie." Thompson just looked at him like he was a dog turd stuck on the sole of his shoe. "A fucking liberty, man, so it is. Even when they're grown up you still care about your weans, eh?" Days before, brandishing a baseball bat, McGraw had chased his own son, Winkie, out of the family home for being back on the smack. "When somebody tries to hurt them it just gets my goat. My fucking goat, Ah tell ye." After a few days on the street, Winkie was spotted by Paul Ferris, taken in, cleaned, slept and fed good meals. They had had a few interesting conversations with Winkie offering that his father was nothing more than a police grass. "Ye'll want to know who's responsible eh?" McGraw looked this way and that, watching that no one was close enough to hear him. "All Ah'll say is that Paul Ferris is one bad bastard." He was speaking in a hoarse whisper. "And his pals. Nobody would blame you ye know."

"What?" Now he had Thompson's attention.

"If you hurt them real bad."

Big trouble was just around the corner.

39

BOUNCERS, BULLETS AND BACKSTABBING

Drew Drummond was McGraw's good pal, had been since child-hood. They had robbed as kids, moved to London, worked the BarL Team together and much more. Now Drummond was doing what he had always planned – running pubs and clubs – and doing it well. But not so well as to avoid trouble. Lethal trouble.

The night before, in his club called McKinlay's, there had been a fracas at the door. Nothing unusual in that except this time was different. Glover and Ferris' and Hanlon's women had gone for a night out and, instead, ended up being manhandled and thrown out by a big bouncer on the door.

As soon as they heard, Glover and Ferris asked Drew Drummond to meet them. Late that night he did so, still dressed in his tuxedo work outfit. Drummond was a big man and violent when needed. Smart as he looked, there would be a razor sharp knife tucked into the back of his cummerbund.

Drummond wasn't the man to fear in that motor. That was Ferris, whose reputation was well established and upsetting his woman rated high up there on the punishment charts.

With Ferris driving, Glover in the passenger seat and the hulk of Drew Drummond locked in the rear, they took off through the east end and on to the M74 heading south. All the while Glover was berating Drummond for what had happened while he apol-ogised and promised to sack the bouncer pronto. Meantime, the car was going faster and faster through the night, heading towards the vast tract of Strathclyde Park, an anonymous place where anything could happen.

"How far are we going, Bobby?" Drummond pleaded of Glover.

"How far do you want to go?" Ferris asked back quietly.

That did it. Drummond somehow managed to scramble over the front seat, across Glover's knee, yanked the door open and threw himself on to the motorway. The last Glover and Ferris saw of him, he was bouncing across the tarmac through swerving cars, the beams of their headlights playing zig-zag on the dark sky.

Now Ferris and Glover were heading McGraw's way. McGraw knew they would be. A distraught and battered Drummond had phoned him from a call box asking for a lift home.

McGraw and Joe Hanlon hadn't made it to his car from The Caravel when Glover and Ferris pulled up. He had known Bobby Glover for years, liked and trusted him. He was capable of violence but he wasn't going to tackle McGraw. Was he? It was Ferris who terrified McGraw.

When cornered, McGraw did what he usually did. Apologised, grovelled and made promises to harm those others who were to blame. It didn't wash.

Moving right up to him, toe-to-toe, Ferris said into his face, "If I can get this close to you, McGraw, if you were going to be dead, rigor mortis would already be setting in."

It was a let off – for the moment – but McGraw had to have Ferris sorted. Had to have him taken off the street.

Later that night, after The Caravel closed, McGraw decided to have words with Drew Drummond.

"Kill ye? Of course, he was going to kill ye," he insisted. "Bastard came round here to wait for yese. It was me that talked him out of it. Right, Joe?" Joe Hanlon didn't like what he was hearing. He liked Glover and Ferris having grown very close to both and had no grudge against Drummond. Now here was McGraw lying to and about them and asking him to back it up. Why? There was only one way to find out. He nodded his agreement.

"Bastard was going to kill me out in the dark, Tam. He really was." Drummond had had a very bad night.

"Ah know but you're safe from him now cos Ah talked him down."

"Thanks, Tam. Thanks a lot." Drummond meant what he was saying. "Ah owe you."

"Well there is something you can do for me," said McGraw knowing their chat would lead to this point. "In return like."

"Anything, Tam. Just ask."

Out in the cemetery behind The Caravel, the three men stood in the dark. This was the same graveyard McGraw used to hand over illegal weapons to the cops in return for favours. From a black plastic bag under one fallen gravestone, McGraw pulled out a .45 automatic.

"Just need to check it, Drew," said McGraw. He lifted his arm out straight, aimed at a dark shape he knew was backed up by a railway embankment and fired. The crisp, clear shot rang out and echoed in the night. "Perfect." McGraw filled the gun with bullets as they walked.

"Where we going, Tam?" asked Drummond.

"Go and deal with this," McGraw said to Joe, handing him the pistol.

"What?"

"Bagan."

"Fuck off," said Joe spitting. "Ah want nothing to do with this business."

"Drew?" asked McGraw.

"What?"

"Anything, you said. You'd do anything. Just wait till he turns his back." Drummond was caught. He took the .45 and stuffed it into the back of his trouser waistband.

Bagan was a late night man. When the three men knocked at his door it was answered in seconds. Some sat and drank some tea, others had a can of beer and chatted.

"Come on, Joe," said McGraw after half an hour. "We've got a hard day tomorrow." The pair left leaving Bagan with Drummond all tooled up.

Two hours and too many cups of tea later, Drummond left the house with Bagan still alive and breathing. It must have been a very long two hours for Drummond running through his mind what would happen if he missed, if he was caught, if he was jailed – all leading to the decision to leave with the gun not fired.

As he left the flat a pair of eyes watched him from the shadows, below them a gun, the safety catch off and the trigger ready to be pulled. From two blocks away Ferris had heard the shot in the night, got tooled up and slipped out of his home in time to see McGraw and the other two leave the graveyard. From a nearby school playground he had watched Bagan's flat, waiting for gunfire, waiting to exact revenge.

It wasn't that he liked Bagan, not then. He and Glover had fallen out with Bagan and split in their business enterprises legal and illegal. There was bad blood between Bagan and Ferris. A great deal of bad blood but not so much that Ferris wouldn't take Bagan's side against McGraw.

If Drummond had fired that gun he wouldn't have lived to leave the flat. Next in Ferris' list was McGraw. He knew where he'd be – all wrapped up at home, walking the floor, unable to sleep, worrying about his money.

That's what Ferris would have done but that didn't mean he understood. McGraw and Bagan seemed to be working together okay. Bagan was involved in many things with McGraw and had seen the man's business inside out. So why have him shot? Did he now know too much? Was that it? The same reason Arthur Thompson and Fatboy had set Ferris up with the cops?

That night McGraw got himself a new enemy and knew sod all about it. Paul Ferris was now out to get him though he wouldn't let on. Not yet.

A few days later, Ferris paid Joe Hanlon a visit at The Caravel during closing hours. Only McGraw and Joe were in as Ferris guessed they would be. Somehow he got the conversation round to Bagan about the trouble he had caused him business-wise, hoping that McGraw would do the same. No chance.

"Ah hear that it's bad problems you're having with Bagan," McGraw offered.

"Yeah, we need to sort it," replied Ferris.

"Ah can see to it that he's no here for a while," suggested McGraw. "Take him out."

"Kill him? Do you mean fucking kill him?"

"Naw, naw," McGraw had his hands out in front of him signalling that he would never think of that. Ferris and Joe knew better. "Ah'll just have a wee word with one of my polis. So his motor gets stopped one night and they find a bag of smack. Enough to get him twelve year inside."

This was worse than Ferris expected. Wanting to kill man was one thing but admitting that he could easily set him up with cop-planted smack and him to go to jail for something he didn't do was something else. Especially admitting he had all those bent coppers at his beck and call.

"I don't know about you," Ferris said to McGraw, "but I don't work that way. And I don't work with corrupt cops. In my world we sort problems man to man." Ferris wanted to pull his gun and shoot McGraw. Wanted to badly. But McGraw's police would come tumbling down not just on his head but on that of young Joe Hanlon too.

"All I meant, Paul, was that . . ." McGraw was ignored.

"Joe." Ferris stood looking at his young pal. "Is this really the kind of filth you want to work with?" He didn't expect an answer. "You want to walk away, you know you'll be welcome with us."

As Ferris left the pub, Hanlon said nothing. Though he had made a decision. He would work with McGraw for a few days more, collect some wages then leave to team up with Glover and Ferris.

McGraw stood and fumed. He had to have Ferris taken out and taken out soon. The problem was that he couldn't find anyone willing to take the hit no matter how much he offered to pay. A few had taken payments then did sod all. He was going to have to find another way.

McGraw wouldn't have long to wait. Fatboy was about to be freed.

40

A GLASGOW SEND OFF

"Listen up," Fatboy shouted to a packed Provanmill Inn. "Youse will all want to hear this." It was his hit list.

Fatboy Thompson had been free a matter of hours. Not for him getting lost in the arms and bed of his woman after all those years apart. He had business to get on with.

That morning, one of his father's men drove him around Glasgow stopping as and when directed. Behind him two cars travelled cautiously following him, both sent by the same man – McGraw. Two cars were used in case one lost him in the busy city centre traffic. It didn't seem the most exciting of trips. Who gets excited by ironmonger's shops? Fatboy, that's who.

Thompson's oldest son was buying the parts to make himself a range of shooters and ammo. He was going to need every gun he could get.

His regular source of guns, Andrew McCardle, was in trouble with the cops. For years he had dealt illegal shooters to every team in Glasgow without interference from the cops. But now he was being investigated and heading for jail for sure. Fatboy had other sources of weapons but McCardle was the easiest and the best. What he didn't know was that McGraw had had a word in the ear of one of his polis telling him McCardle's MO. Public spirited? No, defending himself knowing Fatboy was soon to hit the streets.

Once back in Blackhill it was time for a pint at his local and that announcement. Chatter in the busy pub died instantly and all eyes and ears were on him. For years now he had been drafting and redrafting that list. Almost everyone in the city had heard of it at one time or another but it didn't seem to change much. Just the order moved around a bit.

That day it read:

"McGraw. Doesn't pay his debts. Not fucking one.

"Bagan. The double dealing bastard.

"Paul Ferris, the wee shite.

"Willie Gibson. He cannae hide.

"The Irishman, John Friel.

"Jaimba McLean."

On and on the list went with each name being followed by a brief reason or some insult. He was going to have them all killed in that order and fast.

Fatboy had hardly finished reading out his list when word was spreading through the city. Trouble had arrived.

One of the men from the two cars tailing Fatboy had been in the pub listening. They soon skedaddled back to report to their boss.

Calls were put in early doors to Bagan, Ferris and every other face in the city. There was difficulty reaching Ferris. He was on a flight from London where he was spending more and more time these days working up his relations with the Adams family and others. When the tom toms started beating he was flying home, having a few drinks on the plane with a young guy called Gary McCrae, and Karen, his girlfriend.

Willie Gibson probably didn't get called. He was an ex-mechanic for Fatboy and was blamed for grassing him up years earlier for keeping guns in his garage in Maryhill. Scared witless, Willie had taken his family as far south as possible to live. On a rare visit back to the area a few years before, Willie, his father-in-law, sister-in-law and brother were all shot on a bridge crossing the M8 but survived. Paul Ferris had been tried for attempted murder and found not proven. What was known was that Fatboy and his wee brother, Billy, had watched the whole scene throughout and obviously hadn't forgotten the score to be settled.

Those on the list would pay most attention, of course. But it wasn't just them. The remaining couple of members of the Welsh family would have been looking over their shoulder worried that the Fatboy wanted to avenge their twenty-five-year fight with this father.

Then there were his dealers who had moved to work with McGraw or on the Maryhill, Possil and Milton side with the Lyons family. They would have all been on their toes.

That night Fatboy and his wife went to Café India with his mother and father for a curry. It was Glasgow's favourite food and he had been denied it for years.

Back home, he sat in with his father for a while, chatting as a free man. Or at least temporarily free. This was his first weekend home and he was due back in the jail on the Monday. It was preparing him for the day soon when he'd be released. Soon, but not yet. Someone wasn't willing to wait that long.

Out in the dark he only had to take a few steps to be home from his parents' house. He didn't make it.

"Get yer old man to bail you out of this one, you fat bastard," said the man in the long woman's wig.

"Just a minute," stuttered Fatboy. "Ah'll get my Da." He started turning, heading for The Ponderosa when the first bullet caught him on the cheek with a dull, soundproofed THUMP, spinning him round and dumping him on the ground. Whimpering, Fatboy got on his hands and knees and started crawling to the house. Then the second bullet caught him in the rib cage, bursting a lung. Quickly, with the long barrelled pistol held in two hands, the hitman delivered the final shot – a bullet straight up the arse. An insult but deadly too as the bullet crashed though vital organs. In Glasgow it was called a Send Off.

It took a minute and the hitman was in the car with his two back-up men, Londoners with rifles on their laps, and speeding away to destroy the motor and all other evidence. Within two hours the hitman would be heading south, the Londoners well on their way back to the Big Smoke. By the time Fatboy was rushed to the Royal Infirmary nearby he was declared dead. It was three and half hours after he'd read out that hit list.

Farther out east in The Caravel, the phone rang. McGraw was quickly handed the receiver. The call only lasted seconds.

"A round of drinks on me," he shouted to the bar with a big smile. The crowd turned and stared at the mean man suddenly turned generous. "We have celebrating to do. Come on, let's party."

By bedtime, the whole city held its breath. It was August 1991 and Glasgow was going to burn.

41

FIT UP

"You'll need to help, Tam," said Laurel looking deadpan serious.

"But ye know it's him," McGraw spluttered. "Everybody knows it was Ferris." All he was doing was reflecting back to the cop what he and his bosses had assumed as soon as they had heard of Fatboy's murder. But assuming and proving are two different things.

"We need some solid witnesses," said Hardy.

"Let's face it," Laurel butted in, "any fucking witness."

"There are more cops on the streets sniffing into this than in your worst nightmare, Tam," said Hardy. "But we've never met with such silence. No one, I mean NO one, is saying a bloody word."

"That's because they're scared of him. Ferris. And who can fucking blame them eh." McGraw was chain smoking, anxious, constantly looking out of his window and checking his CCTV. With Ferris free anything could happen. Anything.

"Ach, we know, man. We know that."

"And so you want my help eh?" he said, staring at them as if he couldn't believe their nerve. "So I take the fucking risks right? Are the polis no paid to do that eh?"

For a couple of hours the three men argued and tossed insults and parries back and forth. The cops were in trouble. They couldn't even grumble too much about newspaper headlines predicting that Glasgow would go into meltdown once her organised gangs started the inevitable all-out war.

Everyone was watching and waiting. The McGoverns in the north. The Daniels in the west and south. John Healy and his sidekick, Specky Boyd. The Paisley mob. Even experienced guys like Bobby Dempster were getting a bit edgy. Would Rab Carruthers come back from Manchester to claim his place? Or would they all leave it to Ferris and, if so, would that produce wars?

Street life had been relatively stable for a long time. Now, The Godfather had been challenged by his own son getting slaughtered at his own front door. There was bound to be big trouble.

"Okay, okay," McGraw sighed. "Ah think Ah can help ye. Just give me a couple of days."

"You're some man, Tam," said Laurel.

"Aye, so ye are," Hardy agreed.

"Just one thing," McGraw added. "If Ah pull this off Ah'll be looking for a wee bit come and go on a project Ah'm thinking about."

"Aye, and what will that be?"

"Later, Ah'll tell you about it later."

McGraw already knew exactly what it was. He'd been talking with big Gordon Ross and Chic Glackin about an idea they had been working. A few times now they had taken cars into Amsterdam and filled the panels full of good quality dope, driving it back and crossing the ferry without mishap. The pair had done it so often they could tell you the profit in a Volkswagen Golf, BMW or an Audi load. It was counted in the tens of thousands. Good money.

Ross had more ambitious ideas using the same method needing someone with a team and also some cash. Yet there was a problem. Ross had been quite close to Ferris and had gone to him for some advice. Ferris told him not to work with McGraw, warned him in the strongest terms. Trouble was that Ferris seemed to be spending most of his life in London so Ross was getting a bit frustrated. As soon as this business was over and Ferris in jail for Fatboy's murder, McGraw would run with the idea. That would take a wee bit of help from the cops though. Surely jailing Ferris was worth that? It was only dope.

As soon as Laurel and Hardy had gone, McGraw was on to some of his men.

"Get tooled up. We have a few visits to pay," he said.

"Who to?" one asked.

"Just you fucking drive," he growled. "Ah know where we're going."

William Gillen was their first port of call. A few months before, McGraw had wanted to find Blind Jonah McKenzie claiming that Jonah was stealing some of his drugs territory. Jonah simply wasn't in the city but Gillen said he knew where he was and would take him there for £50 and some Valium.

After several hours driving round Kilmarnock, it was clear that Jonah was nowhere to be seen. On the way back, Gillen kept rabbiting on with more excuses and McGraw lost the plot. He ordered the driver to pull in at a lay-by and see to Gillen. He was promptly kneecapped, left bleeding on the ground and finally warned that if he whispered anything about this the next bullet would be higher – in his brain.

Sure enough, Gillen had refused to tell the cops who had shot him but now McGraw was about to change his mind.

"Was just wanting to be sure you recall what happened that day," he had said to Gillen. "That day you were with Bobby Glover and Paul Ferris and Ferris kneecapped you. Remember?"

Gillen soon remembered having been sweetened by a couple of hundred pounds, some free Es and the promise that he'd be in police protection till long after Ferris had been jailed.

The cops were delighted. This was all they needed to arrest Ferris and Glover on something. They didn't reveal their game plan to the investigating officers. Simply made sure that they got the message that Gillen might be worth a visit, make it seem as if was their breakthrough. He was in police protection by nightfall and the cops were out to arrest Ferris and Glover.

With Ferris in custody it didn't take McGraw's men long to hook in two others. Wee Barnie Docherty was an Irish junky who lived in Blackhill and was more than happy to testify – for the regular bags of quality smack McGraw's men would provide.

"Thirty grand," he had said.

"What?" asked McGraw.

"Ferris offered me thirty grand to help him murder Fatboy Thompson." His face had been poker straight then he added with a wink and a smile, "Sure he did."

The car thief was harder to turn. McGraw's men soon found players who had used a Blackhill man before and a few garages who had bought cars off him to ring and sell back into the market. They also knew from the cops what the suspect car for the hitman was that night – at least the model and make.

"You say it's a Nissan Bluebird he asked you to get for him, right." David Logue said nothing. "Or else some cops will be visiting you with regard to some stolen motors you handled." He still said nothing. "And so will we." He was shown a gun in case he missed their meaning. Still saying sod all. "And if you don't we'll have Ferris told you wanted to stick him in." That did the trick.

The cops now had some witnesses on Fatboy's murder and the means to arrest Ferris and Glover. McGraw felt very pleased with himself. Soon, Ferris would be locked up, maybe for the rest of his life. Bobby Glover might be too but, friend or no, that was life. McGraw was going to make a lot of money out of this deal. A great deal of money and there was nothing he loved more.

He would do anything to secure more cash. Anything. He was about to be tested on that.

42

WORRYING AND WARNING

"It's fixed up. Don't worry so much." Billy Manson couldn't be bothered with McGraw's fretting. Manson was an old school type with one principle – if you couldn't fight you were nothing. And he knew McGraw couldn't fight.

"But this can't go wrong, Billy," said McGraw for the umpteenth time. "And it's costing me a fortune."

"A fortune is it, you cheap bastard? Ah fucking told you Ah was doing this cheap because of old Arthur. A fucking fortune my arse." Arthur Thompson had had a word with his old time associate. That's all, just asked. Now someone else was making this happen. McGraw.

"But it's fifty grand, Billy. Fifty fucking grand."

"Aye, but that's mainly for my men."

"Your men? Who the fuck are they?" McGraw demanded in an outraged tone. This was really getting on his nerves. He hadn't slept for nights.

"A hit on a very capable boy? Think Ah'd do that on my own? Are you fucking daft?"

"Ah've arranged for the cops to be called off though."

"Aye or Ah'd no be doing it with them watching round the clock. Ah'm angry, Tam, no kamikaze."

"So tell me."

"Tell you whit?"

"Who the fuck's your help?" McGraw asked again. Manson looked at him across the table, a large vodka and lemonade in one of his hands, a fag burning in the other. He didn't trust that man. Not one bit but they were in bed together on this and he was paying for the job.

"Well, Ah've scored lucky on this one."

"How's that?"

"Ah'm related to a pal of theirs."

He explained he meant William Lobban, his sister's boy. McGraw decided to keep to himself the well-known rumour that Billy Manson wasn't just the boy's uncle but was also his daddy. That maybe explained the boy's strange, almost neutral face, his incredible body power as well as him being a selfish little bugger with a habit of dressing in women's clothing as a means of escaping the cops. Or so he said. It was enough to get him the nickname Tootsie.

McGraw knew all about Lobban. He was on the run from being jailed after an armed robbery and had come to Glasgow to be hidden. When he got fed up being stuck inside a wee flat and moaned so much, Bobby Glover and his wife agreed to take him into their home. He'd stayed there like one of the family for months till eventually his moaning got to them and he had to be moved on.

A pal? Maybe aye, maybe no. McGraw just hoped that Bobby was in his usual forgiving mood for the less fortunate.

"William came cheap," said Manson. "Ten grand and a decent watch." He didn't reveal to McGraw that he'd had to negotiate with Lobban who wanted a ransom. That he'd thrown in the watch knowing it wasn't the genuine article but a good fake he could buy for a few quid. "The other guy cost more but I had to buy quality."

"Who's that then?"

"The Iceman. McPhie." The name seared through McGraw's being like a white-hot poker.

"Ah don't want McPhie knowing that Ah've got fuck all to do with this," he started and kept going for as long as his breath held out. When he stopped to suck in air, fag smoke and vodka, Manson told him it was too late. He'd already been briefed and that included McGraw and The Caravel. He had to be briefed. He wouldn't have worked otherwise.

Now McPhie knew that McGraw was behind the Doyle murders and setting up this one. He knew too much. McGraw was going to have to have him dealt with and soon.

"Just one more thing, Billy," said McGraw.

"What's that?"

"Glover, right. Just Glover gets it and no one else."

43

BETRAYED

"Ah've got to go to a meeting, hen," Bobby Glover said to his wife. She had just answered the phone and it was a man's voice asking for Bobby. He hadn't given his name but she knew that voice anywhere, had lived with that voice. That was William Lobban.

"Will you be late?" she asked, wondering about something to eat later on.

"Ah'll no be late and Ah'm going to have to phone Joe."

"Joe?"

"Aye, no motor." The cops had his car for forensic tests to do with the kneecapping of William Gillen.

Eileen wasn't a worrier but worried about Bobby every day now. With Fatboy murdered, Paul Ferris in jail and Bobby charged too, it was all in good cause. She even worried that, though charged with the kneecapping along with Paul, Bobby had been released unlike Paul. Why was that? Were the cops up to something?

Joe was a good pal and he'd take care of Bobby. Poor Joe had had his troubles this past year. Shot and stabbed in his groin, his ice cream van busted up, it was as if someone was out to get him and get him large. But the young guy was tough and still smiling. He'd look after her Bobby all right.

Then again the same cops followed her man every minute of the day. They even parked at their door all night. To begin with that had annoyed her. Really annoyed her but not that night. That night it meant that he was safe. That night they would protect him.

Hours later in a field off an isolated road near Gartcosh, William Lobban, Billy Manson and a bloke called Paul Hamilton stood holding guns and watching Frank McPhie train his shooter on Bobby Glover and his good mate Joe Hanlon. Close by was Bobby's Ford Orion. Earlier on the two mates had met Lobban as arranged, near the cemetery at the back of The Caravel, and been forced to drive out there at the end of McPhie's shooter. It was as if The Iceman didn't care about the cops and didn't know Bobby was under twenty-four-hour surveillance. Good call – they weren't that night.

The difficult part of the operation was over now. All the gang had to do was wait. Wait for someone they were expecting.

McGraw had said just Glover, Manson recalled, but on a job like this you couldn't rule out others getting hurt. What should they do? Offer to let Joe Hanlon go? Aye right. He'd fight them with his bared knuckles and teeth and probably win. Joe had to go and he didn't give a fuck what McGraw said.

A strange car pulled in to the field and slowly rolled towards them. At the wheel, Arthur Thompson.

Back at his house a cop car with two plainclothes sat right at his front window. Ten minutes earlier, Thompson had made a show of being seen at that window, skipped downstairs, through the tunnel to Fatboy's, out his back door and away down the lane to where this car waited. He'd be home again in another ten minutes.

Maybe Bobby or Joe spotted the old man coming. Maybe they knew what was about to happen. Maybe they tried to make a break for it. That's when they were both shot dead.

Thompson leaned over the bodies one at a time, cursing and swearing, wanting to hurt dead men. He fired his gun, once, twice then turned on his heel back to his car and away.

The two cars travelled separately to a workshop cum garage in the east end. The young guy who owned and worked them had been ordered at gunpoint to close down for two days and leave them the keys. There, under cover, they transferred the bodies to the back of Paul Hamilton's van. Next they were heading to The Caravel.

"Ah told you. Just fucking Glover." McGraw was spitting blood. It didn't last long.

He recalled a few days before, Joe Hanlon being in The Caravel and losing it with him big time. Calling him a grass in front of everyone, getting him by the throat and ramming him against the wall. Joe had been spending too much time with Glover and Ferris. Maybe it was just as well that he had been shut up.

"Two for the price of one, " McGraw would later joke, any fondness he had for young Joe long forgotten. With Bobby and Joe laid out in The Caravel, Billy Manson left the pub. Frank McPhie had split long before. His work was done. William Lobban had been sent on his way too even though he griped about wanting to be paid. That he had just been involved in the murder of a man who had taken him into his own home didn't seem to register with him. The remaining small group sat, smoked and waited.

Manson returned in the early hours with company – Billy Thompson. The runt strutted around the pair spitting and swearing, then left. He had a big day starting in a few hours – his brother's funeral.

At her home, Eileen Glover sat sleepless and anxious. Bobby hadn't come home. Hadn't phoned her or anything. If the cops had arrested him again she would've known by then. Wouldn't she? Then there was a knock at her door.

It was about eleven in the morning and McGraw stood there.

"Eileen, have you heard?"

"Heard what?" She thought that McGraw looked as if he had been up all night like her.

"There's a car outside The Cottage Bar. Joe's car and there are two dead bodies in it. It's Bobby and Joe." His voice oozed sympathy and his eyes heartache.

Outside The Cottage Bar police had sealed off the area surrounding Joe's Ford Orion. Alan Cross, the bar manager, had discovered the bodies when he had arrived for work. There they were, Bobby laid out across the back floor. Young Joe had been crumpled entirely into the driver's footwell. The cops could see that but didn't know who yet. They were still trying to find out who the two dead men were.

"LET ME PAST," said Eileen Glover pushing through the cordon of cops. One grabbed her and held her telling her she couldn't, it was a crime scene. "Please," she said, "let me through. That's my husband, Bobby."

"How do you know?" he asked curious that she knew when they didn't.

"I just know." That comment was enough to lead to her arrest. To have her interviewed all day and all night as a suspect in the murders. Why? Because McGraw had told her who had been killed even before the cops knew.

It was 18 September 1991. Glasgow was about to change big style.

44

PLANTED AND PLANKED

McGraw had nothing to do with it. The burning papers stuck under the door, the lights on all night or flashing on and off for hours. Segregation in Barlinnie's Wendy House was bad enough without that torture but it was down to Thompson's paid screws not The Licensee.

Paul Ferris had a strategy to deal with that and the other indignities. Pretend he didn't care. Some days he would demand access to the toilet every fifteen minutes so the screws would have to get all rigged up in their riot gear, batons and shields, fetch the two dogs from the kennels and do him an eight man walk all the way with him ambling so slow he'd almost fall over. Just for him to say that the notion had left him as soon as they'd arrived and they'd all have to traipse back.

Other times they'd keep the lights off for hours. When some screw decided to enter his cell they'd find him sitting up, a book in his lap reading intently in the dark.

The strategy annoyed the screws one and all and made Ferris laugh. He always felt better when he was fighting back. But on the 19 September he had no strategy.

Front pages of every Scottish newspaper were shoved under his cell door. There it was splashed – his two best mates were dead. Had been killed. Executed.

For once Ferris prayed for the dark as he sat there under the glaring white lights and wept.

There was no accident about where Glover and Hanlon's bodies eventually ended up. Not only was it outside The Cottage Bar – Bobby's pub – it was slap bang on the route of Fatboy's funeral that day.

Old time street players the country over immediately assumed they knew what had happened. At the funeral, Cockney, Geordie and Scouser accents would roar out.

"A great send off, Arthur. Well done." They didn't mean the funeral. Most of them he had paid to come along anyway. They meant the killing of Bobby and Joe. Glasgow faces knew that it was more complicated than that. Much more complicated.

One man who didn't need paid to be there was McGraw. He and his crew turned up and he felt as if the day was his. He had finally joined company with the big teams from all over and he was going to be bigger than them all. Who was going to stop him now?

Anger drifted through other parts of Glasgow that day. The three young men had many friends and supporters and most were intent on some act of revenge. One idea was to drive into the cemetery with a machine gun. Another to lob a few hand grenades into the crowd. At least one man was intent on scaring The Godfather since they were all blaming him for Bobby and Joe. Just him. That day at least.

The area was mobbed with police. They had already planned a major security exercise but with the killings of Bobby and Joe home leave was cancelled and extra troops called in from the country areas and other forces.

All the revenge hits were called off. For the moment at least.

One problem did bother McGraw that day. His task had been to dispose of the guns used in the killings. He had promised they'd be smelted in some big furnace he had access to but he never really meant it.

In the boot of his car he had a bag, zipped up and ordinary looking. Giving it to one of his men as arranged, the man disappeared into the funeral crowd where he met the man he was looking for.

"Ah'm needing something looked after for a while," he said after the usual social chit chat. "Nothing sinister. Just the usual."

"Ah think Ah know a place," replied the man, "though Ah'll need to check first." Five minutes later he returned saying that he should follow him.

The walk from the cemetery to Moodiesburn Street, Blackhill wasn't far. There he left the bag in the capable hands of David and Bridget Allan. They would store the bag away, not touch it or look at it and get a few quid every week for their trouble. It was an old time practice, one with little risk and they knew they could trust the couple. After all their son-in-law was John Morrison, a hard man from the area and occasional henchman of Arthur Thompson.

McGraw had a plan. The guns in the bag might come in useful some day. Maybe some day soon if they happened to be found and still covered in certain fingerprints and the bullets matching the wounds in Bobby and Joe.

He wouldn't have to wait very long.

45

PREPARATION, PREPARATION, PREPARATION

"You don't have to worry, Tam," Laurel said.

"So you say," he replied, not believing a word of it. McGraw was Olympic standard at fretting.

"Nah, seriously, Tam," said Hardy. "They're planning something special for the wee man."

"They'll need to be very special for Ferris," said McGraw. "He's a fucking Houdini that one."

"Would a confession make you feel better?"

"What? You going to set the boys on him one night? Torture him to fuck and get him to write it all down?" His eyes were raised. "Naw, didn't think so."

"He's going to get a new neighbour soon," said Laurel. "A man with special ways about him."

"It's true, Tam. He's got a good record of the same," added Hardy.

"His name?"

"Come on, Tam."

"Aye, you don't bloody know, do you?"

Christmas of 1991 had come and gone, Hogmanay was past and here they were, no further forward. That's how it seemed to McGraw anyway. Ferris would be going to trial for the Fatboy murder but not yet. Meantime, McGraw had his own problem – Frank McPhie.

The Iceman was going around letting people call him the killer of Bobby and Joe. It made McGraw nervous. Very nervous.

With the Ferris trial outstanding, there was a list of people who would keep their lips zipped whatever pressure they were put under. Maybe it was time to call in that card.

The armed cops hit Bridget and David Allan's house big time. They'd had an anonymous report that there was a bag in there with guns. Sure enough, they found two pistols but more. A sawn off shotgun and a stack of jewellery clearly worth a lot of money.

All the media heard was that the two people had been arrested suspected of having illegal guns. Full stop.

Chief Constable Leslie Sharp had written to all the editors asking that nothing else be reported. There was a good reason it seems. One of the guns might be linked to another high profile murder case, or so Leslie Sharp said.

"One gun," thought McGraw when he was told this by some cops. "They're meant to have both."

The forensic team had already worked out that a Smith & Wesson .44 Magnum and .38 revolver had been involved in killing Glover and Hanlon. As to what the Allans had in that bag – it would take another year to get close. No one was going to be tried on that till the big trial happened. The one everyone was thinking about. Ferris charged for Fatboy.

McGraw's plans to trap McPhie fell flat on their face. A full year later no charges would be pursued against the Allans and their son John Morrison would walk free on related charges. What did McGraw expect? Nice clean prints on those guns left there by McPhie? The Iceman being careless?

There was someone else he hadn't thought about properly – Billy Manson. Old timers like Walter Norval who had led the XYY Team and whose trial for many robberies had caused the High Court to be bombed knew that Manson was a cold blooded hitman.

One thing that Manson wouldn't tell him was who killed Glover and Hanlon.

"That's too dangerous to know," Manson had said but had he shot one of the men? McGraw simply didn't know.

Another man was making him nervous – Paul Hamilton. He

was putting it around that he was one of The Godfather's lieu-
tenants. A man capable of anything and up to every trick. Who
wouldn't refuse a job for old Thompson. Even murder.

He was getting too lippy, McGraw thought. Too full of himself.
As far as he knew Hamilton was nothing more than a Fagan, a
reset man who sold knocked off gear from his second hand shop
on Alexandra Parade.

McGraw was going to have to take care of all these people and
soon. But first he had to sit tight through Ferris' trial, make sure
he went down.

"There's an easy way to avoid being a witness," he said one
night in his front room. "Just sit in the court from day one."

"But we're no meant to," replied Gordon Ross. Ross had been
a good mate of Bobby Glover's as had his company that day, Chic
Glackin. Knowing Bobby meant that they had an introduction to
other folk, like McGraw, and they had been chatting to him about
their drugs trafficking racket.

Ross had worked out that the panels of cars have a lot of empty
space. Clear them out properly and they could pack many kilos
of dope in there. So far they had done a few runs to Amsterdam
but they had ambitions to go further south to Spain where they
could buy direct from the North African traders. Better quality,
lower price and so more profit for all. With Bobby dead and Ferris
in jail, Ross and Glackin were now talking to McGraw exclusively.

"No meant to?" McGraw laughed. "No you're no but what are
they going to do about that? Rap your knuckles?" Ross and Glackin
had been listed by Ferris as defence witnesses. They didn't know
what they were expected to give evidence about but they weren't
happy with the prospect. "What would you rather have? A kick
up the arse or be in the hot seat in front of the judge and the
media?"

Witnesses weren't allowed to sit in a trial before they were
called in case they heard evidence that biased their testimony. It
was a simple ploy, an old one but still effective.

McGraw was giving out advice freely but he wasn't telling the whole story. He had been listed as a prosecution witness early on, a ploy to make sure the defence didn't call him and call him they might.

Ferris faced twelve charges and McGraw had been implicated on at least two – the kneecapping and an attempted murder of a guy in Rutherglen. For most people that would've led to charges. For McGraw it wouldn't even lead to him appearing in court. Now, content that he was safe, he was happy to dish out advice to Ross and Glackin, especially if that meant Ferris had two less witnesses to call.

What he didn't know was that the man in the Wendy House was playing his own games. Ross and Glackin had been listed as defence witnesses to test them. Yet Ferris had no intention of having them called but simply wanted to see what they were going to do. He wouldn't be disappointed.

Karen Owen, his girlfriend, delivered a brand new designer suit, shirt, tie, underwear and shoes to Barlinnie for Ferris, as she would do every day. Now he was dressed for the part and the biggest trial in Scottish criminal history was about to start.

McGraw sent in two spies who would sit in the court every day and report back to him. Now he was ready.

McGraw was going to enjoy this – or would he?

46

THE HANGING COURT

Two men were missing from the trial. Two dead men. Glover and Hanlon.

Ferris' trial of 1992 was seen as being for the murder of Fatboy, even though he faced eleven other charges, every one very serious. He was accused of killing Fatboy in cahoots with Glover and Hanlon. Two men who weren't there to defend themselves or Ferris. Never would be.

Prosecution lawyers considered it an inspired move. Ferris thought it an injustice. McGraw had a good laugh.

Every day, Ferris would be driven from BarL in an armoured meat wagon surrounded by armed police. Outside there would be a convoy of police cars with their lights blazing, outriding motorcyclists and the cop helicopter hovering above. Every day, twice a day, they would shut the roads down as he was swept to and from the High Court. Every day, people across Glasgow heard their message. This is one very dangerous man.

His trial would take place in the old High Court in the Saltmarket where every infamous trial in Glasgow had happened for over a century. The grand building stared out on to Glasgow Green where once upon a time, judges sent condemned men and women to be hung in public.

Hundreds of witnesses were lined up and slowly they appeared in court. Some claimed openly that they had been threatened by the cops if they didn't appear then they refused to give evidence at all. Almost all reported receiving an unofficial letter from the Crown.

A few weeks before the trial, letters on Crown Office headed paper and addressed to Paul Ferris in Barlinnie started being shoved through people's letterboxes. It read:

Dear Sir,

I refer to the letter of 12 January, 1992 (sent on your behalf) which was passed to the Lord Advocate who acknowledge's the assistance given by you to the Stathclyde Serious Crime Squad over several years.

However inquires have shown that your prior assistance was for 'Monetary Consideration' and not 'Public Spirited'. Accordingly the Lord Advocate feels unable to intervene in the matters outstanding against you.

Yours faithfully,

Mr A. Vannet,

Deputy Crown Agent.

McGraw was laughing fit to spit at this. An official letter saying that Ferris was a grass – that would put his witnesses off for sure and make his life a misery when in jail. It hadn't been his idea but it was a cracker. The type of game he'd play.

Paul Hamilton was put in the witness box and asked about the letter. He said it had arrived without an envelope and, due to the spelling and grammatical errors, he had dismissed it as a hoax after a couple of reads. He had no idea who had produced it.

Thompson's lieutenant? He was so close to old Arthur that he didn't even know what he was up to.

It was Arthur Thompson's idea in an effort to put Ferris' witnesses off appearing and convince the prosecution witnesses they were dealing with a police grass. McGraw reckoned that him and the Godfather had a lot in common. He wasn't wrong.

Hamilton's point of view wasn't needed when later the Defence led by Donald Findlay QC produced Alfred Vannet himself who dismissed the letter as a poor fake that had certainly not been signed by him.

Still, dirt sticks, McGraw knew. There were thousands of those letters doing the rounds all over Britain, all saying that Ferris was a grass. Maybe one day it would come back to haunt him at the sharp end of a bullet or a blade.

Hamilton wasn't finished with his evidence. He claimed that the night Fatboy was killed he had been at a social event in Rob Roy Football Club in Kirkintilloch, recalling it well since he'd been involved in a fight with others and ex World Boxing Champion, Jim Watt, had tried to break it up.

One week later he had been in The Caravel bar where he saw Paul Ferris standing in the company of three other men. He recalled that night well since he had been attacked and it was Joe Hanlon who had rushed to break up the trouble.

Trouble was the dates from the Rob Roy Club didn't tie in with Hamilton's dates. He had offered to give evidence for Ferris covering that night of 26 May and ended up sticking him in the deep end just as McGraw had advised him to.

Wee Barnie Docherty, the Irish junky from Blackhill, had to be marched into the courtroom. He had promised McGraw's crew everything. He'd swear that Ferris offered him £30,000 to help kill Fatboy. McGraw had promised him regular bags of free smack.

Trouble was McGraw had got mean and the smack soon dwindled away to zero. Bernie had got on his toes and ran away till the police found him and held him. In the witness box he was a mess, cold turkey crawling over his skin.

David Logue gave the evidence he said he would. He'd been asked by some guy called Gary to steal a car for a job. That's when he stole the Nissan Bluebird that the cops reckoned was used in the hit job. That night he was asked to get rid of the car and paid extra money to do it well.

Of all the witnesses, the star that the media and McGraw were waiting for was Arthur Thompson for the prosecution. He was breaking the so-called honour of the street by giving evidence against Ferris. There was more. One of the charges Ferris faced was trying to murder Thompson by running him over. This could only have happened if Thompson had cooperated with the cops. He was desperate to get Ferris and get him good.

Thompson was master of saying nothing and meaning something. He denied raising £100,000 a week by protection rackets alone, denied any association with crime. He was just a struggling businessman.

Then Donald Findlay asked him who he thought had killed his son.

"We all know who did it," he said. "I think so." As the words left his mouth he looked at the jury then swivelled round to stare at Ferris. He might as well have pointed the finger of blame.

"Ya rasper," McGraw would say later. "How was the look in Thompson's eyes? Fucking flame throwers Ah'll bet ye, man."

Then came the cops' star witness, Dennis Woodman. He was a prisoner in the Wendy House who claimed Ferris had confessed to killing Fatboy while they played chess by shouting out the moves to each other. Every street player shook their heads in disbelief.

"Ferris? Confess? Never mind confess to a stranger? What shite."

But McGraw knew that juries weren't made up of criminals just ordinary, honest people. Who would they believe?

Ferris and Findlay had unsolicited help including letters from Woodman's family saying that he had done this before, setting up relatives. In the Wendy House an English prisoner recognised Woodman from down south. He had done this several times to many people, always getting a result. He was the police's pet collaborator and had been drafted north to catch the big one.

Later Donald Findlay would say that Woodman's jail transfer could only have happened with the authority of the highest power. Even the politicians were colluding to convict Paul Ferris.

When Woodman accused Peter Forbes, Ferris' ever straight solicitor, of trying to bribe him then was caught out swearing on his two young kids' graves – kids who were very much alive – Woodman's credibility was shot to pieces. He had done this before but never against a QC like Donald Findlay.

In spite of reports from the court every day that Ferris was done for, McGraw didn't like how things were shaping up.

"The bloody trial has lasted fifty-five days, Tam," said Laurel. "The longest criminal trial in Scotland's history."

"Aye, and he's facing twelve charges," added Hardy. "That jury knows he's an evil bastard and they're bound to get him on several offences."

"Relax, Tam," added Laurel. "Ferris is going down."

McGraw couldn't relax. All that work and effort, all that expense and risk now hung in the minds of fifteen jury members. They thought they were in that room deciding on simple things like murder. It was more important than that. It was McGraw's existence. His future. It was all ME, ME, ME.

Hundreds of people gathered outside the High Court waiting for the result. When word started being whispered out that Ferris had been found not guilty on one, not guilty on two, not guilty on three . . . not guilty on twelve, a roar went up.

An hour later Paul Ferris walked out into the sunlight and waved with a wry smile.

Later, a senior police officer would give a press statement thanking "each and every witness" for their help. That included the liar Woodman. They would charge no one else with Fatboy's murder or any of the other eleven offences.

Out in the east end, McGraw cancelled a celebratory party and sat alone, at his wits' end. What the hell was going to happen now?

47

ROBBING THE DEAD

"I want a word with you." McGraw almost jumped in fright as he heard a voice he recognised.

Ferris had disappeared for a while after his trial. Relaxing, having fun with Karen and catching up with his young son, Paul. The things anyone would do when they'd spent so long in jail and came so close to spending the rest of their lives there. All the while he grieved for his two pals. Grieved as they had never allowed him to when he was locked up in the Wendy House. He let himself go and felt the pain. Outside was a welcome break from inside but it was a lonely place now without Bobby and Joe. Now he was back and it was business as usual. Or was it?

"Paul, good to see you," said McGraw, his eyes jumping all over the place betraying his real mood – pure terror. Well he might be frightened.

Ferris wasn't tall, well built nor possessed any of the usual traits of a hardman. What he did have were nerves of steel and the capacity to use the utmost violence without thinking about it. He could be talking to you all friendly one second and slashing your throat the next. Had he come looking to kill McGraw?

"We've got things to sort out," Ferris said wandering up to McGraw in The Caravel. "Best said in private." McGraw didn't want to go anywhere with him on his own.

"Ah'm a bit busy here, Paul," McGraw lied. "Any chance we could have a word over there?" He nodded to a seat in the corner where it was quiet.

"Nah, this will do." Ferris stood his ground and smiled at McGraw who didn't like this at all. As soon as Ferris got the not guilty verdicts on everything at his trial, McGraw had been dreading the worst, running over the options of what Ferris might get up to. Trouble was, walking into his pub on his own and shooting him right there and then was Ferris' style. Especially since his best pals were now dead and buried. "It's about Joe's car."

McGraw sighed with relief. This wasn't end game but a chat about a motor. McGraw kept in touch with Sharon Hanlon and Eileen Glover. He'd been a pallbearer at Joe's funeral and attended Bobby's, making sure they both knew he would help them in any way. "And his ice cream van. And Bobby's pub. And . . ."

McGraw had taken Joe's car when the cops had finally released it. Sharon obviously wanted nothing to do with it so he couldn't say no to a decent motor. A free decent motor. Trouble was he'd put it to work as a taxi in the east end.

"Taxing a tragedy," someone had said in McGraw's hearing, the play on words meant as a jibe not a joke. He didn't care. A good motor was a good motor.

"First his car," Ferris continued. "Get it the fuck off the road." McGraw now wished he had gone some place quiet with Ferris. He didn't want any of his punters to hear this conversation. "Do you know what that does to Joe and Bobby's family every time they see it? Well fucking do you?"

Ferris moved on to the other things. Men were working Bobby and Joe's ice cream vans and no wages were going back to their widows and young sons in spite of best promises by McGraw. It was the same with The Cottage Bar and a number of other business concerns they had.

Eileen Glover and Sharon Hanlon were heartbroken, shattered, weakened beyond the organisation needed to run these concerns but McGraw had assured them,

"Don't you worry about all that. Ah'll make sure they're working and the money keeps coming in." It sounded like a kind offer at the time but McGraw had reverted to type. It was important that he let Eileen and Sharon know publicly that he too was hurt but that they could rely on him and his people to keep things going so he was sending out the right message. Yet when it came to actually handing over cash he just couldn't do it. After all, Bobby and Joe had long since stopped being pals in his mind and just become two men who got in his road. And they owed him.

"It's no quite as simple as all that, Paul," McGraw had started, then explained in deliberately confusing detail how he was in partnership with Bobby and Joe. That they both owed him money and he was just trying to get back his just rewards. "That's all. There's no profit in this for me," he pleaded, lying again.

"Have you any paperwork? Like contracts? Bills of sale?" asked Paul. For the first time, McGraw noticed that Jaimba McLean had wandered into the pub and was standing on his own having a peaceful drink. It was the only thing Jaimba did peacefully. He was one of the most dangerous men in Glasgow and had been close to Ferris since he was a young, underage teenager and ended up in an adult jail because it was the only place that could hold and try and control him. Even there he was losing the place, fighting his own shadow if it moved the wrong way. Ferris had looked after him and Jaimba had rewarded that by doing anything he was asked to do often with two shotguns tucked in his coat. The same long coat he was wearing that day.

"Naw, of course not." McGraw was just telling Ferris what he already knew. "It was a gentleman's agreement." At the other end of the bar, some old timer started to sing 'He'll Have to Go' in a reasonable copy of Jim Reeves as in sad, depressing and twangy. Ferris looked at McGraw and wondered if the song wasn't a sign.

"So sort it," Ferris said. "Or Ah will."

"Paul . . ."

"The car is off the street today. Like now. Don't give a fuck what you do with it as long as it's far, far away." Ferris looked round, eyeballing Jaimba, making sure he was okay. The Caravel could carry enemies of his. "As for the rest I reckon this would fix it." He handed McGraw a note on which he had his sister type the businesses in question with figures next to them, some earnings by week, others buy-off totals.

"Fuck sake." McGraw almost choked, feeling as if he was being robbed standing there in his own pub.

"And a couple of grand up front for them. Today." This was coming to a head, McGraw could see that. He was going to have to give Ferris something for the women or risk trouble.

"Ah could manage a grand," he said, "it's all the spare cash Ah've got on hand." McGraw was lying, of course, but he wanted to buy time and hang on to his cash for as long as possible. Ferris knew he would.

"Fine. Give that to me for the families. The other grand by tomorrow and the rest by Friday."

"Aye, okay, Paul," McGraw sighed with some relief. At least he had bought an opportunity to talk these figures down. The next day he'd visit Eileen and Sharon separately and give them another few hundred. While he was there he'd chat about what he considered a reasonable deal. It would almost work but it didn't. McGraw would end up paying across most of that money. It was either that or a war with Ferris as well as Bobby and Joe's families – something he could do without.

"And those weekly figures."

"Aye."

"There's nine months' arrears due. By tomorrow too."

With McGraw's money in his pocket, Ferris strode out of The Caravel heading to Eileen and Sharon's places to hand across the cash. But already he knew he'd be back. He had another problem to fix. Behind him Jaimba strolled out watching everyone in the pub at the same time. Ferris' big mate had a problem. McGraw was going to fix it, whether he liked it or not.

Meantime someone else was in trouble. Big trouble.

48

DEAD AND BURIED

"He's useless to us now."

"You think so?"

"Maybe worth one last round. See what we can get from him."

"Think he's going to bring in more in the state he's in?"

"I think so."

"He just doesn't seem to care about anything. Anything at all."

The conversation was taking place deep in Pitt Street, the HQ of Strathclyde Police. The two people talking were senior officers from the cops and MI5. The subject of their concern? Arthur Thompson.

Thompson had changed since the trial. Most of his time he pottered about at his businesses, was drinking more than ever and seemed to keep his own counsel. He looked just the same but was acting like a man waiting to die.

For years the cops and security forces had worked Thompson. He had helped them with inside information on the gangs in Glasgow, Newcastle and London. Then he'd helped with Northern Ireland using his links with the Loyalists.

Now he looked as if he couldn't help himself, never mind MI5. They met with Thompson and put him under pressure.

"We could let your Loyalist pals know what you've been doing with us all these years," they threatened when he told them bluntly he wasn't interested. He looked back at them with uncaring, lifeless eyes. "All we want now is the lowdown on the Glasgow gangs. The Daniels, McGoverns, Demptser, McGraw, the Paisley people and John Healy. Oh yeah, and Ferris, of course. Always Ferris." At the sound of his name, Thompson looked up, fire in his eyes. The closest the men had seen to pure hate and they'd seen many angry men. "Surely you could do that without leaving your house?"

In truth, Thompson didn't know what was going on with most of that lot now. They were a new breed who kept to themselves unless they were going to give you trouble. He knew about Ferris, made a point of knowing but what he knew he was going to keep to himself. For that time soon when he'd pull the trigger on the man. He'd pull the trigger, no other bastard.

Eventually they could see that his son's death and the failure of his bid for revenge on Ferris had killed something in the man. They were good not God and knew he was beyond fixing.

"There's one thing you could do for us then." Thompson still didn't look up. "One last thing." Now his eyes were raised. "Find us a man who could help us with the Glasgow gangs. Just the one man then you can go."

Arthur Thompson knew the very man.

The red Cavalier pulled up outside Baird's Bar in the Barrowland. The watching men tensed and got ready. Out of the passenger seat stepped the man they were waiting for, Arthur Thompson. But there in the driving seat was a woman, his daughter Tracey. They all knew what they would do now – nothing – but still the signal went up to pull back. Guns were relaxed, safety catches put on, they stayed and they listened.

"Thanks, hen," he said to his daughter.

"No problem, Da," she replied. "I'll be back for you later." In a few seconds he was in the pub as Tracey sat there and watched. Of all the nights for Thompson to get a woman to drive him to his regular haunt it had to be that night. The men were there to sort an injustice not to create another by harming a woman or shooting some innocent drinker in the bar. It was a call off – for the moment.

Inside the pub Thompson would meet with old pals. Men of the street and men of the Orange. Some were just pals, others were handy, tooled up and ready to shoot or slash at the first excuse. It's a place where he felt safe. That's why he planned to meet someone else there that night.

At the time Joe Hanlon's Irish cousins were going to gun down Arthur Thompson in revenge, Ferris was sitting in a city curry house with a few friends.

At the time Arthur Thompson was going to be gunned down, McGraw was round the corner from Baird's Bar. He had a meeting that night.

"There's some people Ah'd like you to meet," Thompson had said to McGraw that night. "Useful people for you." He didn't reveal that all he wanted was to get the cops and MI5 off his own back. Why should he?

"Sounds interesting," said McGraw, "can you no tell me more about them?"

"Whit? Here?" Thompson whispered coarsely.

"Okay, when?"

"In a couple of weeks."

"That long?"

"Aye, Ah'm going away for a wee while. Rita needs a fucking break from all of this."

McGraw knew exactly what Thompson meant. He and Margaret had been going to Tenerife for years and had recently bought a house there at the Playa de las Americas. These days it was the only time and place he felt relaxed. He'd get out once, maybe twice a year but Margaret had taken to going more often. Why not?

The next day Thompson and Rita went to their house in Rothesay. The same house where the cops had arrested Ferris and claimed to have found that heroin. They had a house in Spain but Thompson didn't like to go too far away. This was far enough.

Then came a report that two men had been arrested at Euston Station in London with £50,000 cash, guns and directions and details on him. With Thompson out of the city the gossip wheels spun that he was frightened and in hiding. He couldn't have that.

A couple of days after his return he went for a drink at the Provanmill Inn. He sat in his usual seat but wasn't feeling great. Not great at all. On his way home some old guy said something to him so Thompson slashed him. He wasn't even sure what the man had said but didn't like the look of his face. That was Thompson's way.

Two hours later he was in bed and in agony. Pains across his chest. Sweating. Feeling sick. Rita dialled 999 and the ambulance arrived at speed.

"Heart attack," they said wiring him up to the defibrillator. It didn't work. There was a problem with the batteries not charging with many of these machines. The paramedics had done their job but the batteries were faulty. Still they bundled him into the ambulance and sped him the short distance to the Royal Infirmary.

Arthur Thompson was dead. The Godfather of Glasgow who had ruled the streets of the city was no more. It was 13 March 1993. Now what was going to happen?

With his youngest son Billy hooked on heroin and incapable of fighting his way out of a paper bag, Thompson had no heir. The man who had held Glasgow for thirty years died with few troops, less friends and no hope for the future. With Thompson's death, the Thompsons died.

At his funeral they were all there from all over Britain. No one needed backhanders this time.

A bomb scare in the cemetery held up proceedings for hours and needed a controlled explosion to end it all. That didn't bother most of these guys. They'd been through worse.

McGraw and his troops were there. He tried to catch the eye of the big names from the south and got scant reply. They didn't know the man.

"Imagine an old gangster like him dying in his fucking bed," said one of his crew.

"Ah know eh. That's the way to go," McGraw replied, drawing deep on a fag. "But his timing was shite though."

"How's that?"

"He was meant to get me to a meeting with some guys this week," he replied. "Cunt didn't even tell me who they were."

"Took the secret to his grave eh."

"Aye, that and a few other secrets."

"Wonder who is going to take over from him?"

"Aye, well maybe you'll be surprised," said McGraw with a smile.

Before that it would emerge others were in for a surprise. Not the pleasant kind.

49

ZAPPED NOT ZIPPED

"GET THEM."

The two men hit the car at speed, baseball bats and choppers in hand. Billy Manson was chibbed in the head and pulled from his seat. Two minutes later he lay on the ground stabbed twenty times and his every bone battered, bruised and many broken. The two men walked away.

Inside the car, Manson's working partner, Graham Scott, sat shaken but unscathed. The hit had been for Manson alone. Well not entirely.

McGraw sighed at the news and waited to hear of Manson's death. He thought he knew who had hurt the man. Friends of Glover and Hanlon learned quickly that William Lobban had made the Judas phone call leading them to their deaths. Lobban didn't have the initiative or gumption for that on his own. Manson must have put him up to it so Manson was punished.

The hard nut survived and McGraw was well pissed off. Worse, Manson was a broken man physically and mentally. Now he wasn't out earning money, able to look after himself. Everyone needs to earn. Would Manson be tempted to talk? To the cops? To a journalist?

Not as long as he has some quality of life, McGraw concluded. Bad enough being in daily pain but to be in daily pain in jail was the lowest of the low. He'd keep his lip zipped for the money McGraw made sure one of his men delivered now and then. Not much. Just enough to keep the debt man from the door. Still, he was worth the watching.

Someone else should have kept their mouth shut.

Paul Hamilton was behaving like some cat with his head stuck in a carton of double cream. His fifteen seconds of infamy at the Ferris trial had gone to his head and came rolling out his gob. His big-headedness was enhanced again when he was pulled in as a suspect in the murders of Glover and Hanlon then promptly released. He was talking large. The trouble with a city like Glasgow is it's full of folk happy to listen – for good or ill.

In the right pub and right company Hamilton would boast that it was his van that was used that night to move Bobby and Joe's bodies around the city.

"Fucking amazing, man," he'd blabber when full of booze. "There's me with two dead bodies in the back just driving through Glasgow knowing . . . I said knowing . . . that the cops wouldn't stop me." Hamilton thought he was among friends. Big mistake.

Strathclyde Police had made a public apology for "losing" Bobby and Joe that night. Yet, later, officers would talk of being stood down and being taken off the streets. Having been on a high alert since Fatboy's murder the cops were that night ignoring the east end.

Now here was Hamilton boasting about being involved in a double murder. What would he be doing next? Listing everyone else in on the killings? He was giving McGraw the jitters and he ordered his men to do something about Hamilton.

"Start by making sure that Glover and Hanlon's people know what he's saying. Right?" McGraw was talking to a group of men who had been offered a bounty for shutting Hamilton up – permanently. "Like exaggerate it a good bit. If that doesn't work," he made the sign of a shooting gun with his hand.

The pals of Bobby and Joe were out to avenge their deaths. Who would get to Hamilton first?

The Daimler screeched this way and that trying to flee the chasing car down Dee Street in Riddrie. The other car was smaller, fast and the driver was good. A shot rang out, then another. It's difficult to drive when you're trying to keep your head down. The Daimler skidded again and again and ended up against a wall.

The man was out of the other car running to the Daimler. For a second he stood, the gun pointed at Hamilton's face letting the horror sink in. Then Hamilton cringed and turned away. That's when he got the bullet in the back of his head.

Paul Hamilton had been shut up permanently.

Who got to Hamilton first? The Glasgow cops thought they knew. A male relative of Ferris was arrested and interviewed. Later he was released without charge.

Glasgow cops were worried. After Ferris' trial they had stayed geared up waiting for the city to explode yet nothing much had happened. No street war. No St Valentine's Day type massacre. Nothing.

Eventually the cops had tooled down and went about business as usual. It was November 1993, eighteen months after that trial. Had the faces bided their time? Was the war starting now?

50

SHOOTERS IN THE CEMETERY

"Guns. He does it all the time," said young Barney as they hung around Jagger Motors, Ferris' new car firm. "Been doing it for years."

"And there's no catch, Barney?" asked Ferris.

"None that I could see – apart from paying for the guns."

"That goes without saying."

Ferris' pal Jaimba McLean was in trouble. He had been to some pub and had a fall out with some guys. Not one to leave it at that Jaimba had gone home, picked up two sawn off shotguns and daundered back to the pub. In the door, he started blasting. Three of the gang were hit and badly wounded. Now the cops were after him for attempted murders.

Ferris had hidden Jaimba in a safe house in London when the heat went up. That was all right for a while but couldn't last forever. Jaimba was too well known by the police in Glasgow to show his face at a window never mind risk walking the streets. He wouldn't leave town permanently either, not without his wife and kids. For a big guy who could be so violent, Jaimba was a close family man.

If he got caught and tried, Jaimba was going away for many years.

They had to find some way of having the charges reduced. Anything to reduce the matter. That's when Ferris talked to Barney.

"Ah'm a car addict, Paul, in love with driving fast. Have been for years. Last time Ah got charged Ah was going to lose my licence and do some bird big time. That's when Ah spoke to McGraw."

When Ferris met McGraw they had a quiet chat. The game was simple. Either they could produce some illegal guns and hand them in to a named DI at the Pollok Police Station or McGraw could sort it. What happened with the guns if he did? They'd get left at a named grave in the cemetery next to The Caravel. A couple of days later the cops would give the nod that all was sorted and Jaimba could go home.

"It's a straight trade," said McGraw. "We give them some shooters and they drop a charge or two. We buy them from some dealer – so they gain. The cops show them off as dangers taken from the street – so they gain. And Jaimba can sleep with his wife at night." It all seemed so simple. Too simple. "Where's the problem?"

"Have you been doing this for a long time?"

"For fucking years." McGraw was in his element, showing off his power.

"Who else has it worked for then?" Ferris was almost as curious about that as he was keen to get Jaimba off the hook.

"Billy McPhee walked free for two chibbings," McGraw smiled. "George . . ."

"George?"

"Aye, McCormack."

"You mean fucking Crater Face."

"Aye. He beat the shit out of a guy one might and was heading to jail. Could've lost his job, his taxi licence, the lot."

"Worth the money for the guns then eh."

"Fuck, aye. Then there was Gordon almost losing his licence too. We couldn't . . ."

"Gordon Ross?"

"Eh aye."

Ferris looked at McGraw and wondered about Ross. He had been very close to Bobby Glover who did nothing but support him and give him breaks. Now Bobby was hardly cold in the ground when Ross was all pally-wally with McGraw. Not that it surprised Ferris much. Ross backstabbing him at his trial told him everything he needed to know. "We couldn't have him losing his licence eh." What McGraw meant was now that they were close to running their dope trafficking scam into Spain and North Africa, he fully intended that Ross be one of the drivers and he wasn't about to let that slip through his fingers for a two hundred quid bundle of shooters.

"Just one thing," Ferris added, "no way am I going to a cop shop holding a bag of guns. Understood?"

"Understood."

The deal and the price were set up one day, the guns dropped off the next and the following night Jaimba was back home a happy man.

Things like this were happening all the time, keeping Ferris' attention on his loved ones. He had set up Jagger Motors and now Premier Security providing bouncers for pubs and clubs and watchmen for building sites. That and his London connections were keeping him busy and often out of Glasgow. The war the cops feared wasn't going to happen – not with Ferris leading the troops. McGraw could see that too. He was off the hook.

But could he keep it that way? Could his troops?

51

CLUBBED AND CHIBBED

Loud music, scantily clad young women, the booze flowing – it was yet another perfect night out in Victoria's nightclub. Why not? The place had a killer reputation.

Victoria's or Viccies was the choice of Old Firm footballers, young models, actors and actresses for the best of nights. Anyone with the money was welcome whether they were blowing a week's wages in one night or spending small change on bottles of champagne. It was January 1994 and Victoria's was the place to be.

For those with money, count gangsters on the make. After all, those other celebrants want a good time and that includes drugs. In the early 1990s cocaine was the in drug for those with money to burn. It was more expensive than vintage champagne and cooler than the most expensive designer gear. Want drugs? Find a gangster. Got money? Look beside you.

It was just another deal going down in the Gents. The surfaces in Victoria's toilets were ideal for cutting a line of coke two minutes after you bought it.

Some ordinary looking young guys wanted a couple of lines and had found the man. Trouble was they weren't willing to pay the price. Walking away was okay but arguing? That was asking for trouble.

The fight started without warning. A young guy was getting a doing and it showed. Others went to help. Alex Donnelly was slashed and stabbed fourteen times for his pains and tried to hide in a toilet cubicle to escape more damage. On the floor lay Alex

Harland with serious brain damage. Graham Thomson was there for a piss but couldn't just let that happen. He went to rescue Alex Donnelly. Thomson was only twenty-three and fit. Not fit enough for these guys. He was kicked, stamped and stabbed repeatedly.

Five minutes later one young guy was badly brain damaged and another lay still, blood seeping from his wounds, his eyes shut, his pulse low. Later he died in the Royal Infirmary. A murder hunt was on.

Four men had been spotted leaving the scene in a hurry. Stephen and Alan Moffat, brothers from Easterhouse, John McCall from Cranhill and one other – the bold Billy McPhee.

Calls went to the cop cars. Murder suspects wanted. Arrest them all.

"Ah need a lift and some place to clean up, Tam," said McPhee down the phone.

"What the fuck you saying that on the phone for?" McGraw screamed down the line. "Do Ah fucking know you?"

"Tam . . . Tam . . ." The line was dead. Who else to call? Who else would help?

"Paul, I'm in a bit of a state." McPhee didn't need to explain to Ferris as his voice cracked with heavy sobs. It was a mobile to mobile phone call, still rare in those days but not among those who lived outwith the law.

"Where are you?" he asked and when told turned his car in that direction. As far as Ferris was concerned Billy McPhee was just another lad, a free agent who would work for anyone at anything if it paid. He wasn't close to the guy or even fond of him but he had been pally with Joe and that made him okay for Ferris. He would help him just as he'd help most other blokes in the same situation.

"Sorry about this, Paul," said McPhee sitting in the passenger seat of his car, tears streaming down his face.

"Fuck sake. Where have you been? A slaughter?" McPhee was drenched in blood. His face, his clothes, his hair. None of it his.

"A wee scrap at a club."

"A scrap? Looks worse than that, Billy."

McPhee was a fighter, Ferris knew that. So he'd take care of him. Get him new clothes, a bath, some grub and a safe place for the night if he needed it. Looked like he did.

As McPhee cleaned himself up he talked through his sobs. Some coke deal he had been trying to do in Victoria's ended up in an argument. He'd sorted that guy out then this other one started acting the hero.

"Like Superman," McPhee tried to laugh, "except his Y-fronts were under his trousers." McPhee had pulled his knife and just went for the lot of them. "Ah got some help but," he said. "The Moffat brothers from Easterhouse were there."

"Stevie Moffat?" Ferris asked. "And Alan?"

"Aye, that's them."

Ferris knew Stevie Moffat. A sound guy as far as he could see. Stevie was big on martial arts, fit as anything and had lethal fists and feet. He was the only Easterhouse hardman that never carried a weapon, ever. Didn't need to.

Later that night, Ferris dropped McPhee off at some point in the east end where he had arranged a pick up to take him out of Glasgow. On the short car journey he continued crying and repeating, "Ah've done him in. He's a goner." By the time he woke late the next afternoon, Ferris could see the problem. Graham Thomson had died after that fracas at Victoria's and two other guys were badly hurt. All of them had been knifed. No wonder McPhee skipped town. He was the knifeman, not Moffat who fought with his body in absolute control. Moffat knew how to hurt someone but not kill them. McPhee just went for their gullet with a blade.

That very night the Moffat brothers had been arrested and charged with murder after they had been nabbed trying to sneak out an exit. One man could help them. One man had to help them – Billy McPhee. But no one had seen him.

"He's out of town for a while, Paul," said McGraw. "You know. Having a wee break."

"He needs to get himself back here," said Ferris. "Only he can help the Moffats."

"The Moffats?" he asked.

"Aye, that killing in Victoria's."

"Does Billy know something about that?" His voice all amazement. "Fuck me. Ah'd tell him to come back but Ah don't know where he is," McGraw lied. McGraw had known about it all along and set it up. Why? Money.

Stevie Moffat had started a small taxi rank right at the back of The Caravel. As far as McGraw was concerned that was his area, his business and his profit to be made. Moffat wasn't going to give it up easily so McGraw had to play his dirty cards.

Out near Strathaven in rural Lanarkshire, a farmer had new help. He was a big man, young and strong looking. It was Billy McPhee.

The farm was owned by Jim McMinimee, a policeman's son fallen into bad company. Having lived in the east end for years before moving to the farm, McMinimee knew the McGraws and all their people including McPhee. When the call came from McGraw to see if he could put someone up for a while the answer was simply yes.

As it happened, McPhee could prove useful to the McMinimees. Local youths had been giving the incoming family a bad time driving McMinimee to the idea of violence. McPhee liked that prospect but went one further. Why don't they get knives and smear them all in cattle dung. Whoever they knifed wouldn't just get a wound, they'd get a nasty infection too.

McMinimee liked the idea but never had to use it. Word spread that he had company, some dangerous guy from Glasgow and the young hardmen stayed away.

In July 1994 Stephen and Alan Moffat were found guilty of the murder and sentenced to life. They had pled not guilty but were in deep trouble. Stevie had picked the bloody knife off the floor of that toilet after McPhee had dropped it. His prints were all over the murder weapon. Found guilty or not they still declared their innocence. A few weeks later, Billy McPhee handed himself in to the cops. A short while later another man, John Paul McCall was arrested.

McPhee hadn't appeared to talk about the Moffats and clear them. He was too late for that. Deliberately too late. He hadn't been planning anything apart from his own freedom. The Moffats had refused to talk about McPhee's part in the killing and still refused even though they had been sentenced to life.

Outside, McGraw had been at work. McPhee had been with other people later that night – Gordon Ross, George McCormack and scores of others. A murder? He had been at a party.

As usual, McGraw spoke to his cops. Telling them that McPhee was innocent.

"Besides," he said, "you have two guys for that. The older one is pally with Ferris. Did you know that?"

Charges were dropped against McPhee and McCall but McCall was going to have a trying time.

Two years later while walking near some kids out playing in Easterhouse in the middle of the day, a car pulled up and shots rang out. Eighteen hours later he was dead.

His pals reckoned they knew why. He knew too much about the murder of Graham Thomson. Knew what had really happened. Knew that Billy McPhee was the knifeman. The killer.

Other people came forward with evidence from that night. People who had been in Victoria's and were convinced the Moffat brothers were innocent. Someone was paying attention and death threats started being targeted at Stevie Moffat's four-year-old daughter, Chelsea. Someone wanted to be sure that Stevie Moffat didn't talk. The authorities didn't listen. The Moffat brothers stayed in jail and served their whole sentence.

Back in 1994, McGraw had other work to be getting on with. His pals were going abroad.

52

A TRIP TO THE SUN

"Why take cars when you can take buses?" McGraw asked Gordon Ross.

"We'd look fucking stupid driving empty buses through Europe, wouldn't we?" Ross replied. This was his game, his plan and he wasn't going to let McGraw or anyone else jeopardise it.

"Empty? Screw empty. How's about bus loads of kids?" Now he had Ross' attention but he was going against advice other close people had given him. Keep it tight and small, they had said. Get big and you'll have all the cop forces after you, they warned. You get a good profit so why risk it? But now McGraw and his people had come up with an idea that just might work.

Gordon Ross and Chic Glackin had been trafficking dope in cars for years. Just one car at a time bringing in eighty to one hundred and fifty pounds of good quality gear every time. Their trips meant the price was low, missing out on the traffickers and middlemen who always took their cut, and the quality was good.

They had figured that dope was practically legal now with hardly anyone going to jail for a bit of personal or even dealing small time. It had also undergone a surge of popularity. Everybody they knew took a few joints now and then and they knew a lot of straight guys – bank managers, businessmen – who did just that. Never mind the kids who were mad for the stuff.

The risks were low and the profits high – just the way to run a business.

Ross was ambitious, however. While he was making a decent

living from the dope and the various other scams he worked, he wanted to have enough money to retire and retire well. He was young, strong, full of energy – now was the time to try.

"What does it take to convert a bus?" McGraw was off again. "Hollowing out the panels, adding an extra compartment or two under the floor – no problem for those with access to the skills and equipment." Ross knew he was talking about himself. Or rather Margaret McGraw, his wife, and other business associates.

Through them, McGraw now controlled over fifty ice cream vans and had the back up to fix and repair them. He also owned Mac Cars, a huge company that monopolised most of the east end. He was a man who wasn't short of a mechanic or two.

"What about the kids though," asked Ross, "where would they come from?"

"Do you like football, Gordon?"

"Aye."

"So do most boys." Ross looked at him puzzled till he explained. They would become local benefactors, running boys' football clubs into France and Spain for small tournaments against other clubs. Maybe they could also set up trips from youth clubs taking young kids to Spain for a break. "Would you search a bus full of weans? Well would you?" Not if he could help it, paid cop or not. "Everybody enjoys a trip to the sun. And Disneyland?"

"What?"

"How many visitors are there to Disneyland Paris every year?"

"Christ, more than Ah could count."

"Spot on, so it could be a kind of stop off point for youth clubs, community groups and so on."

"You've been thinking about this eh?"

"Fucking right Ah have." McGraw always thought about ploys that offered good money.

They decided it was a goer. After all they had a good team. Manny McDonnell with his background was well used to smuggling. Ross and Glackin had been doing it with the dope. Trevor Lawson was a safe pair of hands. Then there was Willie Hassard and John Templeton, maybe they cold join in but they needed more. McGraw's brother-in-law, John Healy from the southside was the man. He could bring in some of his troops and maybe be involved in getting the bus and buying a few cars as well. Perhaps organising the football groups and youth clubs. Best to keep that well away from McGraw's patch if he could.

McGraw? What would he do? Put in some money. Oversee the laundering. Connect with Glasgow's five big dealers and start getting orders direct. The other teams would have to put the money up front so all that his crew would do would be the middlemen. Going, buying and bringing back. That's where all the risks were, of course, so McGraw wouldn't be doing any of that and their cut had to be high.

The benefit of being Scottish is that you find Sots everywhere. The beauty of being involved in crime is that there is always someone looking to make a big easy buck. In the south of Spain they found more exiled Scots than they needed.

Pat McCadden was high up on their list but his brother Tommy's links to the London Adams family made him too hot a target for the Security Forces in McGraw's view. What he didn't realise was that MI6 were tailing one of his own men, Manny McDonnell, given his links with Irish terrorists.

Former Glasgow milkman Wattie Douglas was also a possibility and certainly had the form for moving drugs all over the world. Yet Douglas was hunted in so many places he had to have plastic surgery and was so much on the move he was nicknamed The Tartan Pimpernel. Too much risk there too.

Instead they settled for a man who used to be one of the big names on the Glasgow drugs scene till Fatboy, Arthur Thompson's son, had him chased out of town. He had the low profile, the connections and was asking for the right money. He'd do.

Within a few months they had converted a white Mercedes bus, established connections in the south of Spain that could sell them hash straight from north Africa and set up a community group to go on a trip.

"We can't fill the bus," McGraw was almost screaming at Healy and Ross.

"Fuck sake, we could fill the bus three times over," said Ross. "They're mad for this idea."

"Aye, well we can't. You know the weight of dope we'll be carrying? The fucking bus will never make it up a hill."

"What the fuck will we say to them?"

"Say there'll be other trips and their names are first on that list."

"You sure?"

"Well let's hope so eh."

The first bus rolled out and headed south. The men all had their orders about security and checking while seeming to be relaxed, on holiday. There would be no rushing on this trip. Who goes abroad for two days? Almost every step of the way they were wary, expecting to get pulled in. It didn't happen.

They were back in Glasgow and the drugs unloaded. They had just made their first fortune from dope trafficking. Many more would follow. At last McGraw could smell the easy life. What he didn't know was that someone just round the corner was about to make his life hell.

53

SACRIFICED?

The security man had had enough. Sawn off shotguns or no, the robbers weren't going to get away. He jumped in a van, turned the key and headed out to confront them.

The security van hit the red Rover square on the side. The three masked men jumped out, waved their shotguns at the driver, grabbed their bags of loot and set off on foot.

They seemed to know Motherwell where they had just robbed a security van outside a bank.

'Must be local,' thought the security man as he took off again, following them. He saw them up ahead, moving their loot into a white van. Two minutes later, security man Robert McCulloch rammed that too.

Cop cars arrived in numbers. Off they went chasing them through the schemes. One of the robbers stopped a taxi and hijacked it waving a gun in the face of a driver. Once again cop cars were on his tail. Eventually they cornered him, guns at the ready. He was masked and in his hand was a big automatic pistol. For a few seconds he aimed it a cop. Just a few seconds. Slowly he placed it on the ground. Nearby, one of his team trained a shotgun at the cops and took longer to put it down.

It was September 1994. Tam Bagan had just been arrested for armed robbery. It wasn't going to end there.

At his trial for the theft of £283,000 in April 1995, two witnesses were missing. Two defence witnesses – McGraw and Ferris. It soon became clear why.

Bagan's lawyer politely pointed out that his client's defence was a special alibi of incrimination. McGraw had been angry at a story Bagan had given to the newspapers and had got Ferris in cahoots to teach Bagan a lesson, so he claimed.

Ferris and Bagan had fallen out over their double glazing company and a few other illegal games. There was bad blood between them now. So bad that street players predicted a shoot out. Had Ferris plotted another way to punish Bagan?

Ferris, Bagan claimed, had asked to borrow a white van that he used in the double glazing business. Of course, Bagan agreed. It was dropped off by Ferris and a man called Donnie McMillan in Motherwell that day, as requested by Ferris.

When Bagan went to get the van he realised that masks, guns and bags of money were stowed in the back. Clearly, he claimed, Ferris had just robbed the security van and had set Bagan up. Then he panicked, trying to get away.

Why was he wearing a mask then? And carrying a gun?

He feared the Glasgow mob might still be around, still after him.

Why were McGraw and Ferris not in court?

His lawyer had tried and failed to contact them. That much was very true. McGraw simply ignored all approaches and temporarily moved out to Spain. Good for his suntan and better still for setting up drug deals.

Ferris was spending much of his time in London, living in different hotels. Or up in Manchester hanging around with Rab Carruthers, the Glaswegian who terrified Arthur Thompson as well as his adopted city's vicious Mac-10 teams.

The Lanarkshire cops issued a warrant for McGraw's arrest. It was a warrant that was never used, even as he sat chatting with the cops in his Mount Vernon home.

It took the High Court jury a mere thirty minutes to decide that they didn't believe Bagan and found him guilty. He was sentenced to twelve years. His two accused, Gordon McLeod and James Scougal, both got eight years.

Tam Bagan was dispatched off to jail, not a happy man. He felt let down and betrayed. Set up and sacrificed. He knew McGraw's games and had watched him play them. Seen them first hand at close quarters. No sacrifice was too big for him as long as someone else paid the price.

Tam Bagan wasn't going to stand for it any longer. He was going public on McGraw and his corrupt coppers.

54

THE TWO JOHNS

The two men entered calmly and quietly. There was none of the camaraderie and banter that usually happen when men like them visit. They weren't well known cons, they were cops. The problem was who they were visiting.

Bagan had started talking and embarrassed Strathclyde Police into taking him seriously. At last the cops had agreed to investigate allegations of corruption among their numbers. The Met and Merseyside had always been quick to investigate such claims and act when they could. Strathclyde simply ignored them or dealt with dodgy Bobbies on the quiet, in private. Now two cops were on the case and public action was promised.

Superintendent John Neilson and DCI John Malcolm had been visiting Bagan every week in Shotts Prison and interviewed him over hours in the privacy of an interview room.

He had told them the lot about McGraw. Naming names and ranks of the corrupt cops who worked with him and for him. Blaming McGraw for unsolved murders and backing it up with who, how and why. Detailing his earnings from different scams every year and asking why he wasn't investigated, the taxman on his tail. Listing warrants and implications in major crimes when he was never even charged.

On and on Bagan went, in more detail than any cop needed. McGraw knew, of course, and McGraw wasn't happy.

"Twenty grand for him," he had instructed his colleagues

privately. "To be paid any way and to anyone they want. Get the word out. Ah want that cunt dead."

It was a threat that was soon evident. Bagan had been a loner, still was. He didn't do friends, just relied on his own gumption and wit. He had loads of both. But now that meant Scottish jails were peppered with people who would take him out with a jail made blade. It was a threat he didn't bow down to.

When he was jumped and stabbed, young James McCann was the one lifted and thrown into solitary. But Bagan played by his rules and made no complaint. He understood what was going on in men's minds. In McCann's case it might not have been the bounty on Bagan's life but more likely an old score he had to settle with The Licensee, with McGraw for a severe battering his father had taken years before.

If so, McCann had the wrong end of the stick. The hefty doing was dished out by Joe Hanlon when he worked for McGraw, not by Bagan. And Bagan had, of course, split from McGraw in the biggest, most public way.

When the interviewing cops had first arrived, Bagan had made sure they knew that he was only talking with them because they were "internal". That is, they were investigating other cops. At the start of every interview the two officers would switch on the tape recorder. Tam Bagan always said his name, his purpose and stated that no deal had been made with the police. He didn't do deals with the cops. He didn't want his sentence reduced or any favours at all. He just wanted McGraw and his pet polis arrested.

Bagan listed the cops he knew McGraw had in his pocket by name and rank. There was a chief inspector, three inspectors, two sergeants and one detective constable. Long gone were the days of giving PC McLean a bottle of whisky yet he was involved with even more cops and most of higher rank. Bagan knew that but he simply couldn't give first hand evidence of McGraw's contact with them. Then he advised his two coppers to "follow the money". Examine the officers' quality of existence, their bank accounts, any big payments and ask the simple questions of how and who from.

He also warned the police that McGraw had taped these officers accepting bribes. Had been for years. They would know that by now and weren't about to give in easily. That meant they had to get McGraw. Had to get them all. After all, he was responsible for a score of murders, had heroin and dope sold on Glasgow streets, owned brothels and street girls and was involved in every other scam they could think of. Yet he hadn't been convicted and jailed for twenty-one years. Not a bad idea to arrest McGraw, was it?

Bagan had convinced the two Johns that there were serious concerns though they didn't admit that to him. After a year of listening and asking, they went off to write their report.

Chief Constable Leslie Sharp had announced that "allegations of this nature must be taken very seriously" and promised that they would be "vigorously and relentlessly investigated". How could there not be proof? Bagan had been there when money was handed over to the cops, when details of hit contracts were pulled off their National Computer, when team members had charges deleted all for the sake of a body or two. He had even given them details of McGraw's illegal earnings from many of his scams. There had to be a public inquiry. The matter was put in the hands of the Glasgow Procurator Fiscal. Now all the others had to do was wait.

While Bagan was waiting for Strathclyde to make up its mind, he was visited by a group of high-powered politicians and civil servants. Bagan was articulate and bright. He had convinced many people that he should be listened to and they listened for three hours.

"If what you say is true," said one senior politician after he finished, "if half of what you say is true, then there is no justice in Scotland. We are ruined."

"We are ruined," said Tam Bagan.

Tired of the wait, Bagan agreed to talk to some of the press. He told them everything. They wrote up their pieces without naming McGraw. Some just called him Mr Big. That was because Margaret

McGraw had roasted McGraw's ears. Go public, she told him, and threaten to sue if anyone claims you have done something that you haven't been convicted of. He did and they backed away.

Ferris was interviewed by the media and seemed to be in two minds. On one hand Bagan was a fantasist a bit like Dennis Woodman at his own trial when accused of the murder of Fatboy. On the other hand Bagan did know a thing or two about McGraw.

"Corrupt cops working with McGraw?" said Ferris. "Yeah, I've heard them called The Dirty Dozen."

Would Bagan ever be able to go public?

"No chance," said Ferris. "He'll be dead before he opens his mouth."

McGraw agreed to an interview with a Scottish newspaper. During it he was calm and considered though not as fluent or as articulate as Bagan or Ferris. As the journalist was leaving, she noticed that Zoltan, the McGraws' beloved Rottweiler, was ill. Twenty minutes later he died, breaking The Licensee and The Jeweller's hearts.

Later, Gordon Ross would reveal to Ferris that he had got fed up with the dog always barking and snarling at him. He'd fed him a deadly speedball in a wrap of raw steak and watched as the poor mutt went into a big time fit. Two hours later he had died. Ross thought it was a laugh. McGraw grieved for the rest of his life. Zoltan's death broke the heart of a man who would have people snuffed for a debt or jailed for life for crimes they didn't commit.

In 1996, McGraw had increased the bounty on Tam Bagan's life. Thirty grand. Forty grand. A lot of money from one of Glasgow's meanest men even if he was rich. Yet still there were no takers. The prison service suddenly intervened and moved Bagan into a protective, isolated cell. It was what they did with the child sex abusers, jailed ex-cops and the grasses. Bagan hated it and demanded out. They refused.

The heat was coming down on McGraw too. For the first time the tax people came after him and after an expensive battle he had to pay them £250,000. McGraw hated parting with money but close allies could reveal that he was delighted to have got off so lightly.

The papers got other news. He had been nabbed in Heathrow, fresh back from Spain and had £150,000 confiscated. Drugs money they called it. They weren't told when a few months later the money was returned under the official guise of his intention to invest in a business abroad. Aye, okay, but in cash? Then a few weeks later, in July 1996, came the bombshell, not with a bang but a whimper. Strathclyde Police quietly announced that no action would be taken against the cops named in Bagan's report. Very few newspapers or TV stations covered that part of the story.

All Tam Bagan's risks, his isolation, his turning his back on the only life he had ever lived had come to nothing.

What did the two Johns, Bagan's two cops, think about the outcome? They never did say. Did it make them give up faith in their careers? Or did they go on as usual? Either way it had made no difference to the world. Their job was done now and would never be tackled again.

Throughout Glasgow, street players scratched their heads and asked, "Is there no way to get McGraw?" Maybe not with so many high ranking cops on his side. Then again, maybe yes.

Two ghosts were on their way back to haunt him.

55

THE DEATH OF A GOOD MAN

"Have Campbell removed to hospital if he looks like he's dying. He must not die in prison." The letter was clear. But the move to hospital wasn't to save a life but to end it. The British government didn't want a martyr and they didn't want TC Campbell to live.

The letter was signed by the Secretary of State for Scotland, the top politician in the country. It was a new office bearer but it was the same position under Malcolm Rifkind that TC Campbell successfully sued for his maltreatment by the screws at Peterhead Prison after they delivered him to hospital with his back broken, a breath or two from death.

It was back then that TC realised he had to fight in any way he could. Not with his fists – though he would always take the bastards on – but with his brain and another being, his partner in no-crime, Joe Steele.

Joe was much younger. On the day the jury was going to return with their decision in the Doyle murder case, he had managed to get hold of two knives and smuggled them in to the High Court. He was about to be found guilty of a horrendous crime he didn't commit. If so, he'd go mental, pull the blades and strike out here, there, everywhere. It would be a blood bath.

A kindly court screw spotted the blades and talked Joe down. The High Court had been ten minutes away from the biggest disaster it had ever seen. Joe Steele might have been young but he was passionate and innocent.

Campbell and Steele joined forces. No harm they didn't like each other before this. They were in this together now. Fighting together made sense. They were twice as strong and specialised in different things.

TC concentrated on the legal work and raising a campaign. "Win the minds of the public and press and we're halfway there," he would say.

Joe had a different speciality. He escaped from jail, any jail, then a few days later would have someone phone all the media and tell them where to find him. On top of a high tower next to Barlinnie jail, even if he did suffer from severe vertigo, or superglued to the gates of Buckingham Palace. When the word spread through the prisons that Joe had escaped yet again, the chant went up:

"RUN, JOEY, RUN."

The cons were on their side. All they needed now was the courts.

Radical politicians and writers began to pay The Glasgow Two attention. Tommy Sheridan, red-hot left wing politician, was invited by Campbell to meet them. He left the jail convinced of their innocence.

Outside, Sheridan started raising people's awareness of the details of Campbell and Steele's convictions and calling them to demonstrations. Many of his colleagues argued with him.

"Why are you supporting two of the most evil men?" they'd ask.

"I've met them," Sheridan would reply, "and they're innocent and in jail."

The issue came close to having Sheridan thrown out of left wing political groups but he won. The demonstrations grew bigger and one occupied government buildings in Edinburgh. Every time Sheridan and his fellow travellers appeared in the media, a former working class boy from Barlanark now turned millionaire would curse and sleep less. McGraw wasn't happy and he wouldn't forget. It was an issue that would come back to haunt Sheridan many years later.

Glasgow gangsters don't shoot politicians. But someone else closer to home was annoying McGraw even more.

"Enjoying your freedom, McGraw? A wee drink with the boys eh. Good night for it, you Licensed prick." John Linton didn't hide how he felt or care who heard. Often it would go further with McGraw's minders forced to pull Linton off their boss and give him a kicking – or try to. As far as Linton was concerned he always knew that Campbell and Steele were innocent and knew the man who really ordered that fire at the Doyles' – McGraw.

Now, twelve years later, he had given up his life of crime to lead their campaign, a campaign that was gathering strength every day.

Linton had made sure press releases swamped the media at every chance. He broke into the House of Commons one night wandering around putting FREE THE GLASGOW TWO leaflets into MPs' drawers.

Meantime, TC Campbell had gone on hunger strike. By April 1996 he was approaching his hundredth day of not eating food and was fading fast, close to death. Thus the letter from the Secretary of State ordering that he be moved to hospital to die. Anyone who knew Campbell knew he'd go the whole way.

A month or so before, Linton had arrived at the campaign office to a letter. It was from a new landlord saying that the rents were being tripled. The campaign couldn't afford that type of money so they had to move out but Linton used his own place as did members of Campbell's family. No office didn't mean no campaign.

Years later it was discovered that the firm who owned that block of offices had been bought by McGraw. Officially under someone else's name – someone who would go on to front many enterprises for The Licensee.

Since that ploy hadn't worked, McGraw had to think of something more effective. A bullet would do and the chance fell into his lap.

A tough Scouser gang approached him one day wanting some

help in recovering a debt. An east end guy had failed to pay them for thousands of diazepam or jellies, popular among Glasgow's junkies, and they wanted payback.

The Licensee could help them by getting not him but his partner in front of them. Or so he lied. Seeing to him might encourage their man to cough up the dosh.

One night John Linton went to a boxing match in Garthamlock. He loved boxing and anyone who knew him knew he'd be there. After, a pal invited him to the Roadhouse pub for a drink. It had to have been a close pal – Linton was wary of traps by McGraw's crew at that time. It was a safe pub for Linton especially since it was owned by Jim Steele, Joe Steele's brother, a man who he considered to be an ally.

Around 8pm, John Linton was sipping his first drink when a pal invited him out the back to discuss something confidential. It had to be a close pal. Linton wouldn't have left for that dark place with just anyone.

Through the darkness of the night he spotted them. A bunch of angry Scousers and east end faces he knew. Guns went off from every side and John Linton lay dead.

Ten minutes later, Billy McPhee arrived at The Caravel where McGraw had been in company all night. A whisper in his boss's ear, a quiet smile then a large drink for the bringer of good news.

A good man lay dead and The Licensee was celebrating.

Jim Steele was the cops' number one suspect. He went on the run, passing messages back to the press that he was an innocent man.

In prison the bad news was whispered to TC Campbell. He painfully pulled his emaciated body up from his cot and announced that he was done with the hunger strike.

"With John gone," he said, "how will we prove our innocence? With me dead? I don't think so."

Jim Steele eventually gave himself in to the cops. After a short while they announced that he wouldn't be charged. No one would be charged, ever. John Linton's murder remains unsolved.

But the truth might emerge on six other murders. TC Campbell and Joe Steele had been granted the right to appeal and were freed from jail. Meantime a cop passed The Licensee bad news.

A team of detectives were back on the Glover–Hanlon case. Life was about to get difficult for McGraw.

56

PARADISE GAINED

"They're not the usual guys," said Laurel to McGraw.

"Fucking secret sort," said Hardy. "None of the men like them."

"So they're not on social invites," growled McGraw, "what's that to do with me?"

"It's just we got a whisper," Hardy went on. "From one of the forensic guys."

"They're going to hit The Caravel."

"The what? My fucking pub? After all these years?" McGraw wasn't happy.

"It's five years, Tam, since Glover and Hanlon got it." It was Laurel talking in a quiet voice, knowing McGraw had a habit of shooting the messenger.

"Glover and Hanlon? What the fuck has my pub got to do with them?" he demanded. Both cops looked at him, a bit embarrassed that he was continuing the charade of innocence.

"Seems they've had information that the men's bodies were laid out there," said Laurel waiting for an explosion. None came.

"Who from?" McGraw was talking through gritted teeth.

"Seems Tam Bagan has stuck that one in front of them."

"The backstabbing cunt."

Trevor Lawson wasn't expecting the visit. With his money from the dope trafficking and his building business doing well he was enjoying his life. Then McGraw appeared.

"You've got to do this for me, Trevor," McGraw insisted. "The price of saying no might be too high to pay." He left a silence. "For you to pay."

Lawson wasn't really one of the players. He was a hard working man who would bend the rules and break the laws now and then for a few quid but he wasn't into working with bent cops, setting up hit jobs or any of those larks. He had needed McGraw to bring in a few quid and was grateful for that. Also McGraw's extension into buying plots of land and building flats all over Glasgow had brought him a lot of work. All good stuff but he knew what McGraw meant. Had done enough wrong that McGraw could slip to his cops. Could be set up with a boot load of smack and a visit from the Drugs Squad. He had seen McGraw do all of that and worse before.

Or was it worse? Did he just mean that some night as he was driving home a car would pull up alongside with a gun blazing? McGraw had done that and worse too.

Did he know that Lawson had been frustrated by how slow the drugs trafficking was going and been doing a little moonlighting? Just a car or two now and then but did he think those earnings should be his?

Lawson knew The Licensee well enough to know how upset he got when people took his money. Upset? He turned lethal. Lawson had no option but to do the work.

"Just one question, Tam," Lawson asked. "Why knock it down and why in the middle of the night?"

"Mags has a thought of building houses there," he replied. "And if Ah knock it down now Ah'll get an easy ride from the local council."

Lawson wasn't daft. He knew the reasons McGraw gave were rubbish. He knew that Glover and Hanlon's bodies had been in there. Knew all along that he had been asked to help McGraw cover up.

That night Lawson and a small team were hard at work. By morning The Caravel had gone. Every lump of wood, roof slate, every brick and piece of broken plaster created out of the newly demolished pub had been taken away and dumped in numerous different locations. All the forensic team could check now was a stretch of wasteland.

With the bricks and mortar had gone any threat from the secret cops. Bagan could shout all he wanted about Glover and Hanlon. They'd not find The Caravel never mind find evidence inside it.

The Caravel hadn't just been McGraw's HQ. It had been a popular pub that had made him a good bit of money over the years. Now it was gone and so were the earnings. But that wasn't to last long. He was about to open another bar.

The west coast of Ireland is beautiful indeed. Nowhere more so than Donegal. Better still, people there like a drink. A magnet for tourists, people of all nationalities swarm around the area most of the year. Money changes hands from one currency to the next and, if you want a boat for some private sailing, where better to go?

Putting £135,000 into buying the Paradise Bar in Donegal was a no brainer for The Licensee. The pub was bound to make a profit. If he needed to launder some cash, he was in the ideal set up as well as moving some drugs quietly in and out of the country. A no brainer.

Officially the owners were John and Mary Hughes, a Glasgow couple. They could run a bar all right but were short of the readies. That's where McGraw came in.

With the bar refurbished what they needed was a grand opening. Through his legitimate business contacts and his good Irish pal, Manny McDonnell, McGraw made sure that a line up of top Celtic stars and Coronation Street actors were invited, paid and they came. The locals loved Celtic and his wife, Margaret, loved Coronation Street. That was good enough for him.

Swanning about in that company made McGraw feel good. This was the life he had worked for and was working still. After the party, they'd fly back to Glasgow, pack a case and catch a private jet heading to Spain. He knew that even as he was enjoying himself, his white Merc bus would be heading off for Spain too, its seats almost filled with school kids. By the time their break was over, the bus would be home and have deposited another £1,000,000 in his coffers. That's how it should be. That's how good his life had become.

But the Paradise Bar would not stay a paradise for long. McGraw's holidays had to end. There was trouble at home that would need to be attended to.

57

THE CARTEL AND SPECKY

"Bastards." McGraw was in a filthy mood. He always got that way when TC Campbell or Joe Steele were on the TV talking about proving their innocence. He was going to have to ruin all that.

Campbell was the one he feared. The man simply wouldn't lie down. He was the energy and the brains behind their campaign and if he was taken out or disgraced, they could handle wee Joe. Give him and his wife some money, get him on the smack. Easy. But Campbell, he was going to have to be cracked once and for all.

What McGraw decided to do was draw together some local boys, some people who were into the heavy duty action. Like the Steele brothers and their team. Not that they'd know it was a set up. Not all of them. They'd just see it as an invite to make some money.

The Steeles Campbell had known all his life. The same with most of the team as well-known Glasgow faces. If they could have Campbell in possession of a bag of heroin or maybe some coke, Bingo. The rest would be easy.

The group were part of what had become known as The Caravel Cartel or The Cartel for short. It was a group of east end faces who had split the area up. They split the streets and markets up and let no one else in. Some of these men dealt in smack and speed. Of course, McGraw was taking a cut of everything.

McGraw knew that Campbell had blown all his money on his legal defence and campaign. Now he had been freed pending his

THE CARTEL AND SPECKY

appeal, he was forced to live on benefits. Not good. Maybe, just maybe, he could be tempted into drugs just the once.

After he had some people speak to the Steele brothers, McGraw didn't sit back and wait. His brother-in-law, John Healy was involved in his dope trafficking exploits and through him he had met an interesting guy, Stewart 'Specky' Boyd.

Boyd was small, tough, acutely intelligent and called Specky since he relied on his glasses all the time. It sounded like a school playground nickname but no one should have judged Specky on that. He was a killer all right.

There was something else about Specky that McGraw liked – he and Paul Ferris didn't get on.

Specky ruled the south side of the city from Pollok to Carnwadric and beyond to Barrhead. It was one tough patch but one with a big smack problem and therefore big profits.

Some people thought of him as John Healy's deputy but McGraw knew better. Specky Boyd was his own man who would work on jobs that brought in the biggest profits and that included looking after Healy's interests. He ran a tight team, disciplined any miscreants and was ambitious. Specky had the know-how, all he needed now was back up from someone with contacts and the money to bankroll big jobs. That's where McGraw came in.

The pair were involved in a number of scams with McGraw investing some cash, Specky the rest but also taking the risks. It was an arrangement that made a lot of Specky's troops uneasy, something he knew fine well. They were the southside team and they didn't work with the east enders is how they saw it. Specky thought that was old fashioned. Teams should work wherever and however they could to make cash. It was business plain and simple. The same view as McGraw.

Apart from a few quid every now and then, McGraw was after something else from Specky – gun power. He was aware that his life of crime was going too well, that he was getting very rich. That was the very time someone else like the Daniels or the McGoverns or Ferris might try to take it off him. If the east and the south of the city combined – they'd need to call in the Army to get to him.

McGraw asked his business associate for a favour.

"Ah've got trouble with that murdering bastard, TC Campbell," he had said. "No way should he walk free. Now a wee bit of coke planted on him . . . that would be the business."

Specky said he'd see what he could do and was promised a daily breakdown of Campbell's movements from McGraw via his spies and taxi drivers who trailed Campbell every day.

Specky had problems at home though. Robert 'Piggy' Pickett had witnessed a shooting by Specky's team and refused to give evidence against them. Specky got close to Piggy and wanted to reward him. This put the noses of major players on his side out of joint. Specky didn't stand for that type of grumbling.

Drew McLaughlin got it first by accident. Some gunman had mistaken him for an enemy of Specky's and he paid the ultimate price.

Then Brian 'Cocky' Cochrane was blasted as he drove his car down Glenlora Drive in Nitshill, slap bang in Specky's territory.

Billy Weatherall was killed and dumped at a caravan park near Erskine.

They had all been Specky's men who paid the price for grousing about their boss's fondness for Piggy Picket. But there was more.

Specky was in cahoots with Paisley faces who were well organised. Paisley was a troubled town with a high murder rate and frequent feuds involving shooters. The government had noticed this and was providing State money to set up a lot of community projects including security firm, FCB. Except FCB didn't provide much security. It was run by hoods involved in the protection racket and was a front for money laundering.

When local people complained, Irene Adams MP went public big time, naming names. Specky didn't hesitate. He put a hit contract out on her and made sure she knew. He was the very man to kill an MP.

Strathclyde Police, MI5 and NCIS were crawling over Paisley.

Adams' house was filled with security and armed guards patrolled her street for months. When the armed cops were called off, Irene Adams' daughter's car was torched in her driveway. That same night a strange man cornered her in a nightclub and warned the young woman that her "mother better keep her mouth shut".

Specky Boyd was very busy at home but not too busy to help McGraw. Neither were The Cartel. Campbell was about to feel McGraw's wrath.

58

DANGEROUS DEMONS

On a flight back from London where he had been to visit his brother, TC Campbell was sitting across from two attractive young women, wearing short skirts, low cut tops and having a laugh as well as a good few drinks.

"You're TC aren't you?" said one smiling sweetly. "It's good to see you free."

"High time," her pal agreed and they offered him a drink. They were good company. As they traipsed off the plane the women suggested that he come with them to a party. Things at home between Campbell and his wife, Liz, weren't that great at that time so he was tempted. They had picked up their bags and a pal was coming to give them a lift. He was a young man who was delighted to see Campbell, who thought nothing of it. He'd been on TV so almost everyone recognised him.

As he was walking out the airport with the three young folk, one woman got close up to him

"Will you carry my bag for me, TC?" she asked sweetly.

"Sure," he said with a smile. She was a bit drunk, a bit unsteady on her feet. Anything to be helpful.

"Do you like a wee line, TC?" she asked. "You know a wee bit of coke?" He simply smiled back at her and decided not to start on his usual strong words about heavy duty drugs. He hated them. "Cos I've got a kilo of pure Colombian marching powder," she smiled up at him, "in that bag." It was the bag he was carrying. TC grabbed her hand, put the bag back in it, turned around and walked as fast as he could away from them, into the first taxi and off home.

Later that evening the two women reported their failure with the fit up to Specky. He wasn't best pleased. Neither were the Drugs Squad cops that McGraw's people had waiting at the airport door.

Back in the east end, the crew McGraw was trying to use to fit up Campbell were having problems. He simply wouldn't touch any smack. They were going to have to be clever and there was someone close by who could be of use – Campbell's upstairs neighbour.

'Kelly' Kelso had been out of jail for a year having served eleven years for stabbing a guy to death who had caught him stealing a leather jacket from a party in his house. Campbell and Kelso knew each other from old. That's what the crew intended to use.

Kelso was down on his luck. During his years in jail the drug market had sprouted and he had been counted out with no one letting him in. That was, The Cartel wasn't letting him in. All he needed was one big deal. But would he shop Campbell in the process? That was the cost of his entry ticket.

At first he wanted to leave a bundle of smack in Campbell's house till he got shown the door. Then he delivered ninety tenner bags of speed to Campbell's grown up son, Tommy, for safe keeping for his Da. The helpful young guy was obliging and was piling them up in a cupboard when his father arrived for a visit. The bags were binned pronto and TC was out of there and fast. Half an hour later, the cops arrived but the boy was still arrested for sediments found on work surfaces.

As it turned out, some bent bobbies had been faking arrest warrants to give cons hassle. One of those had been used and the young man was freed on his first visit to court.

When a local dealer arrived with a big bag of heroin for Campbell he told him who had asked that it be delivered before he took it away. Kelso.

A good kicking from Campbell didn't calm Kelso down. Instead he started trying to bug Campbell's phone and hung out at night, camouflaged in bushes near his front window. The man was so desperate he seemed to be losing his mind.

Finally, The Cartel dealers relented and gave Kelso a delivery of heroin. That same night the Drugs Squad raided his house. It was okay though. He had his alibi – the one The Cartel had given him. TC Campbell had climbed up the short distance at the front of the building and planted it in his house. Hadn't he just?

What he didn't know was that Campbell and his wife Liz had separated and he had moved out. He was elsewhere that night, a long way away in the company of others. It felt to TC that Glasgow was full of people after his blood even though their bundle of tricks came to nothing. McGraw was spitting teeth.

The Licensee continued to try and trip TC Campbell up. He couldn't use the old method of simply paying someone to top him. Through the media and the campaigns the man was too well known for that. Still McGraw had nothing to fear.

In 1998, when Campbell and Steele returned to the High Court on a procedural matter they were amazed to hear the three appeal judges debating the issue of William Love. He was the man who had claimed to have heard a confession from Campbell but had since retracted it privately, publicly, on TV and had even signed an affidavit. Two out of three judges said no, the evidence on Love couldn't be heard. The only one saying yes was Lord McCluskey, highly respected by laymen and lawyers alike.

Campbell and Steele were returned to jail that day. Joe Steele was offered a deal. A quiet jail, great conditions and free in nine months. He insisted that Campbell was brought into the room. There was no deal being offered to Campbell. Joe said no thank you.

Months later it would be revealed that one of the judges had nine pages missing from his papers. Nine pages that might well have changed his mind. It was too late now though. Campbell and Steele had to give up or keep fighting. They chose the latter, of course.

Meantime, some of McGraw's pals were in big trouble and he was about to dish the same deal to some others.

59

BETTER OFF DEAD

Billy Manson wasn't in good shape. Ever since that attack back in 1992, his body ached more and more every day. Maybe, with that pressure, he was getting ready to talk. McGraw was going to have to do something about it.

They were cheap dates. Once every week or so, McGraw's men would visit Billy, pass him a few quid and stop for a while for a cup of tea and a chat.

Had he seen William Lobban, his nephew? Not for a while. Lobban had been jailed for an armed robbery on the Pipe Rack Pub. He was grassed up by Eileen Glover now convinced that he had led her man, Bobby, to his death.

In Perth Prison he was terrified for his life, convinced that McGraw or Ferris was going to get him. Not sleeping or eating in case of poison, he finally took a guard hostage pretending a silver pen was a blade. That got him banged up in solitary then shifted south to an English jail for his own protection. Funny enough his food that very night had enough poison in it to kill a dozen.

Glasgow faces, Mick Healy and Ian 'Blink' McDonald robbed a bank in Torquay. The robbery had gone belly up and Healy was arrested soon after. Blink, the getaway driver, had gone on the run and was arrested paying a sneak visit back to his wife. They had met in a Chinese restaurant where all the customers were armed cops. It had been 1993 and the technology of tapping phones had improved.

Lobban appeared at their trial but not as himself. He was called Witness X and spoke from behind a screen, shading his face from the court. It didn't work. Everyone in Glasgow knew who he was. The point of his evidence? To blame Ferris for the bank job, for every murder and the prospect of World War III. The court didn't believe him.

Lobban was back in jail again. The two things Manson's nephew could do were spend money and get caught trying to steal some more. No, Manson hadn't seen him and he didn't want to either.

What about big Frank McPhie? Heard anything of him?

"Ah thought he was going down for Worm Toye. Ah really did."

William 'Worm' Toye was an axe killer who had chopped down a guy in the street who was due to give evidence against his own brother. In Perth jail he set himself up as a drug dealer – till Frank McPhie joined the company. The pair argued and fought over who should have control of that hall. Toye held his own and threw a good couple of punches. McPhie stormed off screaming, "Ah'm going to finish you."

Five minutes later, two men wearing sacks as hoods rushed into Toye's cell where he was chatting to some men and stabbed him to death.

McPhie and young Neil Munro were charged but walked free from their trial. Case Not Proven.

"Ye know he's been to a wedding since? A fucking usher, man. Guess what? The groom was murdered. Ha. Fucking murdered. Hah. Ah think The Iceman has turned greedy."

McPhie had been out of prison for only two months when he was flown to Dublin to be an usher at his pal Christopher McGrory's wedding. He'd met McGrory through another pal, Colin McKay, who was best man at his wedding.

Young McGrory was well-to-do with interests in horses and a frequent visitor to Ireland. Yet rumours were circulating the Glasgow streets that he was into trafficking cocaine between Scotland and Ireland. Only two weeks after his wedding he was found half naked and strangled to death out in an isolated spot near Dougalston. The cops put out a full alert and didn't have far to look.

McPhie was scarpering all over the place looking for something. At one house in a well-to-do suburb, he'd sit outside all night watching. Every night. When confronted he had said that McGrory had buried something in the garden that belonged to him and demanded the right to dig the place up. It was refused. For the second time in a few years, Frank McPhie was about to be arrested for murder.

"Have you heard about Ferris, Billy?" they'd ask just to see what Manson was picking up.

"Nah, nothing," he'd reply.

"He's not been to see you?"

"Nuh." This was the bit they didn't like. Manson saying nothing about the man they all feared most. Ferris was hanging around with some names from down south and seemed to be getting too big for his boots as far as they were concerned. Every now and then he'd float back into Glasgow and they'd put a tail on him. Trouble is he always spotted them and lost them too easily.

Was Ferris seeing Manson? Was he collecting information about the killing of Bobby and Joe? McGraw didn't like this at all and decided to cut the risk. Manson had to go.

The visit started as usual, nice and friendly. There were two men that time. Manson was taking his painkillers more and more these days and some lay by his side on his chair. McGraw's men knew what they were and had found some easily through one of the old women who got bogus prescriptions off the GP to sell to drugheads.

Without a word, one held his head and the other pushed pills down his throat. Not whole pills but crushed pills, the ones they brought. Wash it down with some water and stand back and wait.

"Cunts," he murmured trying to get to his feet. "Bastards." They gave him some more.

In a few minutes he was out of it. Hours later he'd be found dead. Overdose was the official finding. McGraw knew better.

Did he smile when told of Manson's demise? If so it wouldn't be for long. First an old enemy was going to end up in big trouble then so would he. Trapped in a place where people wanted to kill him.

McGraw was about to be in not too good shape.

60

THE LONG ARM

Armed cops surrounded his car. He waited for a gun to go off, to end his days. Instead his window was smashed and he was yanked through it. Ferris thought he was a dead man but he was only arrested.

He had gone to pick up some plates for making counterfeit notes. He needed months of persuading before he had visited the flat of London illegal arms dealer, John Ackerman. Ferris would run a few examples, have them tested by experts then set out on a scam that could make him millions. But those boxes didn't have plates. They had Mac-10 machine guns and ammo.

Up in Glasgow a party was happening with the host, The Licensee. For the last few years he had feared Ferris and had tried hard to get him.

Late one night in 1994, he sent out Trevor Lawson and Manny McDonnell to check up Ferris' usual haunts. At Premier Security in Rutherglen they had gone into a tenement across from the business and climbed a couple of floors. From there they had a good view of Premier's yard from the gate to the door. Ideal for a hitman.

Out in Croy they stopped off at the Celtic Tavern, now known as the Croy Tavern, but then with close associations to Ferris. It was after midnight and the place was shut. They checked the windows and all around the building looking for escape routes and dark places close to where cars would be parked.

Out in the east end of the city, they drove up and down close to where Ferris' pals stayed then on into the city centre where they checked out the area around his flat, down on the riverside looking on to the Clyde.

Hours later they went to the Marriott Hotel, picked up McGraw and headed south through the city. The Thornlie Arms was closed but not empty. Inside, the owner, John Healy, and Specky Boyd, waited. All they knew was that McGraw had some business to put Specky's way. Healy left them alone to chat.

"It's a hit, plain and simple," said McGraw looking at Specky. "At Premier, very easy, but you'll need a good sniper. At Croy, easy too. Close up job with a fast car waiting."

"Who's the target?" asked Specky.

"Ferris."

"Fucking Ferris? Are you crazy?"

At that time, Specky Boyd didn't like Ferris but he respected the man, had sense of his power and on trips he'd taken down to London people were telling him that he was getting stronger still. "Fuck sake, Tam. He's mates with Bobby Dempster and Rab Carruthers. Then there's the Adams mob. Do you think they'll just ignore someone shooting Ferris?"

The answer was clear to all in the room. No.

Specky was getting on well and didn't need to attract more grief. Killing Ferris would bring down hell. Yet there was money to be made in this venture, perhaps, so he didn't let go there. The dope trafficking that McGraw, Healy and others had kicked off looked to be a winner. Could Specky get in on the action?

McGraw's answer was no. It wasn't that he didn't trust Specky. He did. Yet he wasn't sure of some of his team and those would be the men sent into Spain. They had only started to run that bus a few months before and it was already proving a big money earner. No way was McGraw going to risk that. It was something that Healy would agree with. After all, the more who were involved, the less of a cut for him.

It had been a wasted night, or so it seemed. McGraw decided to look outside Glasgow for a hitman. Maybe some of the big

English cities, maybe over in Ireland using Manny McDonnell.

The English hitmen approached said no. They had heard of Ferris through other gangs in their area who respected him. They weren't about to invite that grief.

McDonnell said he'd ask in Ireland. Trouble was that McDonnell had problems. Not only was he on some Republican foot soldiers' hit list suspected of stealing dough, but at least two Loyalist groups thought he'd cheated them. He wasn't going to be telling McGraw that but he would struggle to get in and out of Belfast alive let alone find the right men to kill Ferris.

The night had been a waste of time for McGraw. As he was driven home towards the east end, two other men followed at a distance. They were a special drugs squad and their night had been fruitful indeed.

The cops had launched an international Drugs Squad in February of that year when some Glaswegians got into trouble. Two cars, an Escort and a Volkswagen Golf, had been nabbed on the Spanish–French border at Le Perthus in February of 1994. In the cars were some 340 pounds of top quality Moroccan hashish with a street value of £1.2 million.

Willie Hassard and John Lyon had been good pals of Bobby Glover's. In the other car, another pal of Bobby's, John Templeton, was there with a long-legged blonde, Caroline Dott, Gordon Ross' girlfriend. The three men were working for Ross, that's how they saw it. Ross and Glover had been pals, they all had been. They were really working for McGraw.

This was Dott's first run. She had just suggested going along after Ross had told her about his scam, trafficking drugs. It would look more natural with a man and a woman travelling together, she reckoned. She was right but after they had arrived at Disneyland Paris, Ross had stayed on there sending her with Lyon to pick up the drugs. He had also sent her through the most drugs aware border post in Europe. Sent her in her own car registered under own name.

As soon as Ross sussed the teams had been nabbed he skipped home to Glasgow under his false passport.

Ross had promised the team the same as him, £5,000 for being mules. He was getting his five grand okay but also a percentage of the profit as they sold the dope on to the big Glasgow dealers.

Street players who had heard of the scene shook their heads. Ross had been keeping too much bad company. Too much time spent with McGraw.

Later, McGraw would put it about that Dott had been released and subject to a strict curfew. Having phoned Ross back in Glasgow, McGraw's men managed to get her a passport that looked very much like her, had it delivered to the airport along with her ticket and some cash and so spirited her home. The truth is a lot more boring.

After a few days of listening to her pleas that she knew nothing about the drugs, the authorities realised that Dott was no major player and simply released her.

While Caroline Dott was treated in a terrible way by McGraw's men and Ross, her own boyfriend, some other people were paying attention. The British cops knew about the three men arrested, knew that they were Glasgow players. The dope had also been stored away professionally inside the hollowed out panels of the cars. There had to be more trafficking going on. It was time to watch the crew, especially McGraw.

For three years the drugs squad watched, bugged, taped and photographed McGraw and his team. It was a drugs squad who spoke to no one else so his own cops were clueless. Besides, like Arthur Thompson before him he had been told by the cops that some drug dealing was okay but to keep it under control. A million quid's worth every trip wasn't their idea of control.

In December 1997 they came for McGraw. It was jail time again. The question is, would he survive unscathed?

61

PARADISE LOST

McGraw was screaming at the cops. Absolutely howling.

"What the fuck am Ah doing here?" he demanded. "Did you set me up? Well, fucking did you?"

He was in Barlinnie Prison in a room upstairs in the staff area, miles away from his team in the halls down below. Out of earshot, in other words, and he was using that to the full.

It was Laurel and Hardy he was meeting with. The two men had said repeatedly that McGraw being lifted came as big a surprise to them as it had done to him with one obvious difference – they went home at night.

If they had known more of the story then maybe the chat would have taken a different turn. That mouth of his had let him down again.

McGraw had put himself right into jail big time. He had been sitting in a Chinese restaurant in the city centre talking with two of his team. He was saying that Benidorm would be the pick up point and detailing the best route back for the bus. Exactly the route they followed and exactly how they had lifted three men with a massive load of dope.

The man who often sent spies out to earwig on others had been beaten at his own game and so had most of his crew.

Billy McPhee, Gordon Ross, Manny McDonnell, John Healy, Trevor Lawson and others like Graeme Mason who looked after the bus under the name Geoffrey Balmer, southsiders John Burgon, John Wood and Michael Bennett, the driver. None of them were happy.

The cops had nabbed the busload that McGraw had been talking about and found £236,000 of dope planted in the panels. What the cops didn't know was that another car had safely completed the trip with even more dope on board.

As well as watching the crew night and day the police just pulled an old trick – they followed the money. The scale and frequency of the operation meant the team had pulled in many millions over the three years of operation. At least four of them were millionaires, none more so than McGraw. But that was part of the problem.

None of them had fallen into the trap of suddenly spending large. That would give the game away. But down in Spain the banks simply couldn't cope with the amount of Scottish bank notes floating round their coffers.

Even though the North African dealers had bribed several bank managers giving them a good cut, their head offices wondered how the Scottish notes had increased so much over the past three years.

McGraw's efforts to have the Scottish dealers pay only in pesetas didn't work that well. These were men who hid their money and didn't carry it into a bank asking for an exchange rate into pesetas.

The men had also been watched as they passed from Scotland to go abroad. Even McGraw was followed when he and Margaret flew by small jet directly to Benidorm. When you're fighting the security services you are up against it.

Down in the secure unit in Belmarsh prison Ferris was learning the same lesson. From his legal papers he discovered that he had been followed by NCIS and MI5 for at least two years. How can you fight the government like that?

Worse, Ackerman had turned Queen's evidence and was about to put him and his two co-accused right in it. Once he had given his evidence Ackerman would be given a light sentence, never mind that he'd been selling illegal shooters to all England's top teams for years. Then the Home Office would announce that he had died of some heart complaint only for him to reappear in

Amsterdam under an assumed name living off a fat government pension.

Ferris was going down for the guns. First for ten years reduced to seven on appeal but there was no party in Glasgow hosted by McGraw. He was too busy trying to save his own neck.

When the Irish cops announced that they had seized the Paradise Bar in Donegal, he thought the whole world was out to get him, especially since the Irish had not consulted with Glasgow cops knowing McGraw's relationship with them. Some £200,000 was taken from its bank account as well as a load of cash lying in the bar. A few weeks after it had been seized, the bar was auctioned and sold for £215,000. The owners, John and Mary Hughes, were going to jail unless they cooperated.

For months they disappeared off the scene, in reality living under police protection under false names. They were going to appear at his trial to give evidence against McGraw about how he used the place for money laundering and reveal all the well-known faces he had met there. McGraw was in deep trouble and he knew it. He'd do anything to gain his freedom. Anything – and that had to involve the cops.

It was an accident. One of the accused had been sent up to see the medic when it wasn't the ordinary surgery time. While he was waiting at the door, McGraw came down the stairs accompanied by two well-known faces – two of Glasgow's top cops. Why the hell was he meeting with them? Is that who he went to see most afternoons when he was called away? He told them it was his lawyer but his lawyer seemed to spend an awful lot of time with him. Much more than theirs. McGraw was in trouble.

"Are you doing a deal?" asked big Gordon Ross.

"Playing your games as usual?" demanded Trevor Lawson.

"See if you are, Tam, Ah'll cut your throat." It was the usually loyal Billy McPhee making a threat that everyone knew he would keep.

Worse than the threats was when they stopped talking to him

but clearly were talking about him. He had no option but to keep seeing the police telling them everything he could.

The ins and outs of disgraced ex-cop Paul Johnston and his security firm Guardion that was protected by Specky Boyd. The addresses of some of the Daniel family, one of the strongest mobs in Glasgow, and who they bought some of their smack from. Titbits on Goofy Docherty and rumours about how Frankie 'Donuts' Donaldson had intimidated some Rangers star into leaving the club. He went on and on as long as it was necessary. He had to get out of jail, preferably alive, and that's what started to plague his days and nights.

In his cell he couldn't sleep for worry, real worry that one of his team would visit him with a blade. Then there were all those others who he had hurt or who knew people he had hurt. He couldn't eat or even drink tea made by someone else. He had arranged for enough inmates to get poisoned in his time and knew how easy that was. Every time he walked through a hall or went to the toilet his eyes were peeled, his heart thumping waiting for the inevitable assassin. Showers, forget those. He wasn't going to take that risk. His bowels had stopped working because of the lack of food and those bloody nerves.

It only took one month for The Licensee's health to go downhill fast. He had lost stones in weight and his face was thin and gaunt. Red blotches had broken out on his skin. His eyesight was deteriorating fast. He had to get out. He had to get protection.

The only place the jail system would offer him was Saughton Prison – the nonces and ponces unit. It was where all the informants went, ex-coppers serving time and sex abusers, particularly child sex abusers, for their own protection.

Ordinary prisoners would refuse to go. McGraw went there in a flash. But still he couldn't sleep for worry. Still he couldn't eat. It cost £100 to have someone poisoned in a prison, any prison. The only benefit it had for him was that an unexpected blade in the ribs was less likely. Still possible but less likely.

In May 1998, the trial of all the defendants started. It was going to take a long time. The accused were ferried to the High Court in Edinburgh every day in a long convoy surrounded by cop cars, outriders and a helicopter or two hovering above. As they traipsed into the court the cops carried guns and twenty stayed there on guard.

This was one huge security exercise and sent the message that these were dangerous men. It sent another message: another mob might just try to kill them.

In the event it was a long drawn out trial without incident. They had pulled all the men's phone records. For McGraw, the so-called brains, there was a surprisingly long collection of numbers from four registered phones. The records gave the cops a problem or two. The most called numbers were directly into Baird Street and Pitt Street, the cops' shops.

Every day McGraw looked weaker and weaker. On the forty-fifth day, two men were released by the judge, no case to answer. On the fifty-fifth day the jury came back. McGraw was found Not Proven, as were most of the others. Only three men were jailed – Graeme Mason for eight years, Paul Flynn for six and John Healy for ten. None of them were McGraw's men, who had all escaped the wrath of the law. But Healy wasn't pleased. He believed he had been set up.

Out on the street the man with the hunted eyes stood and stared. If they would kill him inside who would take him out now? Too many and he was too weak, too scared to defend himself. He ran for his life.

McGraw was free. How long would he last?

62

LOOK, NO HANDS

McGraw was ill, even he could see that. That spell in jail not eating, not sleeping, had almost killed him. Had it damaged him permanently?

Margaret McGraw believed in psychics, Tarot card readings, the lot. She had told her husband that he would be coming home at the end of the trial and she was right. Straight home he went to a big plate of mince and tatties. He could only eat half and spent the next three days on the toilet crapping for Scotland. He was going to have to build himself up again, slowly.

The good news was that his team had forgiven him. Freedom compared with ten years in jail can do that for a man. It did it for them all. After all he was only making sure they were all okay. Wasn't he?

The even better news was that he was finally rich. He'd been well off for years and with Margaret investing their money had got even richer still. Yet by his own admission the dope trafficking had netted £35,000,000 profit in three years. He claimed the top men pocketed £5,000,000 each. Safe to say his earnings were more than double that, never mind his fortune from elsewhere.

Yet he had paid a huge price. As soon as it got close to dark at night he had to be home, locked up, the security system set. All roasty-toasty and safe. Still he couldn't sleep much. Dreams of men hurting him kept floating into his mind. He had tried sleeping tablets from his doctor but those zapped him and made him scared that he was weak. Vodka was always on his agenda but he could sip that for hours, getting slowly drunker and drunker yet not have one yawn to stifle.

It took two years for McGraw to begin to recover his body strength. Meantime Snaz, his brother Willie and his now smack free son Winkie, ran his business – legal and illegal. The financial guidance was still from Margaret and her touch was spot on.

Their property portfolio stretched all the way through Glasgow, down through Spain and the Canaries and even to the former East Germany where EU funded rebuilding was massive. In every EU grant there was an easy scam and that meant easy money.

Even as McGraw was recovering he was getting richer and richer. Yet that's not how the State saw it.

After the investigating cops licked their wounds on failing to convict most of the accused on the dope trafficking they began to tally the cost. The trial alone had cost £10m. The investigation well over £2m. Then there was Legal Aid available to help those with no cash to pay a lawyer.

McGraw as usual had pled broke. His lawyer, Donald Findlay QC, had claimed £218,000 fees from Legal Aid. His major partner, John Healy, had played the same game and his defence cost £228,033. The total Legal Aid bill for all involved was more than £1.6m.

All in all it had cost the State almost £14,000,000 to jail three men and allow another seven to escape.

Around that time an accountant in one of Britain's top firms had information he felt he must share. It was annual accounts headed in various names including Cambridge Street Properties. Though none were listed in his name, that was the cover name McGraw had for many of his legal business interests in Scotland alone. What was he worth? At least £30,000,000.

In spite of all that wealth he still had to apply for Legal Aid. Even when caught with his back against the wall and facing years in jail, even then McGraw still had to save money. Yet McGraw was about to become richer, or at least Margaret was.

For years there had been interest in Mac Cars, then one of the biggest minicab companies in Glasgow. This came particularly from Steve Malcolm and Tommy Wallace. They were both businessmen, very successful, but they kept bad company from time-to-time.

Wallace had appeared as a witness in the drugs trial talking about cars he had sold the gang. His evidence had helped get McGraw off while putting John Healy slap bang in trouble. Now it was time to do business with him.

McGraw couldn't be bothered with the hassle Mac Cars gave him any more and there was a good price offered on the table. Margaret McGraw signed the deal and soon after, Malcolm and Wallace set up a partnership that would net them many £100,000s from the east end of Glasgow every year.

Some people claimed that it was a debt being repaid to Wallace. He claimed he had sold the suspects cars so just told it the way it was. Either way, McGraw was happy, for the moment.

McGraw settled into what appeared to some like semi-retirement. Yet even while he had been in jail his deals had struck death on Glasgow's streets.

John Simpson was a strong and violent young man who had worked for Specky Boyd as his minder and equaliser. Yet Simpson was getting some ideas above his station.

Other Boyd team members were jealous or scared of Simpson – often both. When he started sleeping with one of Specky's girl-friends people said there should be trouble. There wasn't. Specky had several women. When he started dealing drugs on his own and being violent to citizens for no reason, that's when Boyd started to wonder.

McGraw had a grouse against Simpson. During a jail term in BarL he had slashed McGraw's brother, William. The young man had no respect for anyone. It had to be sorted.

Boyd agreed and set up a plan to get Simpson but McGraw wanted it to be his men. Boyd was going to finish the man anyway so was happy that some other crew were going to take the risks.

In 1997, as Simpson lay sleeping on the couch of a relative's house a phone call was made. Two minutes later, two masked men rushed in and blasted Simpson in the head. The main man was Gordon Ross.

Simpson didn't die. The bullet had smashed though his skull, damaged his brain but not in a way that would stop him doing anything he wanted. What it did change was his mood. Now he was always in a foul, aggressive mood. Boyd couldn't have that.

As McGraw and his men festered in jail waiting for their drugs trial, a car drew up alongside Simpson in his home patch of Pollok. A familiar face greeted him. He walked across. As Simpson reached the car a gunman sat up in the back and blasted him to death.

The message was passed on to McGraw that Simpson had been killed because he wanted him dead. In reality Specky Boyd had his own reasons and wasn't finished there. Paranoid that they were next, his team soon started shooting each other and disappearing off the face of the earth.

To McGraw it was just another score settled, another problem taken care of and he didn't even have to be free or ask again. That's how powerful he had become.

As McGraw continued to take it easy, holidaying often in his home in Tenerife, another old problem was about to get his comeuppance.

63

MELTING THE ICE

The headlines were enough to get campaigners on to their feet. Who gets charged with murder twice in three years and gets Not Proven both times? The Iceman, that's who.

Frank McPhie and Colin McKay breezed through their trial accused of killing their former mate, Chris McGrory. The cops weren't chasing anyone else. That's police speak for having the right man – they thought.

Now a free man, McPhie was annoying a lot of people. He had always been a braggart and a bully but he had got worse. Maybe it was walking free from murder trials that street players and police alike were sure he had been guilty of. Maybe he thought they could never get him. He was wrong.

McGraw had a message from some Irish people he had linked to when he set up the Paradise Bar. There was a Glaswegian buying smack and dope from them. A bit of coke too. Was he all right?

"Who is your man?" asked McGraw.

"Frank McPhie," they answered. "Do you know him?"

McGraw wished that he didn't. Over the past two years McPhie had been openly boasting about being the one who killed Glover and Hanlon. Maybe he was feeling brave knowing that Paul Ferris was banged up in jail? Then again, didn't he know that Glover and Hanlon had many friends? Some of them Irish too.

"Ah wouldn't trust him to buy my fags," replied McGraw drawing on his next cigarette. "That man will cheat you given half a chance." It takes one to know one some people thought.

McGraw was right. One year down the line and a major transaction hadn't been paid for, other drugs had been stolen and they suspected McPhie. McGraw needed to talk with the Irish mob face to face. For this he pulled in an offer from a new pal, ex-cop turned security boss, Paul Johnston.

Johnston had been sacked from the Glasgow cops over an insurance scam. Shortly thereafter he had set up in the security business as many former cops do. His business partner was his wife, Marie, and many in that game would comment that she was the one with the bigger balls.

The Johnstons had done well helped by Marie running some dating agencies, a fancy name for high-class call girls. Yet it was their security company, then called Guardion, that was bringing in the big bucks. Specky Boyd was in on this company, owning some of the assets and providing a protection service as well. That's how McGraw got to know the Johnstons.

They had several large houses, the biggest being Chapeltoun House in Ayrshire. More a small castle than a home, it was perfect for discreet meetings especially for visitors from Ireland, close as it was to the west coast ports.

There McGraw told the Irish mob a story about McPhie. He included the murders of Glover and Hanlon, omitting his own involvement, of course. What he didn't know was that Johnston had the whole place wired and their every word was being recorded. Or did he?

McGraw went on to say that McPhie's house was perfect for a hit, being across the road from high-rise flats. Maybe he remembered his plans to have Paul Ferris shot in the grounds of Premier Security. All they'd need was a good rifle shot. The Irish found that funny. After all they were a country at war. They had marksmen to choose from.

After that the Irish men went back home and talked with other people. Whether or not they spoke to Joe Hanlon's Irish cousins isn't known. They certainly talked with people capable of doing the job.

On 10 May 2000 McPhie turned up at his allotment to be faced by a group of angry men he didn't know. It was clear they were going to turn very nasty so he jumped in his van and sped off. They went after him.

McPhie led them across the city heading towards the M74 south but still he couldn't shake them. An hour later he was running out of fuel and they were yards behind him. He had no option but to head for home.

Finally, in the Maryhill area he seemed to have shaken them off just a few hundred yards from his house on Guthrie Street. He didn't realise that they had turned off. Job done. Screeching the van to a halt, McPhie jumped out and started walking quickly towards his front door. That's when the sniper bullet hit him in the head.

As he lay bleeding to death on the ground, McPhie clutched his mobile phone and called his wife. She came running out of their home followed by two of their sons in time to hold him while he died.

When the police had arrived and closed the area off, they started a step-by-step check of the neighbourhood. Two floors up in the flats they found it. A rifle, laid down right where the sniper had shot.

Door-to-door inquiries only brought one clue. A red-headed man seen leaving the car park on foot seconds after the shot rang out.

The Iceman had been killed in a professional hit. The same way as JF Kennedy. Only days later detectives would admit they thought they'd never find the hitman. That he had left the country within an hour of killing McPhie. But that wasn't going to stop them having a go at someone else.

The Daniels family had reason to be upset with McPhie. They had argued over drug territories for years and lately he had slashed one of their nephews over a spilled drink in a pub. No one messed with the Daniels like that. Besides, the cops wanted to use every chance they got to upset one of the country's biggest gangs.

In October 2000 they arrested the lieutenant to Jamie Daniels, the gang's leader. John McCabe was thirty-seven and a well-known hardman but had he killed McPhie?

The cops didn't think so when a short while later he was released – no case to answer.

McGraw was getting stronger and reverting to type. That's why on the night McPhie was killed he threw a party in the east end. He didn't like McPhie, that was well known. What he didn't spell out to them was why.

One more problem was ticked off McGraw's list. Maybe he really could retire and soon? Then someone whispered a word in his ear that made him shiver. An old enemy was about to tell the truth in the most public way.

64

BOOKED

"He's going to do what?" McGraw couldn't believe his ears. He thought that he was well finished with him.

After Paul Ferris was found guilty of gun running it pleased McGraw to see that Premier Security had its funds frozen and went bust, that money lying in a safe was confiscated and the cops were still hunting to strip away all of Ferris' wealth.

The media also had a field day. With him guilty of such a serious offence they were printing stories that alleged all sorts of badness on his behalf, all based on nothing more than a drunken call from a pub, if that.

Locked up in an English secure jail, what could Ferris do? Write a book, that's what.

"You need to sort him out," Margaret had demanded of McGraw. How could he? Pay for a hit in Frankland Prison? He didn't know anyone down there.

"How?" he asked. It was a good question. She didn't know how either.

When the book was released all hell broke loose. *The Ferris Conspiracy* was a detailed account of Ferris' trip into crime, working for Arthur Thompson and everything else – including McGraw and how he worked with corrupt cops. He named McGraw. The only people he was banned from naming by the publisher's lawyers were some of the cops.

A best seller and serialised in a Sunday tabloid, the book was an instant success and remained a success.

Overnight, retirement was ruled out for McGraw. As he passed through the streets of the east end he could see people looking and sniggering. Sitting in a pub, men close by would make wise-cracks about The Licensee. He had to do something, but what?

Then he got worse news. TC Campbell, still fighting in jail for the right to appeal against his conviction for the Doyle murders, was writing a book too. That could be the end of McGraw.

One person could be tackled – the co-writer of both books.

The anonymous calls threatening death and destruction rolled in.

"Don't worry," TC had said on the phone. "The ones you need to worry about are the ones who don't contact you at all."

Then two cops turned up at the writer's door. Two constables in uniform claiming that a masked gunman had appeared at a house in the street looking for him. Right surname wrong house, so the gunman had fled but he might come back.

There was something funny about those cops. Their hair was too long. Their manner too scruffy. Their uniforms looked out of date. And who sends two ordinary bobbies to deal with a man carrying a shotgun? What gunman flees when he knocks the wrong door? And those cops, didn't they have the same numbers on their tunics?

McGraw must have been speaking to one of his pet police who dug out a couple of uniforms. It didn't stop the book and *Indictment* gave him his place in the centre of the murder of the six Doyles though TC never claimed that he was guilty, never would. It didn't say he did it but asked why he wasn't tried. It was a question everyone agreed with. Everyone apart from McGraw and his crew.

It wouldn't be the last book that infuriated McGraw. It was a problem that would nag him for years till he finally took action.

Meantime a major problem had just occurred – TC Campbell had been released for another appeal and Ferris would be free a month later.

Trouble was on its way.

65

THE HIT JOB AND HELL

It was a short walk from his house but still he kept his eyes peeled. TC Campbell knew men were out to get him and keep him silent at any cost.

The first few months of freedom had been difficult for Campbell. Everything had changed so much since they last threw him back inside. Mobile phones were tiny. Sugar in cafes came in small bags. They had made the top of Buchanan Street into some monster of a shopping centre and much more.

Life at home was difficult too. He had divorced Liz and married Karen the last time he was free. By the time he was heading back to jail their beautiful young daughter, Shannon, was on the way.

Now she was a toddler and she and her mother had a well-settled routine in their small flat. A routine he was breaking into. But there was more than that. There were the watching eyes and knowing, just knowing McGraw was out to get him.

It was a short walk from his house but still he kept his eyes peeled. At this time he would've been wandering up to collect Shannon from nursery, once a day, every day. He knew that the watching men would know that.

Yet that day Shannon was at home ill and he was going to the chemist to collect some drugs for her. The watching eyes wouldn't know that. They'd just know that he would be there.

It was the strange 4x4 in the car park that attracted his attention. He hadn't seen that car around. Then he was waltzing across to Campbell with a smile on his face.

"How do you do," he said, "Ah'm The Iceman." The knife was out in a flash and parried by TC at the last minute. More knife blows from both hands rained in. TC got up close, grabbing him in a bear hug, clasping his arms to his side.

"You're no The Iceman," he shouted, "you're no Frank McPhie. You're fuck all." It was Billy McPhee, a much younger man than Campbell and used to keeping fit rather than fighting for freedom. But TC Campbell was an old street scrapper.

The fight struggled on for ten minutes till McPhee's knives were broken and scattered. He staggered back to the jeep, collected two more knives and came at Campbell again.

As the men struggled and McPhee struck out, women and kids from the school and nursery gates screamed.

"Ah've phoned for the polis, Mr Campbell," shouted one woman.

"So have Ah," added another. But no police were in sight. They wouldn't arrive for a long time.

Up close, Campbell could feel the bulk of the man. But there was something false about it. Grasping a knife from his attacker, Campbell struck out but the blade bounced off his chest. He was wearing a bullet-proof vest like he did every day.

Exhausted and bleeding, McPhee made it back to the jeep which drove off at speed. Five minutes later it was back. This time the driver joined in the fight – it was McGraw.

For twenty minutes more, Campbell tackled the pair. At one point McGraw smacked him hard on the skull with a golf club. His knees wanted to buckle but he stood up and made his confused brain keep working. He struck out with a stolen blade and it stuck right underneath McPhee's scalp. Fight over.

It took the cops another fifteen minutes to arrive. By which time the area was scattered with knives, broken golf clubs and enough blood to pass any forensic check. There were also enough witnesses.

The following day when TC Campbell was released from hospital a young cop interviewed him, promising him action.

"Don't bother yourself, son," Campbell said, "your bosses don't want my man to be jailed." The young officer couldn't believe what he had said.

Three days later, McGraw and McPhee were interviewed by the cops. No action was taken.

It turned out that all the CCTV cameras at the shops had been switched off. It also turned out that the shops were owned by a man as a front for McGraw.

That golf club had been used before, according to the media. Ferris was out and the world held its breath for the predicted war. Ferris wasn't interested, having announced on his day of freedom that he was giving up crime to write books. No one believed him except his close friends and family.

McGraw had different issues. To try and recover from the state he was in on his release from jail he had been getting botox sessions to give his face back some shape and youth. Then he got his teeth fixed – a full mouthful of screw-in jobs that cost him a fortune and caused him agony for weeks – right when Ferris was being fêted by the media on his release.

That had been a miserable time for McGraw. Physical and emotional pain combined with Margaret nagging him non-stop about what Ferris was saying to the media. Now he was pain free and determined. According to press reports, McGraw and Ferris had a public fall out with knives and that golf club just a week earlier. It wasn't quite that way.

McGraw had made a decision but told it to no one. He had to regain his street credibility or suffer a life of torment and maybe lose everything.

He had started by recruiting some heavies to act as his minders. They had been there since the day Ferris had been released. With everyone predicting war, McGraw didn't want to be unprepared. But war never came so he would step up his game, make his mark.

When his jeep came head-to-head with the car of two young players in the east end, either one had to reverse or they had to have words.

With his three tooled-up heavies in his motor – Serbians he

claimed – he decided to have words. They were Ferris' supporters after all. The type of men who had been laughing in his face.

McGraw bawled and shouted at them calling them every name under the sun. Then he fetched his golf club and started to smash up their motor. That was too much. One was out of there and at him.

Like most street fights it was a quick flurry. McGraw smashing at the guy with his golf club, the other guy stabbing at him whenever he could. His first blows bounced off McGraw's bullet-proof vest so he aimed low drawing blood from his thighs and his arse. Sometimes from his arms.

All the time his heavies sat in the jeep. Not budging. McGraw was back in the driving seat and steering his motor over the pavement. Behind him one young guy was chasing him on foot, roaring for him to come back.

All in all an embarrassing affray for McGraw. By early evening he had done two things. Made sure his version reached the media first through two of his men who had been fostering relations with certain journalists over the past two years. Then he sacked his minders. Serbia might have been at war but Glasgow was too hard for them.

For the next fortnight the media was full of reports of street war and other bad things that Ferris had allegedly got up to. Then it happened. He was being recalled to jail on the basis of a report by Glasgow cops.

To avoid being dumped in a Scottish prison, Ferris drove south with some witnesses. Glasgow cop cars chased him all the way. In Durham, after problems finding a policeman, he handed himself in.

Up in Glasgow McGraw threw a victory party. In the crowd a face sat and smiled and drank. He was watching who was there, who had chosen McGraw. It would be a short celebration. Life was about to turn bad for The Licensee.

66

SCUNNERED

"It's only a hit," McGraw said, trying to sound reasonable. "You've done them before."

"Aye," said one of the men, "but it's who you want killed is the problem."

"Ah'll pay good money," said McGraw and immediately spotted the cynical looks on the guys' faces. "One hundred grand." It was a huge starting offer from McGraw. He must have been really angry or, more likely, terrified.

The pair from the north of Glasgow haggled him up to £150,000 then wangled £25,000 down payment, cash in hand that night. As they drove away from his place they couldn't stop laughing.

"Wait till the wee man hears this," said one.

"He'll pish himself."

Two days later McGraw received an invitation to a party in a private room at The Corinthian. Guest of honour, Paul Ferris, to celebrate his freedom. McGraw never appeared but the party happened and most of that £25,000 was spent that night.

When he had been sent to jail, Ferris had demanded a full medical where he stripped naked in front of a doctor and two governors.

"Have I any cuts or bruises?" he demanded. The answer was no, squashing media reports of his fight. "Please write that down in your report."

When McGraw read of what Ferris had done, one day a small

group of journalists hanging about outside his house were invited in.

"Nae pictures but feast our eyes on this," he said stripping off. "And you, wee man, keep your eyes off my cock, right." He was addressing a recent arrival in the city who happened to be gay. It was no secret but he had only been there a couple of weeks. How did McGraw know that?

Next day the papers wrote up about McGraw's stripping act and how he had no injuries. Trouble was they had the wrong McGraw – not Tam but his brother William. The pair had always looked like each other.

After seven weeks in prison, the Parole Board reviewed Ferris' recall and threw him back out as a free man within minutes. It was a report full of supposition and rumour. No facts and no real concern.

Now he was attending his own freedom party paid for by McGraw. That night in the Mount Vernon home of the family, strong words were spoken and Margaret McGraw wasn't happy. Ferris was making him look like a fool and he had to have it stopped.

It wasn't McGraw who was about to do the stopping.

67

SCARED TO DEATH

Trevor Lawson was a scared man. Word had been passed to him that certain men wanted a word with him. A word about Bobby Glover and Joe Hanlon. He reckoned he knew what that meant – they were going to kill him.

That Lawson demolished The Caravel pub was not in dispute. The question of whether or not he knew why had never been asked of him directly. Did he know that Glover and Hanlon's bodies had been there? How much else he knew had also to be explored. Some men, intent on finding an answer to who killed Glover and Hanlon, wanted to ask those questions and Lawson was their man. Not really a player, no one suspected him of any part in the killings. All they wanted was information and thought he'd be the best route.

Lawson had told McGraw but he just poo-pooed it. McGraw was too busy these days working with Specky Boyd and Paul Johnston. Johnston was giving him clues about the security business and inside information on Paul Ferris who was then working as a consultant. The media kept associating Ferris with a company called Frontline which he denied. To test that out, Johnston got his wife, Marie, to suggest to Ferris that he do some business for Guardion. The trap didn't work with Ferris being keen to take it on as a consultant.

Boyd on the other hand was making sure drugs got through into Glasgow and was supplying McGraw's dealers direct. Boyd was keeping McGraw in funds and McGraw didn't go near the drugs. Just the way he always wanted it.

Lawson was going to have to manage those men on his own. All he had to do was avoid them. Surely that wasn't too difficult? McGraw had been avoiding people all his adult life.

It didn't help Lawson. He might have made a good quality of life for himself being worth several millions and having a great house at Dunipace near Falkirk but these people could end it all in a bang. Each day he simply got jumpier and jumpier.

One night on the way home from Glasgow he stopped at The Pines Bar near his home for a drink. He stood there watching the men around him, trying to find a familiar but unwelcome face. There were two guys in the corner who he thought he knew. Did he?

Suddenly one of the men got into a scrap. That was it. It was the cover for one of them sticking a blade into Lawson's guts, so he thought. He was out of that pub in a flash, panicking and sprinting right on to the M80 and heading for home. The first car threw him into the path of another. Then a third car hit him.

It was March 2002 and Trevor Lawson was dead. An accident, they said. Fear and guilt killed the man.

Not even the paranoid McGraw thought it was suspicious. Lawson was a nervous kind of man anyway. Yet out in the east end some pals were talking.

"One down and three to go," they said.

Life was about to get bloody for The Licensee.

Back in the east end Gordon Ross, Billy McPhee and George 'Crater Face' McCormack were giving the neighbourhood hell. They had always been quick on the draw of a blade or a gun and didn't need much reason either. McPhee had made a lifetime's work of chibbing people, sometimes for money, sometimes for fun. The east is littered with young men whose faces had been re-arranged by McCormack for little reason or none. Ross shot a man simply because he asked him if that's what he was going to do. He obliged.

Now it was worse. Ever since they had walked free from the

drugs trial with money to burn they did what they fancied. Cocaine and booze make for an evil mix and that was their poison.

Reports flooded the streets of old men being slashed, young women raped, young men stamped on till they bled from every orifice. All for their own fun.

Ross was in biggest trouble. His oldest son, also Gordon, had raped at least two women and hurt them badly. Instead of punishing the boy big time and compensating the women as best he could, he just ignored it. Local people saw all this and they weren't happy.

When, one time, another rape victim of young Ross went to the cops, the duty sergeant asked her, "Are you sure you want to go ahead with this? These are dangerous people. They'll burn your house down with you in it." No wonder they felt free to do whatever they fancied.

People went to McGraw – ordinary people, pub managers, taxi drivers – and asked him to get his men under control. He ignored them. Then he heard another report that worried him.

Ross had been freelancing. Bringing in his own gear. When he managed a load of drugs for McGraw he'd cheat on the figures, lop off some goodies and keep the proceeds for himself. This wasn't helped at all by Ross' father boasting in the pubs that his boy was rich, a multi-millionaire for sure.

Rape and pillage if they liked but steal McGraw's money? He was going to have to do something about that.

68

DEAD MEN WALKING

The bar was crowded as usual. Men speaking loudly about football, telling quiet tales of the street, young men boasting of lassies they claimed to have pulled. Over in the corner, a woman of indeterminate age softly sang 'Danny Boy' to herself. Just an ordinary night till someone tapped him on the shoulder.

It was a pal. A known face and one he welcomed. All in all Ross felt safe in that pub, The Sheiling. Why shouldn't he? It was his local, full of his people.

Other drinkers hardly noticed the two men chatting. Why should they? They were known to all and being quiet. A lot quieter than the old dame singing to herself.

One minute they were there, the next they were gone. Nothing unusual in that either. Ross liked to move between pubs. Show his face here and there. Maybe the other guy had gone with him?

Out on the street the men were having serious words. Ross was having none of what the other man was saying. He was raising an issue but not losing the place. He wanted Ross to deal with it but he wasn't budging. The discussion didn't last long, maybe minutes.

Ross took a few steps away from The Sheiling when the first blade struck. He was down and a blade struck again. Seconds later a young crew walked past.

"That's payback, you prick," one muttered looking down.

Across Shettleston Road, a jeep sat back from the canopy covering the pumps in a garage.

"Looks like the young team have struck," said the driver Billy McPhee.

"Aye, local justice eh," said McGraw in the passenger seat. The jeep started up, pulled carefully out of the garage turning right and away.

For the next while, east end people walked past Gordon Ross as he lay bleeding on the ground. Once or twice people stepped over him. They knew who he was but didn't want to get involved. McGraw's men were a dangerous crew. God knows what would happen if they had stopped and talked to the man.

An hour later a passing police car stopped to investigate. Expecting a drunk they found a dying man. Hours later, Gordon Ross died in a hospital bed. It was September 2002. McGraw had just had one of his men killed.

The set up had been easy. Spread the word that Ross had paid a rape victim of his son £10,000 to keep quiet. She had relented and gone to the cops. Now Ross Senior was chasing her or his cash to inflict some hurt. She'd spent some of the money and had gone running terrified.

All true, of course, but the young team wouldn't like it. The young team had had enough.

Billy McPhee felt more special than usual. To be let in on McGraw's revenge was an honour indeed. He had delivered it often enough but this was different.

He had got on well enough with Ross but had never really liked him. The man was too full of himself, too sure that the world owed him large.

That night when he and McGraw hit Ross' house there was a lot of screaming and swearing. He had had to threaten Ross' girl-friend to shut up and tell them everything. Tell them where he kept his money.

McGraw was livid. Ross had just sold a load of smack for him and £200,000 was due. There was no sign of the cash. None at all.

McGraw wanted what was his and everything that Ross thought he owned. After all hadn't he been stealing from McGraw? Hadn't he? Suspicion was enough.

For days McGraw's men trailed the east end looking for secret lock-ups, safes in back rooms, anywhere there might be money. What they found they kept – at least McGraw did. But they didn't find as much as he wanted. McGraw was not a happy man.

But now McPhee felt special and went on as usual. After a fracas with an ex-girlfriend of Winkie McGraw's where he had sherricked her, hurt her mother and humiliated her boyfriend, a young man ran into the Shettleston Juniors Social Club and shot McPhee in the face at point-blank range. Any higher a calibre of gun and he would've been dead. As it was the pump action rat-killing gun blasted his teeth and damaged his jaw.

For months McPhee was out of action, holed up in his house taking care of his injuries. With every day he was getting more and more nervous. Worrying. If the young team could turn on Ross what was to stop them turning on him?

What about that shooting of Jaimba McLean, an old pal of Ferris? He had arranged for him to be blasted in the chest in spring the year before as he had watched and put out word that it was because he was dealing smack and cheating his customers. What if someone had found out the truth?

The time he went to collect a debt for McGraw. Edinburgh pub landlord Billy Sibbald wasn't really a player. Not really. And the debt wasn't to McGraw but to another guy stuck in jail. So he had gone too far and the man died. Would Sibbald's pals come looking for him? Would the guy Sibbald owed the money to?

And the attack on TC Campbell? What if someone fancied some revenge? And the drug deals he had been doing behind McGraw's back? What if he found out?

McPhee had made a lot of enemies and now he thought about those folk. If that ordinary guy could shoot him in the mouth what could a hitman do? It got so he didn't want to leave his house. Then he had to.

It was March 2003 and Ross' body had been released for burial. It was all set up for St Patrick's Roman Catholic Church in Coatbridge. All the McGraw crew would be there and a good few others. Funerals were important on the street. You either attended or people talked about why not. Lethal people.

McPhee had no option but to leave his home and go out.

At the funeral he was a lone man. Around him people chatted to each other. In a corner the usual faces surrounded McGraw, whispering in his ear. McPhee just walked on and was ignored. Well not quite.

"You're next," someone growled at him. He said nothing but just kept walking.

A few days later, McPhee decided to leave his house again. This time to go and watch his beloved Rangers then to go on to a meeting In The Hoops Bar at the Barrowland. A pal was with him, one of McGraw's men, and drove him to The Hoops after the game. At the door McPhee suddenly changed his mind but didn't say why. Did he fear an ambush? Or just bitter Celtic supporters who knew he was a Rangers man? They drove on to The Springcroft Tavern out near his home in Baillieston. It was a local to him. A friendly pub where families with young kids would congregate to eat and play. There was a rugby match on the TV, Scotland versus Wales. He'd watch that and have a few pints.

In the bar his pal suggested he take off his bullet-proof vest to feel more comfortable. McPhee said he would but didn't. At one point his mate went to the toilet. He seemed to be gone a long time. Maybe he had an upset stomach. Then the front door opened.

A tall man of swarthy colour and with a black plastic bag hood walked in quickly, straight up to McPhee and stabbed him again and again. Around him adults and kids were screaming in terror. At least two people were being sick, retching again and again. McPhee pulled a knife and fought back but was bleeding badly from a score of wounds to his neck and head. His attacker kept going, stabbing him low round his arse and genitals. Then he was out of there and gone, into a waiting car.

McPhee lay on the ground, dying. It was 8 March 2003. Another of McGraw's men had just been killed.

When the police cordoned off the place they did a detailed search. The blood of several people was found on the front door handle and scattered outside making forensic checks impossible. In the car park, under stones, around ten knives were found – all had belonged to McPhee. Had he planted them there?

McGraw and his men did their usual search for McPhee's money. What they found they took. McGraw was getting cash rich but people poor.

Three down. The question was, would there be four?

69

THE FOURTH MAN?

Specky Boyd was having a good time in the sun. So he should, living as he was in his luxury villa in San Pedro. It was a business trip, he said, to sort some matters out. Someone else had the same idea but a different target.

Paul Johnston wasn't a happy man. His wife's company, Guardion Security, was in trouble with the taxman. There was worse than that – his old pals, the cops, were after him.

The police wanted to talk with Johnston in connection with allegations of intimidation, baseball bat attacks on competitors and torching other sites. They were serious allegations and Johnston could have been heading for jail, even being held on remand while awaiting the trial. Disgraced or not, he was an ex-cop and ex-cops don't get easy jail time. Then there were all the enemies he had made while in the security business. Any one of them could simply pay a con to stick a blade in his ribs. He left Scotland and headed fast to one of his houses in Spain.

Boyd had gone out to spend some time with Johnston to sort out mutual matters. Friends would say that the two were not on the best of terms. Money had gone missing. Money that Boyd reckoned he was due.

There were few records of that money in spite of Boyd being a heavy investor in several joint enterprises. Boyd got most of his cash from crime and spent periods in jail. He couldn't leave a paper trail for the cops.

Now Boyd was going to have some time off. Friends and relatives were flying out to Spain from Glasgow. His twenty-one-year-old daughter, Anna Nicola Gavin, her pal Louise Douglas and his girlfriend's daughter, three-year-old Helen Williams.

He had picked them up at the airport in his Audi TT sports car and was heading back to his villa. It was a small car for so many people plus their holiday luggage. Especially when several cars were available to Boyd at that time, including a luxury 4x4. Maybe he wanted a fun ride, a good start to their summer break.

Speeding up the A7 motorway close to the mountain village of Mijas, suddenly the Audi veered to the left, through the crash barrier and head on into a BMW 525 travelling at speed in the opposite direction.

The two cars disintegrated into a pile of warped metal then WHOOSH, the whole lot went up in flames. Two Spaniards in the other car were dead. So were the three females in the Audi. So, of course, was Stewart Boyd.

It was June 2003, and one of Glasgow's top players was no more. The question was – accident or hit?

Spanish cops were sick and traumatised at the scene, that's how bad the damage was. It was carnage. A wipe out, as if someone had planned it that way.

A few days before his death, Boyd had been expressing concern about his safety. Not like him. Rumours abounded that he had been involved in two major drug trafficking flops and the Russian Mafia was on his case. The very type of team who could afford to fly in a specialist to rig that car to crash.

Paul Johnston went public a short time later to say that he had driven that Audi TT the day before and the brakes were a bit sticky. Yet Boyd was careful with his motors, knowing how easy it was for them to be tampered with. So why did he cram everyone into that small car? Especially if he knew about the brakes.

On the very day of his death, trouble started. His father, a straight old boy, was sacked from his job as a guard with Guardion Security.

Sacked by people who knew him and his boy as his boy lay dead.

Then there was the fight for money. That Boyd was worth millions there's no doubt. The question was where was it and who had it? Not his family for sure.

Back in Glasgow, people should have been watching more carefully. A curious friendship had built up that might give a clue. McGraw had become close to one John 'Joker' McCartney, Boyd's deputy in the city.

McCartney was known as The Millionaire Dustbin Man since he had kept himself registered in that employment for years, paying someone to clock him in. It was a smart move, keeping the taxman off his back while he earned his real money from crime.

It was one of the few smart moves McCartney made according to the street. They wondered why Boyd had anything to do with him at all. Boyd ran his team, full stop.

As people squabbled about Boyd's money, so some fought for control over the southside of Glasgow. Guns were going off in every corner, blades being pulled. It was war for the turf, a turf that McGraw had wanted for years. A turf Boyd had been keeping to himself whatever it took.

One month later, information emerged that NCIS had been trailing Boyd. It was the same national security mob who had followed and nabbed Paul Ferris. Did Boyd's allies suss this and decided they didn't like the heat?

Given McGraw's business with Boyd, was he the main person to complain? To want to something done about it?

Eventually, Spanish police had completed their forensic and accident analysis and announced it was a simple car crash. Back in Scotland, Boyd had been buried but weeks later his grave was desecrated and wrecked. It was a low life act carried out by one of the many small time players who he used to give a wage to. Now they were fighting each other and the Boyd family.

The questions remain unresolved and the fighting still goes on.

One day, perhaps, the whole truth will emerge about why Stewart Boyd died.

Was Boyd the fourth man? Part of someone's hit list or wish list? Part of McGraw's hit list or wish list?

One other man was about to have a close encounter with bullets.

70

BAD DAY FOR THE PUB

The rain lashed down, driven by the wind. It wasn't the best of days but inside that pub people were cosy, warmed from the inside by booze of their taste. It was about to get warmer.

John 'Joker' McCartney and Craig 'Hairy Hands' Devlin were having a drink. The two had been close for a few years and wanted to get closer in bed together, business wise.

Years before, Devlin had fallen into some money when his wife's family received a massive pay out after the father had been killed in the Piper Alpha oil rig disaster. He had used the cash to invest heavily into the business he had ambitions in – crime.

He wanted to be a drug trafficker big time and a member of some team who could rule the city. He was even trying his hand at the security business. In all this he had teamed up with McCartney. When McCartney was accused of trying to kill Frankie 'Donuts' Donaldson, a life-long enemy, he had pled not guilty and simply blamed a list of others. This included Devlin who was accused of being the mastermind behind the plot. The ploy worked with McCartney walking free and Devlin not being charged.

They were close in other words. Very close.

The door banged open and shut again. No one looked round. It was a busy time for the pub. The man with the hooded top walked in fast, directly to the bar. No surprise there. Many folk in Nitshill needed a drink badly at some point in the day. Then he pulled a gun and started blasting.

The place was full of players like Michael 'Benji' Bennett and

Stephen 'Scudder' Scullion but the gunman knew who he was there for – McCartney and Devlin – and caught them both. Devlin on the arms and McCartney on the arse and scrotum.

In the panic, McCartney hit the deck and scrambled under a table. Bleeding, Devlin ran into the ladies' toilet. Shame he hadn't picked the gents. He would have had familiar company there.

McGraw had driven the two men to the Royal Oak to transact a bit of business. The idea was for them to buy the Royal Oak. Not only was it a good going pub, more importantly, it was well known as Boyd's HQ.

As the turf war for the southside raged on, someone in the McGraw camp felt it would be a psychological bonus to take over Boyd's old headquarters. Trouble is, many folk in the area disagreed with McCartney's plans and someone had heard of the meeting. That someone sent someone to stop it. If they had known McGraw was there, it would have been him they shot.

As it was, McGraw was playing the fruit machine in the corner when the blasting started and did what he was good at – he took cover in the bogs. The gents.

In the panic and the pandemonium in the Royal Oak most dived for cover while others slapped out at the shooter, drawing blood. He took to his heels and ran.

It took another five minutes for McGraw to leave the gents. When he did, he could see that McCartney was in a bad way and Devlin in a lot of pain. He decided to combine two needs – first for him to leave and leave fast; second, get the men some treatment.

It must have been the first time The Licensee had flagged down a cop car. Speeding in his jeep five minutes later he could see that McCartney was in a bad way. When the cops pulled over they saw the jeep driver's face looked familiar. In the back were McCartney and Devlin bleeding fast. A police escort was provided all the way – not unusual for McGraw – to the Southern General – an unusual destination for him.

Both men survived though McCartney took a long time to

recover. His genitals had been badly damaged. In the way of things, a cruel nickname was soon circulating the southside. John 'Nae Baws' McCartney.

McGraw wouldn't be going back into that area for a long while, especially given what followed. A couple of weeks later the Royal Oak was torched at night. Not some accidental fire but a job so professional the building had to be demolished and the site cleared. No one would be buying that pub in a hurry.

Rumours circulated that Specky Boyd's family had been responsible for the shooting. Trouble kept raging as people were shot and slashed and no one was talking to the cops. Eventually, Boyd's young brother, Ross Boyd, was arrested and charged with the shootings.

Two years later, in February 2006 he went on trial pleading not guilty. McCartney was called as a witness and swore that it couldn't have been Ross Boyd.

"He's my cousin," he revealed, "he is the last person on earth to try and shoot me." Outside in the scheme, people shared a wry smile. The Boyds had been hunted since the day Specky Boyd died and they knew by whom. Cousins or no, there weren't good relations between the pair.

Craig Devlin simply failed to appear. He had good reasons – fear. After the shooting, McGraw and Devlin had fallen out big time over drugs money owed. Devlin knew what that meant and skipped the country, going to Benidorm then Malaga where he managed a pub owned by Specky Boyd. A pub that people were still fighting over.

McCartney had to choose between Devlin and McGraw. It was no contest – McGraw was the winner.

McGraw was cited and simply didn't turn up. As witnesses referred to him, they wouldn't use his name, simply saying "the man in his fifties with grey hair". No warrant was ever issued for McGraw. Once again the cops had let him off lightly.

Other witnesses simply said they couldn't recognise the man in the dock. Or their memories since the event had somehow turned vague. It was a typical street shooting – everyone was there and no one saw anything.

With no motive or eyewitness of the shooting the only evidence was that Ross Boyd's blood had been found in the pub. An injury, the Crown claimed, sustained when some people had attacked the gunman. Not at all, was his reply. He had been playing a fruit machine when the shooting started and got hurt in the melee.

Ross Boyd was found Not Proven and walked free from the court.

The trial was February 2006. Back in Glasgow in 2004, McGraw's men were about to be busy. They had to catch Billy McPhee's killer.

71

A LONELY PLACE

Life had been difficult for Mark Clinton lately. It seemed after every hit job in Glasgow he was being pulled in by the cops. Now it was about to get bloody as well.

The jeep crawled up behind him as he walked towards home through the Barrowland one night. Four men jumped out and grabbed him. Big men and strong. They'd have to be to tackle him.

He fought back as hard as he could, gouging an eye, ripping at a cheek with his teeth but they were slashing at his legs with butcher's cleavers and he was weakening.

They bundled him into the back of the jeep and drove off. He knew who they were – McGraw's men.

"You're going down for McPhee," one snarled.

"Think so?" Clinton's voice, all arrogant and cocky.

Beside him two thugs thumped cleaver blades into the front of his thighs.

"You're going down. Right."

"Aye, right."

More cleavers sliced into his legs.

"You better kill me," he shouted. "Because Ah know who you are. Ah'll get you."

Half an hour later he was dumped on the road barely able to crawl let alone walk. His body healed fast but not that fast.

It had been a bad couple of years for Clinton. Two years before he had been arrested, accused of murdering Justin McAlroy.

Shooting him on the front lawn of his Cambuslang villa then leaning down to put slugs into him as he hid under his car. Shooting and killing him.

McAlroy had been a rich boy with a millionaire father, Tommy, who had made his money through building. Rich boy, sure, but he wanted to be a bad boy. McAlroy had got into dealing cocaine, buying sizeable amounts from different players. But he had the habit of consuming his own product and sharing it with pals. That brought trouble.

Everyone on the street knew that he owed McGraw large on a coke deal. It was the kind of debt that would upset anyone never mind mean-minded McGraw.

Approaches and threats had been made but still no cash. Some folk reckoned McAlroy was trying to win some pals that would scare McGraw. He used to be close pals with Specky Boyd but had fallen out with him over some money. He had to make other mates.

That's why he was giving away free tickets for the Red Rose Dinner. It was an annual fundraiser run by the Labour Party in Wishaw and involved such powerful politicians as then Home Secretary Dr John Reid and Jack McConnell, then the First Minister in the Scottish Parliament.

Whole tables of Glasgow gangsters attended that time in 2004. Well, it was free for them. But it didn't work. Two days later, McAlroy bought himself a pistol and ammo. Three days later he was dead.

The cops had pulled Clinton in for that but released him after a while. A man called Willie 'Tiler' Gage was convicted though no one on the street believed it was him. No one.

The cops had even questioned Clinton about Gordon Ross' killing. That was even though they had CCTV footage of him in another part of Glasgow that night. It was as if he was a suspect in every hit job in the city.

Now Clinton had been charged with killing Billy McPhee by stabbing him to death in The Springcroft Tavern. He had his alibi rock solid but they claimed to have witnesses. Ordinary punters lunching in the club ID'd him. Straight men and women who wouldn't lie.

So, why was McGraw sending his men out to put pressure on him? Did he just want to be sure that someone, anyone, went down for McPhee? Or was there more to it than that?

A few weeks later, Clinton appeared at the High Court on a procedural matter to do with his trial. As he walked away from the court, a man started walking beside him. McGraw.

"There's an offer on the table, Mark," said McGraw. Clinton thought of swinging at him then looked behind. Two steps away walked five of McGraw's men. They'd all be tooled up and ready. He wasn't carrying. Difficult to get through security at the High Court with a chib in your jacket. "It's a no brainer."

"Speak to me," Clinton replied.

"Ah can get you off for McPhee." McGraw let his words sink in. "Ah've done it before." No explanation was offered. "Believe me, but you have to so something for me."

"Whit?"

"Fit Ferris up with a load of smack." Clinton acted as if he was thinking about it, asking questions. "And if you don't," McGraw added, "Ah'll bring witnesses in that you haven't even heard of. Witnesses who'll swear it was you that killed McPhee."

By the time he had hailed a taxi, Clinton put a call out to some people who would get a message to Ferris. He wasn't about to fit anyone up with heroin but there was more to it than that. What McGraw was after was a time and place for Ferris. Did he mean to have him killed?

Ferris had confounded his critics when he had done exactly as he said he would at the gates of Frankland Prison the day he was freed. He was writing books and keeping out of trouble. Okay, he was also working as a consultant in the security sector but that was a role that earned him good money, always had. Some newspapers went on and on about how he really owned and ran a company called Frontline in spite of that being owned by a different man entirely. That annoyed Ferris but was no big deal. After all, it was a legitimate company working within the laws of the land.

All legal and with Ferris getting many chances in interviews and the like to repeat his allegations about McGraw and corrupt cops. That must have really annoyed McGraw but annoyed him enough to try and kill the man?

Having given Ferris the heads-up on McGraw's plans, Mark Clinton had to go into hiding. McGraw and his men were out to hurt him. Maybe kill him. While he was waiting for the trial he had the keys to half a dozen houses in Glasgow, never staying at the same one on two consecutive nights. He rarely saw his wife. Would never agree to meet anyone. No matter how close they were, he'd just turn up out of the blue. He'd even had to forgo going to watch his team, Celtic.

Glasgow was his city. A big teeming place full of people he knew. Yet for those months it was the loneliest place in the world for Clinton.

At the trial, he didn't know what to expect. Then he got a bonus.

The first witness couldn't identify him. The second did but then pointed out that he had been shown a newspaper picture of him as he was waiting to take part in the ID parade. The witnesses were the main evidence and after three hours the Crown were in grave difficulty.

Overnight it was decided that the case against Clinton had collapsed. It had lasted three hours – one of the shortest contested murder trials in Scottish history.

What would McGraw do, now that the chance had gone? He was busy enough in other ways and some unusual problems were about to hit him where it hurt.

72

GRASSING THE RUBBER

"We need something big, Tom," said the smooth-looking man in the decent suit. "Very big." They were having the conversation in a secret building in the city centre. McGraw and his new cop handler.

"What in?" McGraw asked.

"Drugs," came the terse reply. "We need a big hit on drugs."

When Arthur Thompson had died, the cops soon worked out that McGraw had to be their new man on the information front. For years they had been working together on a much higher level than Tam Bagan had raised or Paul Ferris had written about. By 1998 they made it official: he was working to a top man. Top men needed top results.

McGraw had the means and the contacts. All he needed now was a group of men with a few quid and the ambition to make a lot of cash.

That was how in 2002 Customs and cops were trailing a lorry from Felixstowe all the way to Glasgow. What was so interesting? £25,000,000 to £50,000,000 worth of coke hidden in rubber bales.

Even ordinary citizens had learned a few things from his own drugs trial in 1998. Bring the gear in yourselves and you can get bigger loads, better quality and more profit. It was the kind of deal the ringleaders could have retired on forever. Except it was never going to work. McGraw would make sure of that.

He knew people who knew people in Colombia. Scottish granny Irene Campbell wasn't caught in Venezuela as coke mule to bring it back to no one. The scale of the deal was fantastic. With the Scots taking care of transportation and all of the risks, the price rocketed down.

Then the Colombians had packaged it in a unique way inside bales of rubber. Rubber that stank. Bales that were so hard to cut open, who could be bothered? They had used the same method all over the world.

When it arrived at Felixstowe by boat, Customs and Excise were waiting. They had their official reasons for nabbing the team, like Britain never bought rubber like that from Colombia, but they had also been contacted and had already reached an agreement with Glasgow cops. They would check that the information was true then allow the truck to travel on to Glasgow, following it all the way. Once the gang tried to open the bales the joint forces would strike. That way they would get the drugs and catch the crooks.

First stop for the lorry load of raw rubber was a warehouse out in an industrial estate near Stepps on the site of the old Black & White whisky store. There the load was emptied and left.

For weeks, cops and Customs watched that warehouse twenty-four hours a day. No one came near. Shame they maybe didn't realise that it was right next door to Frontline Security's office where one Paul Ferris was a frequent visitor.

Two months later, convinced they were now safe, they moved the gear to Kilwinning, Ayrshire. There a couple of local men were paid to lift the bales and start cutting through them. That's when the cops and C&E struck.

It was the biggest haul ever and a great storyline covered by all the media. It's exactly what McGraw's cop handler wanted.

Two small businessmen and two labourers went down big time for the trafficking. No one seems to have asked how the two very ordinary ringleaders could arrange such a heist.

Up near Stirling was the answer. In another warehouse men were busy cutting open rubber bales. Bales that had crossed from the same origin and contained the same goods – cocaine. How did that happen?

Two of the convicted men wanted to talk, separately. They both complained that they didn't know how big this was. One that he didn't even know that anything was going down. They knew there was someone else behind the scam. Someone secret. Their only clue? The letters on the top man's mobile when calls came in. They read TMcG.

McGraw hadn't given up working with the cops. Now he simply worked on a bigger scale and was rewarded handsomely for it. Why did he do that? Did he need the money? Or was he trapped with the cops having him by the balls just as much he had them by theirs?

Other problems were about to hit McGraw. Problems he had never dreamed of.

73

LOST AND FOUND

Back in Glasgow, problems were brewing. Is it ever any different?

New laws had been introduced allowing Scottish cops to seize assets and force the owner to prove they earned them in a legal way. As a very rich man who hadn't held down a job for decades, McGraw could be in the hot seat.

The answer came from a source close to home and confirmed by the authorities. All he had to do was not pay a sweetheart deal with the Inland Revenue. They had been on his case for a long time but had finally settled on a small payment. Buttons to McGraw.

A total of £12,500 remained outstanding. McGraw didn't pay it and was declared bankrupt. As in broke, skint. Why would they chase a bankrupt man? They never did.

Yet other problems were brewing. McGraw was getting more and more paranoid. Every night he'd be locked up in his home early nursing some vodka. Some days he didn't even leave the house. Margaret was keen for them to spend as much time as possible in Tenerife but he didn't want to go. He feared he might lose everything if he turned his back for a second.

Besides, he had played a role in grassing John 'Goldfinger' Palmer, the timeshare fraudster who had swindled thousands of British couples out of millions of pounds. He had heard that Palmer's people were on Tenerife and might not be too pleased to see him.

McGraw was getting to be dull and drunken and it was annoying her. What was the point of all that work, all that money if they couldn't enjoy it? She could. He couldn't. That's when she threw him out.

Margaret had been the love of his life, that's for sure. Yet now in his fifties he was out on his ear, on his own.

Property wasn't a problem since the family owned stacks throughout the city. Suddenly he was on his own in a flat and the rules and bad habits he had lived by all his life seemed to disappear.

For once in his life McGraw didn't have minders. He would drive out at night to local pubs, ones on the periphery of the east side of the city and get smashed out of his brains.

At times he'd talk out loud.

"Don't look at me, you bastard, Ah'll torch your house one night."

"You know who Ah am? Well do you?"

Everyone did and everyone ignored him. They watched and listened but didn't respond.

Now he'd wander into the sex clubs. At times in his life he'd owned saunas – brothels by another name. At another point he had put money into lap dancing and pole dancing bars, making a few quid. Now he became a punter and spent a lot of dough.

With money to splash – Margaret always made sure of that, then there were his massive planks, secret money that no one else knew about – he'd treat the girls well. Spoil them at times. For that some of them would take him home and show him a good time.

It was one of those girlfriends he was waiting for the night a traffic cop knocked on the window of his car parked up a city centre lane. The cop didn't recognise who he was and didn't care. Drunk driving is drunk driving.

Later McGraw would spread the word that he had been at a party commemorating the anniversary of Glover and Hanlon's death. He wasn't. A set of pubs with large vodkas did it for him. He was in court this time being fined £300 and banned for twelve months.

There was a bigger project on the go though. Margaret had always nagged him that he should tackle what Ferris and Campbell, as well as a stack of newspapers, had written in books about him. Now he was going to do it.

Through a close lieutenant he had made contact with a journalist. The book could be written as long as he looked good and it was announced he hadn't cooperated with it. That would do it.

The agreement brought other opportunities. Firebrand socialist MSP Tommy Sheridan was suing the *News of the World* for claiming that he'd had affairs and participated in sex parties. The paper was trying to convince two women from the east end to come forward as witnesses. To help put Sheridan in his place. Could McGraw help?

Of course he could. Hadn't that bastard Sheridan been the one to raise the campaign to free TC Campbell and Joe Steele? Bastard. And he did. The trouble was, as he introduced the pair to one of the newspaper's representatives, two separate groups of people were sitting in the pub, watching and taking notes. There were few hiding places in the east end for McGraw.

The news of the book was good enough for Margaret and they got back together. McGraw was back at home with the woman he loved. There was only one problem – he had a young baby now.

One of his girlfriends had given birth. McGraw was open about it and why not? They had been separated at that time.

An arrangement was made for money to be paid to the woman every month. For the child, of course, but also to buy her silence. Imagine what the papers would make of a McGraw love child.

Now the book was out. The book about him that he had not cooperated with, or so the book's blurb declared. One day at the massive Borders in The Fort shopping centre, slap bang in the middle of his east end territory, the sales assistants spotted him. Walking through the aisles searching for his book. Walking through aisle after aisle stacked with Ferris' latest book. A lost and lonely man.

Was it bad timing? Poor content? Who knows but he knew one thing – Ferris had beaten him again.

McGraw was getting tired. Done, weary. And it was beginning to show. Life had one more surprise for him. The biggest surprise ever.

74

DANCE OF DEATH

"McGraw isn't a well man."

"Too true, he's always been a sicko." The two men smiled at the wee joke.

"Naw, Ah mean he really is no well."

"Couldn't happen to a better man."

The people of the east end had become used to watching McGraw and now they were seeing a different man. There was something tired about his eyes, lackadaisical about his manner. It was as if he didn't care about life.

At home they knew he'd had stomach problems and he was going to have that looked at. A visit to the Royal Infirmary that day, 30 July 2007, was taking a long time. He was going to have a test, a colonoscopy – or tube up his rear end. Not the most comfortable or dignified of medical examinations and there had been a delay. By the time he had returned home he had a headache and a much worse stomach ache. Maybe just the test, they thought.

After a sleep he was no better and asked for tea and toast. The pain had got worse, it was agony and he cried out, "I want to die. Fucking stop it. Ah just want to die."

Margaret was worried. McGraw wasn't like this ever. Then he tried to sit up and slumped over on her, pinning her to the bed.

A long term family pal, Jim McMinimee, had just come to the house and rushed in to the bedroom to help.

"He's having a heart attack," someone said. In the room was

John 'Joker' McCartney, McGraw's new best friend. What could they do?

"Help me," McGraw said. "Please fucking help me."

After dialling 999 the ambulance was there in minutes. With him all wired up they rushed him to the hospital. Minutes after he arrived they declared him dead.

McGraw was fifty-five years old. The last day of his life had been one of great discomfort and extreme agony. It had been the worst of days for him. Some people didn't think that was enough.

"We should go to the house," said one woman, "all of us and take the place over."

"Naw, line the road and throw stones and that at the hearse."

"Ah want to get that bitch by the hair and kick the fuck out of her." She meant Margaret McGraw and like many others couldn't believe that she hadn't known what McGraw had been, what he had done to their men folk or their kids, most of them in jail for crimes they didn't commit or, worse, dead.

Seasoned gangsters and old timers had to talk the angry women down. They couldn't blame them for their fury but a funeral was no place for revenge. Besides, he was dead now.

Even on the day of the funeral, no one was sure if the women had listened to reason. They had a lot to be angry about. They simply called it McGraw.

The night before his cremation a young east end face had something to do. He had found out the route of the hearse the next day and had a calling card to leave. FRONTLINE posters were put up every twenty yards.

It had been the company everyone associated with Paul Ferris. If McGraw could sense what was going on, one of the last things he'd see was a constant reminder of Ferris to take to his grave. If he couldn't, who cared? At least his family and pals could see the posters. It was a message to them too.

As mourners carried the coffin into Daldowie Crematorium, Robbie Williams' 'Angels' blasted out. For weeks the east would reverberate with more appropriate funeral music ideas for McGraw. The Rev. David Locke did his very best to talk sensibly but caringly about McGraw. Locke had himself opposed pub plans by the same man so he knew what he was talking about though didn't mention that on the day, wise man.

"It is not for us to judge the actions of others," said Rev Locke. "God shall be the judge."

That day at that time, Paul Ferris was down by the coast. He had visited his elderly mother that morning and now he was having some quality time with his children. Did he think about McGraw's death? Not much. Did he take pleasure in it? Not at all. It was an episode that had ended and he was pleased for that. Who he knew would never be pleased were the widows and orphans McGraw had created.

As McGraw was heading for the fire, TC Campbell was on guard duty. He had won his appeal, proving his innocence after twenty-three years and got some interim compensation. Immediately he had spent that on a big house with great security. He had grown weary of sleeping with one eye open at night and a big axe in his bed to fend off McGraw's paid assassins.

He bought a house in Riddrie close to BarL. The ex-house of a former BarL governor, Slasher Gallacher, so called because he was sacked after he knifed a prisoner.

Trouble was the government was holding out on the rest of his money. After all those years wrongly spent in jail he was due millions. As it was he couldn't even afford the electricity bills in his big new house. So he was guarding the gate, the electric gates that no longer worked, watching out for bailiffs coming to steal away his worldly goods.

Did he think about McGraw's death? What do you think?

At the cremation the final song was 'Amazing Grace', written, as Reverend Locke explained, by a former slave trader turned good. Proof he said that the worst of men could be saved by the Grace of God.

Some at the funeral might well have believed that. Others

wouldn't care. Out in the world there were people who would think of McGraw and howl for revenge and everlasting hell and pain for him.

He was the man they call The Licensee.

75

LATE LICENCE

War, they said. They got it wrong.

They had misread McGraw and simply didn't understand who he was, mistaking him for some strong leader the east end couldn't cope without.

The business side – legal and illegal – continued as before. Why not? The people who ran it are still here. Snaz Adams, young Winkie McGraw – now the father of two children – and, of course, Margaret, The Jeweller.

McGraw had never been a ruler or a strong man. He had been a talker and a manipulator. Someone who did anything for money. A man with no friends. A man who would betray to earn a few more quid.

It was the others who did the work, some holding the respect of east end folk. They were the leaders, not McGraw.

Some things have changed since his death. Death is like that.

A young woman found that she suddenly didn't get any money. The child is his, there's no doubt, but that commitment ended the second he drew his last breath.

John 'Joker' McCartney isn't seen round the east end much these days. Maybe he thought there was a place for him when McGraw left the world. The others didn't share that view.

Maybe he was the closest McGraw had to a friend but a friendship based on what? Greed?

A small legal matter has been sorted. Margaret has successfully sued Gordon Ross' parents and sons on an outstanding debt of

£100,000 and a bonus of £25,000. The same Gordon Ross whose lover at the time of his death, Kellie Anne O'Neil, was thrown out of their home, penniless.

Then there's a new man in Margaret's life. Jim McMinimee, who had sheltered Billy McPhee all those years ago, had arrived at the McGraw house just as McGraw became seriously ill. It was him who called 999 and followed the instructions on how to treat him till the paramedics arrived. All good things to do for any man. But two months later he had moved into Margaret's bed.

Her family were bemused and upset. Others were disgusted. Why so fast? Then she revealed that they had been lovers for two years before McGraw died. This is the love of McGraw's life we are talking about. Sad, so sad.

Maybe it helps us understand why twenty years ago some of McGraw's cops would openly talk about Margaret naked, about little moles and marks on her skin that would require the most intimate knowledge to know. Was theirs a love story? Or a story of convenience? He made the money and she made it grow. Full stop?

What of McMinimee? East end faces are wondering who the hell he is. Though now he runs three escort agencies, it seems his father was an ex-police inspector. Now there's an irony. Some say that McGraw had got into bed years ago with the cops so why shouldn't his wife?

Then a Sunday newspaper printed some photographs. They are of Margaret and McMinimee in a car, with him dealing drugs, so the paper said. East end players aren't surprised at the pair. They just shake their heads and say, "What's new?"

Margaret then revealed that she was into Tarot card readings and fortune telling. That she had predicted McGraw's death in the manner it happened but didn't tell him since it was inevitable. She did tell him something else though. That he should stop his drug trafficking through Spain back in the 1990s since she'd read in the cards that he was going to get lifted. He ignored her and he was arrested.

In McGraw's estate he left a total of £621.02. Hardly enough to buy the drinks after his funeral. So where were all his millions? Where people knew it always was – in Margaret McGraw's control. Same old, same old.

WHERE ARE THEY NOW?

Adams, Snaz: Still a well-known face in the east end.

Bagan, Tam: Released from jail he now leads a quiet, crime-free life with his wife. Has discovered painting, gardens, beekeeping and sells designer kitchens to make a good living.

Campbell, 'Big' Bill: Having been jailed for pub bombings in Glasgow and that of McGurk's Bar in Belfast that killed 16 people, Big Bill died in the Maze in 1997. He is commemorated by a plaque in Belfast's Shankill Road. His nephew, Jason, slit the throat of a 16-year-old Celtic supporter in Glasgow in 1996.

Campbell, TC: Free at last. TC Campbell is still fighting the state for full compensation for his years of unjust jail time. Last heard, the government was trying to deduct amounts for crimes he would've committed if free during that period. How could they know that?

Caravel, The: Sold off as a development plot a full five years after it was quickly demolished by McGraw.

Deans, David: Was the front for McGraw's interest in taxi companies. When that was exposed he was sent to Milton Keynes where he took over Raffles, a major taxi firm, where he was then accused of bribing taxi inspectors. Back in Scotland running taxi companies in Bathgate and Chapelhall.

Dempster, Bobby 'The Devil': Continues to be a presence in Glasgow and runs Ruchill Security.

Devlin, Craig 'Hairy Hands': Having fallen out with McGraw and struggling after being shot in the Royal Oak, Devlin took off to Spain and hasn't been home since.

Doyles, The: Since TC Campbell and Joe Steele won their appeal against their conviction for murder, the police have not re-opened the investigation into the killing of the six Doyles in 1984. Their murder remains unsolved.

Drummond, Drew: Still involved in running nightclubs. Not so close to the McGraws now.

Elliot, Walter Toe: His murder remains unsolved.

Ferris, Paul: Released from jail in 2002, he confounded his critics by not being interviewed by the cops since, let alone charged. The joint author of four books – *The Ferris Conspiracy, Deadly Divisions, Vendetta, Villains* – he has appeared on a number of documentaries and twice at the Edinburgh Festival. Runs a website: www.ferrisconspiracy.com

Glover, Bobby: His 1991 murder remains unsolved.

Hanlon, Joe: His 1991 murder remains unsolved.

Hardy: Long since retired from the cops. Was last seen driving an ice cream van he had bought from McGraw.

Healy, John: Released from prison. Rumours circulated that McGraw had to pay Healy £1m compensation for him taking the fall in the drugs trafficking trial.

Johnston, Paul: In spite of Scottish cops dropping their investigation Johnston remains abroad. In 2006 took part in the Lisbon–Dakar rally in his own team, Braveheart, but crashed in Mali after completing 4,100 miles.

Laurel: Long since retired. Last heard of, he was a director of a large security company.

Lawson, Trevor: After being killed on 13 March 2002, Lawson left over £1,000,000, a farm with a luxury house, properties in Dennistoun and elsewhere. He didn't leave a will.

Lobban, William: Having been jailed for six years for robbing a Rutherglen post office, spent his sentence in fear. When released, he moved to England before returning to live in rural Inverness-shire. In 2007 he lost a leg due to a blood clot. In the same year he was caught drunk driving and lost his licence for four years as well as his motability motor.

McCardle, Andrew: Having been jailed for gun dealing in 1992, McCardle was free in 2002 when he turned up at a drugs crisis clinic with a gun, ammo and a rope threatening to take hostages. As a result he slashed his throat in the dock of Glasgow Sheriff Court and was sent to State Hospital Carstairs. On Boxing Day 2004, he was found dead in Carstairs. The inquiry concluded that he had died of a heart attack. McCardle's mates insisted there were more sinister reasons for his death.

McCartney, John 'Joker': After three attempts were made on his life in Barrhead in 2008, he eventually moved home. As this book goes to press he is believed to be on the point of buying Rumours, the pub of his former boss, Specky Boyd.

McCormack, George 'Crater Face': Quieter now that his two heavy pals, Ross and McPhee, are dead.

McDonnell, Manny: After a dispute with his son, his house was surrounded by armed cops in 2004. They found nothing.

McGraw, Margaret: It isn't clear if she's intent on taking up fortune telling for a living. Then again, she doesn't need to.

McGraw, Winkie: Now the father of two children, is said to be upset at his mother's plans to marry Jim McMinimee.

McGrory, Chris: His murder remains unsolved.

McMinimee, Jim: Last seen in the papers photographed selling bags of cocaine to journalists. The cause of much laughter in the east end.

McLean, Jaimba: After surviving the shooting set up by Billy McPhee, Jaimba is taking it easy, keeping quiet, living the family life. The shooting remains unsolved.

McLean, PC: Long since dead of alcohol related disease.

McKay, Colin: Is rumoured to have linked up with Ian 'Blink' McDonald and involved in a feud with promoter and security businessman, Barry Hughes.

McPhee, Billy: Stabbed to death in the The Springcroft Tavern, Baillieston, on 8 March 2003. His murder remains unsolved.

McPhie, Frank 'The Iceman': The red-headed sniper who shot him has never been caught. His murder remains unsolved.

Malcolm, Stevie: In 2004 made £1,200,000 profit from Glasgow Private Hire Taxis, a company he and partner Tommy Wallace had created when they bought Mac Cars from Margaret McGraw. In 2004, a pal, David Deans, was exposed as a friend of McGraw's who had moved into the taxi business. In 1993 Deans had been arrested for 120 stolen cars being used by a taxi firm in Paisley, owned by Stevie Malcolm.

Manson, Billy: Overdose or murder? The State says overdose. Who do you believe?

Morrison, John: Settled from a life of crime to set up Provan Security.

Old Barns, The: Having been bombed once by Big Bill Campbell and the UVF, the Glasgow pub was torched again in 1998 on the first anniversary of Big Bill's death. Supporters of Big Bill were suspected.

Ponderosa, The: On the death of Rita Thompson, the house and estate passed to her daughter, Tracey. Selling the house seemed doomed when the media caught hold of the issue. Then, early in 2008 the house was quietly sold. Let's hope the new owners have a more peaceful, trouble free life.

Provanmill Inn: In 2005 it was torched though not destroyed. A month later it was torched again.

Reid, Dr John MP: Now chairman of Celtic FC.

Ross, Gordon: His parents were successfully sued by Margaret McGraw for the return of a £100,000 loan. No mention was made of the £200,000 smack deal he took for The Licensee and was lost at the time of his murder. Knifed to death outside The Sheiling Bar in September 2002, his murder remains unsolved.

Royal Oak: Shortly after the shooting of McCartney and Devlin when they were rushed to hospital by McGraw, the pub was torched and totally destroyed.

Sibbald, Billy: His murder remains unsolved.

Steele, Jim: Remained a close ally to McGraw up to his death.

Steele, Joe: Free and still waiting for his full compensation. Rumours say that on his release McGraw sent him a bag of smack in spite of him breaking that habit in jail.

Steele, John: Author of an autobiography, *The Bird that Never Flew*.

Steen, Archie: Six years after his break out of Barlinnie, was accused of running an ice cream van empire from jail and arranging a hitman to deal with other drivers. No charges were brought due to lack of evidence. In 1995, it was discovered he was parking his own soft top Escort Cabriolet at Perth Prison and using it as transport for his Training for Freedom trips.

Thompson, Arthur 'Fatboy': His murder remains unsolved.

Thompson, Billy: Badly disabled after an attack and a long-term smack addict, he now sells it from his house. When his mother Rita died, he was disowned. In July 2008 John Morrison Junior, the son of John Morrison (see above) was found dead in Thompson's home due to a heroin overdose.

Thompson, Rita: Died of throat cancer in 2006 at 72 years of age. Rumours circulated that she had left money in her will to have Paul Ferris killed as revenge for the murder of her son, Fatboy.

Vannet, A: Was promoted to Sheriff in Airdrie. One of his more famous cases involved former world snooker champion, Stephen Hendry, as a witness in a case of a bar room brawl.

Wallace, Tommy: In 2004 made £1,200,000 profit from Glasgow Private Hire Taxis, a company he and partner Stevie Malcolm had created when they bought Mac Cars from Margaret McGraw. Gave evidence in the 1998 drugs trial that suited McGraw and contributed to the conviction of John Healy. Rumours circulated that he compensated Healy on his release from jail.

Walker, DS Norrie: A few years after the conviction of TC Campbell and Joe Steele, DS Norrie Walker killed himself. At the time, the cops said he left no note. This is now contested by some people who knew him well.

INDEX